A GALLERY OF ZIONIST PROFILES

A GALLERY OF ZIONIST PROFILES

BY LOUIS LIPSKY

FARRAR, STRAUS AND CUDAHY • NEW YORK

© 1956 by Louis Lipsky
Library of Congress catalog card number 56–13175
First Printing, 1956

Fifteen of the profiles in this volume were published in
the *Congress Weekly*, under the editorship of Samuel Caplan.
A number of them have been translated into Hebrew and
published in *Haboker* in Israel.

Published simultaneously in Canada by
Ambassador Books, Ltd., Toronto. Manu-
factured in the U. S. A.
by H. Wolff, New York
Design: Betty K. Crumley

DEDICATED TO SHMARYA LEVIN

With humility and reverence

contents

the missing profile

A FOREWORD BY MAURICE SAMUEL

A gallery of Zionist portraits and Louis Lipsky's not among them! Could anything be more absurd—even if Louis Lipsky is himself the painter? Of course the painter has what he thinks is a good excuse; he is presenting us here with the lineaments of those who are no longer with us and therefore, he argues, a self-portrait would be out of place. But the excuse is merely a cover, we should wait in vain for him to make good on another occasion. The truth is that he will not talk or write about himself; that he never has done. And so the lopsidedness must be corrected as best it may by an inferior hand.

Now this lopsidedness issues from something more than the mere absence of the portrait of the artist. It is a very rare circumstance indeed that the very excellence of a book should constitute an injustice to its author, that the peculiar merit of the production should obscure and even falsify the merits of the producer as a man. But such happens to be the case at the moment. These portraits, generous, shrewd, individual, penetrating, would to a stranger seem to be the work of an uninvolved bystander, as remote as could be from the impassioned participant; "here," he would say, "is a gifted and sympathetic flaneur, not a man of action, a lounger on the periphery, not a leader at the center." And as everyone with the slightest knowledge of Zionist history can attest, nothing could be further from the actuality.

He writes, to be sure: "I was both an observer and an actor in the Zionist Movement . . . I was attracted and repelled by its *dramatis personae* . . . In the shadow of their perform-ances I played the small part destiny assigned to me." The aforesaid stranger would take these last words at their face value; the more so as there is scarcely a hint in the book about the long, often intimate, and sometimes turbulent re-lationship in which the writer stood to many of his subjects, among them the most important figures in their day. Would anyone guess from what is set down in the following pages about Louis D. Brandeis, Stephen S. Wise, Chaim Weizmann, Vladimir Jabotinsky, Jacob de Haas, Abraham Goldberg—to mention but a few—that Louis Lipsky's knowledge of them was acquired largely in the arena of Zionist politics, in shifting patterns of close association, sometimes in a common pur-pose, sometimes at quite violent cross-purposes? You will scrutinize the book in vain for so much as a glimpse of the rages and enthusiasms which attended the great Zionist split of 1921, the founding of the Keren Hayesod and of the American Jewish Congress, the fighting out of the policies of the Zionist Congresses—all the welter of activities which have brought about the creation of the State of Israel; and there-fore, if you knew no better, it would never occur to you that there were such great actions, or that in all of them Louis Lipsky played a leading role.

In another of the few references to his share in Zionist history he says: "If I were to write the memoirs of my Zionist life they would be chiefly concerned with what I remembered of the gifted and dedicated men (profligate and pious) who made the Jewish rebirth so exciting a reality. It does not serve my purpose to give an account of how I was di-verted to its service . . . I was a contemporary of its pio-neers in the United States and followed its development throughout the world with a pertinacity I cannot explain—in all kinds of weather, through all sorts of exaltations and defeats—down to the day when the State of Israel was clothed with sovereignty in 1948."

"It does not serve my purpose" will make the insider smile. It should read: "I don't know how." This is meant literally. I am convinced that Louis Lipsky hasn't the foggiest idea of the important place he occupies in the history of contemporaneous Jewry; I am equally convinced that nothing that I or anyone else can say will have the slightest effect on his estimate of himself: that is, if he ever bothers to make an estimate of himself, which is doubtful in the extreme.

These introductory observations bring me to the core of Lipsky's personality as I see it. Paradoxically he does in fact embody in equal measure the detached observer and the fiercely committed partisan, the inveterate causeur and the man of action. I have known few men who are such willing, pleasing, and illuminating *shmoosers* at a cafe table, fewer still who are, in single-minded dedication to a cause, so capable of sustained, arduous, and masterly leadership. And the paradox is all the more piquant because these irreconcilable qualities, these utterly contradictory temperaments are not at war in him; they do not intrude on each other, or spoil each other; they alternate harmoniously in what seem to be separate existences. The artist-lounger in him does not complain: "I was meant to be a man of action," for he is one; nor the man of action: "I was meant for the quiet, contemplative life," for he has it. It is the only case of schizophrenia I have met which moves me to affection and admiration.

Somewhere of course the qualities issue from a fundamental unity. It is impossible otherwise to understand the nature of Lipsky's leadership. I have known a number of leaders in Jewish life; every one of them, with the exception of Lipsky, seems to me to have wanted leadership, and in most cases the impulse was in one degree or another justifiable. The man had ability, knew he had it, and was determined to create the circumstances which would permit him to exercise it. It might happen, indeed, that more effort and ingenuity went into the creation of the circumstances than into the proper use of the opportunity; but certainly to want and even to strive for leadership is not inconsistent with the honorable use of it. Lipsky has never wanted, let alone sought leadership. The maneuvering for it is wildly alien to his being; he struggles against the status with the reflex actions of a man being pushed over a cliff, and has a profound aversion for its choreography. He regards newspaper reporters as coarse interlopers, and under the prodding of his devoted subordinates submits to interviews with a gracelessness born of congenital shyness. He is astonished when his abilities and convictions bring him to the fore. No matter how genuine the public demonstration for him he always seems to be muttering: "What do you want of *me?* Get on with the business!"

Those who have seen him in the thick of action, as chairman of Zionist or American Jewish Congress Conventions, have carried away an unforgettable picture of what looked, on the surface, like nothing more than superb managerial and parliamentary skill combined with astonishing physical and nervous endurance. Skill, rapidity of judgment, fairness, consistency of purpose, endurance, good humor, the sense of proportion, all were indeed there in abundance; but what chiefly made Lipsky the master of conventions was the universal acknowledgment that his ego was completely absent from the scene. Whatever might be thought of his policies, no one ever suspected him—and of how many others could this be said?—of acting for the improvement or even retention of his personal standing. The welfare of the Movement was for him the sole and continuously applied touchstone, whether in the formulation of a policy or the composition of a committee. Amid the shifting of combinations and intrigues he pursued with unswerving steadiness the ultimate objectives of the Movement, and, himself as innocent as a dove, he was as wily as a serpent in recognizing and frustrating manipulations with a dubious purpose.

But neither his acknowledged selflessness nor his managerial dexterity would have sufficed to give him his unique position either at the conventions or in Zionism at large if they had not had as background a breadth of intellectual outlook and a clarity of expression unequaled on the American Jewish scene both on the platform and in the press. The ultimate objectives of the Zionist and allied movements were for him, always, the enlargement and enhancement of Jewish life, its liberation from restrictions, internal and external, the assertion of its dignity, the release of its creative forces. He sees Jewish life as a whole, and I believe that with regard to the specific Zionist question he has always acted on the principle that what is good for the Jewish people is good for the Jewish homeland, and what is good for the Jewish homeland is good for the Jewish people. He does not separate them, as some extremists do; he cannot; his life and outlook are grounded in Jewish peoplehood.

It will usually be found that when a man of political action passes for a "theoretician" he is not much more than what is called in the public-relations world an "idea man." He thinks up a new little philosophy for each new situation. He will shift his basic arguments according to the opportunities of the moment, so that his followers at last become disoriented as to the ultimate values of the movement. No doubt it is very tempting to whip up enthusiasm for a shift of policy by appealing to a new set of first principles; and no doubt a politician may go very far by this method. He will not, however, create a body of doctrine, or set a lasting example of integrity, or remain a permanent influence. Lipsky, by all odds the foremost political theoretician in American Zionism, has done the first and promises to do the last two. He has, in fact, been the educator of two American generations. His public addresses at the conventions and on other occasions are models which few in Jewish life have been able to follow. They are lucid, architecturally superb, unrhetorical, and filled with a dignity which never lapses into the pompous. Like his articles and editorials they are permeated by a sense of the creative in Zionism and in Jewish life.

Not the least of the services which Louis Lipsky has performed for American Jewry has been to set a new standard in secular leadership. There was a time when that leadership was pre-empted by men of means, or by men who had de-

voted the major part of their talents to careers outside the
Jewish field, or by religious leaders who divided their time
between the pulpit and the platform. This was a heritage
from the age of *shtatlanut,* when self-appointed notables
"represented" Jews to the Gentile world. It is not a derogation of the memory of Louis D. Brandeis, or of Louis Marshall,
to recall that they acquired their standing in the non-Jewish
world and that, having placed it at the service of the Jewish
people, they did not give their entire lives to this service.
Stephen S. Wise, a mighty figure in American Jewish life, had
his congregational duties, and in addition diverted no little
part of his energies—and it was right for him to do so—to
other than Jewish purposes. Louis Lipsky has been the only
one of that stature to confine himself to the Jewish world,
simply as a secular official, and to demonstrate that neither
wealth nor outside recognition are indispensable to effective
Jewish leadership. If there has been some change in this
respect in the Jewish world much of it can be traced to this
example.

I think the strongest single element in Lipsky's attitude
toward Jewish life is the sense of form, but that word must
at once be divested of any implication of formality; form in
the sense of the becoming, the proper (and again without
the suggestion of propriety or stuffiness), the pleasing, form
in the sense of rightness, justice, moral fittingness. It domi-
nates in his public actions, in his general outlook on the meaning of man, and in his outlook on the meaning of Jewry. I
stress this point, in addition, because the sense of form is the
bridge between his two selves.

Before he committed all of his energies and emotions to the
Jewish cause Lipsky was a young and promising dramatic
critic. He has to this day remained a lover of the drama, and
discourses on it—when his "other" self takes charge—with a
fluency, insight and wide knowledge that would make our
stranger take him for a practicing professional. Now in drama
more than in any other literary discipline it is form that
determines the degree of merit. If I say that Lipsky sees the
world, and Jewish life, under the aspect of the dramatic I

must add at once—if this is by now necessary—that he brings
to his vision something of the trained craftsman but infinitely
more of the man of high, intuitive rhythms.

There is another aspect of the dramatist that illustrates for
me the personality of Louis Lipsky as it has impressed itself
on me. The dramatist must be faithful to a theme; and at the
same time his characters must be free, they must be themselves. He must not distort them for his purpose; he must
love and respect them for what they are, and his theme must
grow out of his arrangement of them, never out of a com-
pulsion that he uses toward their inner natures. Lipsky has an
infinite respect for human beings and for their intrinsic quality.
This is not usual in the political leader, whose interest in
persons is heavily weighted by his estimate of the use to
which he can put them for the cause. This innate respect is
evident in the portraits here assembled. It is emphasized by
a glancing remark about himself: "I was an easy mark for
(human) curiosities." He was, indeed; sometimes arousing
thereby the impatience of the less tolerant, like myself.

Although I write here with a kind of glibness about the
basic unity in the two Lipskys, it has always baffled me—it
still does—that this man of the platform, the conference
room, the editorial desk, this director of a movement, should
have alternated so easily with the careless (but not formless)
and kindly bohemian. For it is no use blinking the fact that
the director of a movement, let him be as respectful as you
like of the personalities of his followers, must nevertheless
show firmness and vigor in what I have called the "arrangements." He cannot permit the bore, inane or possessed, more
than his proper share of importance, which is usually mi-
nuscule. And thus it has been with Lipsky the leader. With
Lipsky the artist or bohemian the opposite was the case.
"Easy mark" is a charming understatement. Lipsky's capacity
to endure the company and conversation of bores is a marvelous thing to behold. I am not implying that he is surrounded
by nothing but bores. Far from it. But the proportion of his
leisure time occupied by them is abnormal. He seems to be
able to defend the Movement, but not himself. It may be a

form of expiation. On the other hand, he does not seem to suffer. His liking for human beings overcomes the gravest obstacles. He manages somehow to enter into the bore's love of himself, or at any rate to contemplate it with never-failing benevolence.

It is also very easy to say that it is this absorption in others that has kept Louis Lipsky young, but who knows the sources of these things? One can only record that at eighty he is quite naturally the leader of a dissident group in the American Zionist Movement, and that with the same clarity of view, expression, and purpose as he demonstrated as a young man when he threw himself into the revolt against the Brandeis leadership.

It gives me quite a turn to reflect that only yesterday (exactly forty-two years ago, if I am going to be pedantic about it) I entered the employ of the Zionist Organization of America as a promising office boy when Louis Lipsky was its general secretary and already marked by his devotion and abilities for national leadership. Our personal contacts have been irregular; for years they were daily, for years absent. I never renew them without that early feeling of deep respect. I used to think that part of it at least was due to the difference in ages, but now that I am myself approaching the area of technical venerability, and the difference is of little importance, I see that this has nothing to do with it. As I perused this book and saw the ghosts parade before my mind's eye, as I meditated on those I had known but dimly (there are also a few who had sunk below the horizon of the living before my time) and those to whom good chance has given me closer access, it occurred to me that very few of them occupy as distinguished a place in the Zionist and Jewish tradition as Louis Lipsky. Nor is this explained by the historic record alone. Zionism is not merely doctrine and program; it is something contained in lives, and a special measure of it is contained in the life of the man to whom this imperfect tribute is addressed.

NOTE TO THE READER

These profiles are not put forward as substitutes for biographies. With the exception of the pieces on Theodor Herzl and Chaim Weizmann, they are sketches and impressions of personalities I knew whose lives were implicated in Zionism, more or less—leading it, contributing to its progress or hovering on its periphery. I had hoped to recapture within the form of a Profile the lingering memories of a long life in which I walked in their company.

There are many important omissions, which I regret. Many interesting personalities have become shadows in Zionist history. Some of them I have been unable to revive, for they do not now register or reveal themselves in an arresting manner.

I have tried—not always successfully—to avoid the cliches of memorial or eulogy. It was necessary for my purpose to remove the haze of legend that has accumulated around the Hero or the Pioneer, the Orator or the Propagandist. I ask forgiveness if, in my desire to keep the Profiles within a reasonable frame, there has been a distortion of the reality and if the features of the subject do not emerge as clearly as intended. I have not been a diligent research student. I am sure many of my readers see what I have seen in different colors and dimensions.

Zionism stands in a circle of danger and may become the

victim of sentimentality or excessive reverence. I shall feel amply rewarded if I have preserved for the historian or the casual reader lively human accounts of some of the personalities who—each in his own way—contributed to the renascence of Jewish life and the creation of the State of Israel.

Louis Lipsky

NEW YORK, JUNE, 1956

introduction

The best memoirs of the Zionist Movement are those colored by the lives of scores of unique personalities who occupied the Zionist stage in succession, each in his own way adding interesting chapters to the Zionist chronicle. Much has been written about the philosophy of the Zionist Movement, its achievements, its problems, its partisan controversies. Zionism became more and more vocal and heavily reminiscent with the years. It amassed a tremendous store of archives now resting in the Library of the Jewish Agency. In the last analysis, however, it was the creation of a generation of men of forceful personality and varied talents who, instead of being driven into alien fields, identified themselves with the destiny of their own people and thus were able to live out their lives with more dignity, with greater creativeness, among their own people. They made Zionism and, in turn, Zionism made them.

If I were to write the memoirs of my Zionist life they would be chiefly concerned with what I remember of the gifted and dedicated men (profligate and pious) who made the Jewish rebirth so exciting a reality. It does not serve my purpose to give an account of how I was diverted to its service, how it shaped and guided my life, how it made me feel a pulsating kinship with all things Jewish, good and bad. I was a contemporary of its pioneers in the United States and followed its development throughout the world with a pertinacity I cannot explain—in all kinds of weather, through all sorts of exaltations and defeats—down to the day when the State of Israel was clothed in sovereignty in 1948.

From 1913 onward I moved closer to the international scene and got to know the leading figures at Zionist Congresses—the propagandists, journalists, poets, organizers, the party leaders, the official and unofficial kibitzers who used the Congress as the stage for their self-display. The tenants of the larger part of my memory were these Zionists. I was both an observer and an actor in the Zionist Movement. I was in it at the beginning, and a wondering spectator through the years when, by a miracle, what could so easily have been an unrelieved and consummated tragedy, became the fulfillment of an age-old dream. In that world I lived the larger part of my life. I was attracted and repelled by its *dramatis personae.* They were my companions, my confidants, the objects of my admiration, the butts of my criticism. They fascinated and thrilled me. In the shadow of their performances I played the small part destiny assigned to me.

Leadership in Zionism had many facets. There were poets like Bialik, philosophers like Ahad Ha-am, and social reformers like A. D. Gordon; who exercised a deep influence on the Movement, but were never an integral part of the life of the Organization. There were eccentrics like Herman Schapiro, the fumbling philosopher of Heidelberg, who came to the Congress with various projects and finally subsided (and died) when his proposal for a Jewish National Fund was placed on the agenda. There were men like Davis Trietsch, who brought the idea of having Cyprus serve as a temporary haven of refuge and heckled Theodor Herzl with the proposal at the early Congresses. There were men like the egocentric Alfred Nossig, the sculptor and poet, who crossed swords with Herzl and disappeared from the Zionist stage as if the earth had swallowed him. There were poets and artists who haunted the lobbies and the cafes and gave the Congress the disorderly aspect of a County Fair. Leadership in the usual sense came from the Platform, where Herzl was the first regal dominant figure. That

Platform was reserved for the Advocate who, for the first time in two thousand years, not only aroused the hopes of a people for their Return and Redemption, but established the stage on which the drama of Redemption could be reviewed, criticized, rejected or applauded. The Congress was the World Theater of the Movement.

On the day Herzl first appeared in Basle it may be said that the curtain was raised on the spectacle of an organized effort to realize in modern terms the mystic hope of a long-delayed fulfillment. It seemed as if the ghosts of the ancient past had been exorcised and brought back to the living world as witnesses. The hazy background of the Stage reflected the rise and fall of the Jewish people from the days of Abraham, the Father, to the last struggle of the dying Hebrew Commonwealth. The witnesses in the shadow included Moses, the leader of the Exodus, the promulgator of the Law; Zerubavel, Ezra and Nehemiah who led the return from Babylon; the Maccabeans who fought for freedom against the Syrians; Bar Kochba, the leader of the last revolt against the Romans. Among the shadowy figures were the men of the law, the men of piety, the philosophers and exegetes; the moralists and the preachers; those who gave their lives for *kiddush hashem;* who suffered under the persecution of centuries and taught the Jewish people the arts of patience and restraint, and humility. With the last echoes of the expulsion from the Promised Land, all these heroes passed off the living stage and Jewish life took refuge in the underground, and so far as the world was concerned, Jews were strangers living under their feet, to all appearances plowed under, raising their heads only to be flogged back whence they came.

The French Revolution was the herald of a new day. The emancipation of all the oppressed was proclaimed, but the freedom offered to the Jews was not an invitation to re-create their own freedom in their own land. It was an invitation to join in the equalitarian procession, carrying the banners of other civilizations, merging in a pseudo-freedom which for them meant their national extinction.

The Zionist Movement challenged history. It called a halt to what seemed to be an inevitable trend toward self-effacement. It turned the flow of Jewish life into its ancient channels of self-revelation and redemption. The Jews were organized against the Emancipation through a desperate attempt to recall to life their own civilization hidden under the burden of neglect and obscurity. Instead of adapting the coloring of their environment, their demand was to be recognized as a living, aspiring people in their own garb, with their own language, with their own social conceptions, in their own land. They asked for the right to rebuild their own home in their own image.

The whole Movement converged toward the Zionist Congress—the stage on which the leaders played their parts—heroic, melodramatic, comic, too. There, the vocabulary of an organized people found utterance. In its plenum and committee rooms, in its foyers and cafes, in its newspapers and through their correspondents the vocabulary of the Jewish renascence was created—the clichés of a parliament, the forms of organized debate, the programs of contending parties. A propaganda that encircled the world was given wings. Out of the many languages spoken, gradually one language took possession of the scene. Out of the many legal systems and procedures they got to know a common method through experience. The intellectual conceptions of emancipation, as well as the doctrines of the Marxists, were modified and developed to accord with the demands of Jewish rebirth; for the new life was not to be built on the dogmas of alien civilizations; it was not to be a plagiarism or an imitation; it was to work out its own destiny in consonance with the revelations of its own sages and prophets and poets. The trend of history had to be reversed and brought back to the field of Jewish self-emancipation.

From 1897 to 1948, with brief interruptions caused by war, the history of the Rebirth was recorded in the Zionist Congress. Every issue that arose in Jewish life was exposed and discussed there or in the Actions Committee or in the Zionist press or in the party conferences. Every change in the conditions of Jewish life in Palestine or in the Diaspora found its record there. Every Zionist of note registered his appearance in its proceedings in person or through indirect participation. The Congress took notice of the organization of the Galut, the progress of the Aliyah from decade to decade, the advances and retreats in the political field, the achievements of the budget-makers and the fund-collectors. The portraits of the leading actors were limned in words, descriptions or in dramatic conflict, and the names of the workers in the fields, the builders of the communes and the cities, were called from the rostrum.

In Herzl's day there was grace and dignity in its proceedings; there was majesty which was seldom revealed in later days. The floor was taken by men like Max Nordau, Alexander Marmorek and Israel Zangwill who returned from the free world to the platform of their own people. But the first *besetzung* of leadership soon made way for others. The Russians, the Poles and the Germans came over and took possession of the floor and of the platform. The formidable Ussishkin challenged David Wolffsohn, the merchant of Cologne. The "democratic faction" was swept forward into commanding positions. Then came the World War; Chaim Weizmann, the chemist; Louis D. Brandeis, the American judge who never appeared at a Zionist Congress; and the Balfour Declaration. Vladimir Jabotinsky made his stormy appearances, like the hero in an Italian melodrama. The strident, challenging voice of Robert Stricker was heard. The economist Arthur Ruppin came to plan its economy. The vanguard of the labor movement made its appearance. The general debate developed into a rowdy exhibition; the Labor party to the left and the Mizrachi, just as vociferous, to the right. Leo Motzkin demonstrated his matchless skill as a parliamentarian. In the ferment of events between the two world wars, the stage was filled with men from England like Joseph Cowen, Frederick Kisch and Harry Sacher; Americans like Henrietta Szold and Stephen S. Wise; Austrians like Rabbi Osias Thon, Senator Ringel and Rabbi Chayes; proletarian leaders like Nachman Syrkin, Ber Bokuchov and Berl Katznelson, S. Kaplansky and Chaim Arlosoroff. As the Movement grew, the whole stage became more and more proletarian in manner and method, and party strife brought its divisive problems to the arbitrament of democratic procedures with a great deal of creaking of the parliamentary machinery. The National Home took over more and more of the agenda. The "budget" absorbed more attention. It was the inevitable cause of terrific controversies of class interests. The underground defensive force of Haganah made its presence felt and when World War Two came the State was ready to burst its undercover wrappings, step out into the open and take over the molding of its own destiny.

From the records of that bustling, crowded stage—from the memories of personal experiences of fifty years—I have selected for consideration a score or more personalities, following no order or design, mingling the high and the low, and described them as I knew them, without prejudice. I have tried to give meaning to their lives in the setting of the Zionist drama; less of history and more of personality. In some instances I may have followed a wrong angle; I may have disregarded the conventions and contradicted the official tradition of unrelieved eulogy, and I may have transgressed protocol and social tact.

In my view, however, the subjects shown on the screen of my memory come out of the ordeal of affectionate scrutiny in proportions of far greater human significance than if I had followed the line of least resistance and accepted the stereotypes of the official record. At any rate, once the type is set, the proof sheets corrected, the plates engraved, corrections are impossible. Let them stand as my eyes saw them, as my heart remembers them! Abler and keener portraitists and historians may come to review what I have written, who may regard my work as impertinent distortion. May they find those colors of Truth which I have sought and probably missed.

the first three

THEODOR HERZL (1860–1904)

The writer knew most of the leading personalities of the Zionist Movement for over half a century. But he never heard the voice or touched the hand of the Prince of them all. Echoes of the personality of Theodor Herzl reached us through Americans who met him at Congresses. He was revealed in the records of the early Zionist Congresses and the literature created at the time. He spoke through Manifestoes and public addresses and letters written to persons we knew. His name was the spark that ignited the Movement in the Diaspora. Stories were told of him by American delegates to the Congress. His photographs in various poses were circulated as media of propaganda. A literature about his leadership became available. Fragments of his Diaries were made public after his death. Today there is little of his Zionist life hidden from public scrutiny. The dust found in his grave in Vienna was carried to Jerusalem. For many years after his premature death he was a living influence in the Movement. The writer hovered about the fringe of his Zionist career, touching hands with others who had touched his hands; he himself was distant in time and place from the creation of the Movement but closer

*to the writer in some mysterious way as he became aware of
the varying colors of his life. This profile—if it may be called
that—is an attempt to capture the features of his personality—
to limn him from memory—and to draw in general terms an
outline of his amazing career, which still casts a warming glow
over Jewish life long after his disappearance from earthly
sight.*

In the few years of his Zionist life and leadership, Theodor
Herzl renewed and revived an old Jewish legend. He was accepted by many as the reincarnation of the Messiahs of the
Middle Ages who raised the hopes of their people for a brief
span of time and disappeared in mystery and were forgotten.
It was wondered whether this new Redeemer would stay long
enough to test his Mission. Those who believed in the tradition were disturbed that Herzl did not come from the halls of
learning; that he was not pious or saintly; that he was bred in
a worldly Vienna and was a writer for journals and the theatre.
He never pretended to Messiahship, but his regal appearance
suggested the role he was destined to play.

The story of his life—personal and public—has been told in a
heavy volume written by Alexander Bein; it has been revealed in his amazing *Diaries*. When you have read all that
has been written about him, you begin to understand why the
new Symbol of the old Legend would not be the weird and
futile story of another False Messiah, but the engrossing first
chapter of the modern Exodus which led in 1917 to the Balfour
Declaration and in 1948 to the rebirth of the Jewish State in
the Land of Israel.

There were no indications of his later transformation in the
beginnings of his life. Born in Budapest in 1860, he was matured in an alien environment. He was not part of the main-
stream of Jewish life. His Jewish education came to an end
when he was thirteen. What he knew of Jewish tradition was
packed away in his memory and rarely disturbed him. He
knew of Jewish disabilities only as an affront to an ancient people and as a personal humiliation. He was made conscious of

being a Jew by the society in which he lived. He was educated in the University of Vienna. He studied law and was admitted to the bar. He practiced his profession for a while, and then turned to journalism and literature.

He was drawn to the press, to the theatre, and to the society of the elite. Like most young men of the time, he was first a Viennese, then a cosmopolitan. He looked through a small window into the larger world of culture and longed to be included in it. He was not troubled by the deeper problems of life; he was not "a soul in torment." He became a good reporter and commentator, and a writer of light and easy entertainment in the theatre. His security was assured by the generosity of his father. When he was twenty-nine he married. When thirty-two, he was well known as a journalist and dramatist, and reached the high point of his ambition when he was sent to Paris by the Vienna *Neue Freie Presse* as its correspondent.

Herzl was unaware that for several decades the Jews of Eastern Europe were engrossed in a national revival. They were emerging, in spite of Russian oppression, from life in the ghetto, and were opening their windows to modern thought and aspirations. They were greeting the alien air. They welcomed enlightenment. In the course of their spiritual and intellectual escape, they ran toward the liberating ideals of the Russian Revolution, but at the same time the Hebrew language was reborn and the old ideal of the Return experienced a revival. Hebrew became the medium of a modern literature. It was revived as a spoken tongue. Hebrew schools and academies were founded. Hebrew journals of a high quality created a rejuvenated public opinion. The ideas of Pinsker, who wrote *Auto-Emancipation* in 1882, took the practical form of promoting Jewish colonization in the Holy Land. Societies dedicated to the Jewish revival were organized in all Jewish communities in which Russian Jews had influence. While assimilation was eating away at Jewish values, national aspirations were being fertilized through the medium of Hebrew culture and the work of Jewish colonization in Palestine.

To all of this Herzl was alien. Paris was, in a sense, the birthplace of his conversion. There, slowly, with uncertain steps, he found his way back to his people through the provocations of anti-Semitism. He read anti-Semitic periodicals and books with avid curiosity and rising indignation. He was present as a correspondent at the trial of Alfred Dreyfus in 1894, and saw the ceremony of degradation. He heard the cries of "Down with the Jews" in the streets of Paris. He followed the intrigues and sensations of the Dreyfus Affair as it moved to its revision under the angry challenges of Emile Zola. He was obsessed by an inner unrest. He fell into a mood of feverish agitation which he could not explain to himself. He wrote a play with a Jewish theme in which there was sharp debate about the Jewish "problem." He described the state of his mind at that time in these strange words:

> For some time now, I have been engaged with a work of in-describable greatness. It has assumed the aspect of a mighty dream. Days and weeks have passed since it has filled me utterly. It accompanies me wherever I go. It broods above all my conversations. It peers over my shoulder at the trivial work I do. It disturbs and intoxicates me.

A fascinating description of his agitation is given by Bein in the following exciting phrases:

> Then suddenly the storm breaks upon him. The clouds open, the thunder rolls and lightning flashes about him. A thousand impressions beat upon him at the same time. He cannot think, he cannot act, he can only write. Breathless, unreflecting, un-able to control himself or to exercise his critical faculties lest he dam the eruption, he dashes down his thoughts on scraps of paper as if under unceasing command. So furiously did the cataract of his thoughts rush through him that he thought he was going out of his mind. He was not working out the idea; the idea was working him out. It would have been a hallucina-tion if it had not been so informed by reason from first to last.

His mental state was reflected in the restless inquiries he made of friends and acquaintances as to the validity of his ideas. He was not sure of himself. He even doubted his sanity.

He composed *The Jewish State* in various forms. He sent the first version to Baron de Hirsch; the second was a revision addressed to Baron Edmond de Rothschild. In desperation, he wrote and rewrote the text to get the matter out of his system. He then decided upon the publication of his manuscript in order to validate the creation of his mind and to win, if possible, public support.

Herzl knew nothing whatever of Pinsker or Hess, the forerunners of Zionism. He seemed not to be interested in what had been written on the subject. He was the victim of his own intellectual unrest, his own imaginative adventures, his own dissatisfaction with the position of the Jews in the world. He was led by degrees to appreciate the abnormal aspects of Jewish life. He came to despise Jews of standing in society who could have done much to improve the position of Jews, but who sought instead their own well-being without giving a thought to their doomed brethren in the ghettos. He believed that it was imperative that the Jews be liberated, that the world should be made to see that the solution of the Jewish problem was one of the issues of modern civilization. He became the self-appointed promoter of the cause, and the rest of his hurried life was dedicated to its service.

Herzl's distinction was that he gave the Jewish problem form, dramatic content, and political reality. He provoked a general international discussion. The pamphlet he wrote—*The Jewish State*—was the first public expression of a dynamic concept of how the Jewish people could achieve their freedom, a land of their own, how their redemption could be organized and financed.

With startling self-assurance, on his own responsibility, he proposed the creation of a Jewish State and became its sponsor and advocate. He used all his friends to help him find a way to distinguished supporters. He won the loyalty of Max Nordau, then at the height of his international fame. He met Baron de Hirsch who rejected his plans. He submitted a memorandum to Baron de Rothschild who thought his enterprise would be dangerous to Jews in general. He established contacts with Jews in England, in the United States, in Russia.

At first, Herzl hesitated to identify the territory of the Jewish State. The Charter he aimed for made necessary, however, approaches to the Turkish Sultan, who held sovereignty over Palestine. The pressures of the Russian Zionists forced him to come down to *terra firma*. When he wrote the novel *Altneuland* in 1902 he had beyond doubt landed definitely and forever in Zion. But here he revealed, even five years after the First Congress, that he still had not penetrated the deeper meaning of redemption and rebirth. The Zion he saw twenty years after 1902 was a synthetic composition. It was made of shreds and patches, picked up from alien gardens. The home the Jews returned to was provided with modern furniture not of their own design. It had acquired no distinctive way of life based upon Jewish tradition or Jewish ethics or Jewish aspirations. The garments of the Ghetto were removed, social living was cleaner and roomier, but nothing distinctive had been developed. There was only a faint reflection of a new Jewish spirit. There was no evidence of the renaissance of Hebrew. Children sang Hebrew songs to welcome distinguished visitors. German was very much at home in Zion. The pioneer labor movement had not yet put in its appearance. How the State was created was not described except in general terms. There was no reflection of the spiritual and social ferment Zionism would generate in the process of becoming a state. The Jewish religion was *in statu quo*. The Jewish "soul" was not even under observation. Only in the last year of his life did Herzl realize what creative power was hidden in the Promise.

The publication of *The Jewish State* was the first public step in his great enterprise. It was not submitted as a dogmatic finality. It was not a plan or blueprint. There were many improvisations subsequently discarded, but the objective was clear. It was to secure for the Jewish people the grant of sovereignty over a territory large enough for the requirements of a nation.

The magic title of the brochure evoked widespread interest and comment, rejection and acceptance. It raised the sights of many Jews and made them conscious of their origins, their depressed position, their servitude and the urgency for organized action. It was their first exposure to world scrutiny as a people. It made them feel that the world might be won for the cause of their liberation. It gave them courage and hope and liberated their spirit. It gave wings to their imagination and work for their hands.

When Herzl set out on his mission he had no sponsors or backers, no committee or organization. He was the sole promoter and advocate of an international project, and its leader. It was not his aim to create a mass movement. He was not concerned with democratic forms. His first thought was to seek the cooperation of Jewish philanthropy. When these efforts failed and he realized that political negotiation must be backed either by masses of people or by funds, he called the first Zionist Congress to be held in Basle in August 1897.

Through the Congress the Leader of a people emerged. When he stood on the platform at Basle it was said that "he was like a scion of the House of David risen from the dead, clothed in legend and fantasy and beauty." In the Congress he was the moderator in clashes with persons and parties. He curbed his natural impatience. He was gracious and considerate, sharp in retort, but quick to recover balance. He was aware of the dramatic. His interventions in debate were well-timed, arresting, but controlled. He became a skilled parliamentarian in a democratic assembly in which procedures and languages fought for dominance. He was seldom an orator. He spoke as if he were the First Minister of State. He gave the impression of a man convinced of the validity of his mandate which stood higher than the vote of Congress. Beneath his public calm and reserve a fierce restlessness beat against his strained heart.

All his unrevealed talents converged to provide the audacity to become the first Jewish diplomat, the first to negotiate the cause of reestablishing the Jewish State on practical, political levels. The man of letters became a political strategist and diplomat. He seemed to carry the credentials of an ancient peo-

ple who had regained old political manners and came straight
to the throne of public opinion, seeking not special favors or
mercy, but the righting of an ancient wrong; on the record, not
in secret treaty.

He was not an economist. He was not a financier. But he had
the gift of an extraordinary imagination and an amazing resourcefulness. He was able to find harmony in discord, unity
in diversity. It required great resoluteness at that time to face
an arrogant Kaiser and to plead the Jewish cause with restraint and dignity. The effort to see and influence the Sultan of
Turkey was an elaborate conspiracy of great ingenuity. The
influence of the Kaiser died early, but Herzl played the gam-
bit with the Sultan to the bitter end. The crafty ruler finally
offered him Mesopotamia, Syria and Anatolia, but specifically
excluded Palestine.

Herzl had proposed the refunding of the Turkish debt by a
group of Jewish financiers. The consideration was to be a
Charter for Jewish Colonization in Palestine. His effort to establish contact with the Sultan is a fantastic story of Oriental
intrigue. He had to push his way through the meshes of a cor-
rupt court. His own agents were not to be relied upon. Every
step had to be paid for. Bribery was the order of the day. He
was never sure that his messages were being received or that
alleged replies by the Sultan were authentic. He seemed to be
playing with an invisible adversary. Finally, in 1901 he succeeded in having an interview with the Sultan and spent two
hours face to face with the ailing ruler. In his account of the
interview, Herzl wrote:

"He stood before me exactly as I had pictured him—small,
lean, with a big hooked nose, a dyed beard and a weak, trem-
bling voice. He wore the uniform of the Selamlik, a mantle
above his shield coat, diamond orders, gloves. He gave me his
hand and we sat down. He sat on a divan with a sword between
his knees. He took two cigarettes out of a silver pack, handed
one to me and took the other himself. He said, 'I have always
been and still am a friend of the Jews. I rely chiefly upon
Muslims and Jews. I have more faith in them than in my other
subjects.'

"I complained of the injustices that are committed all over the world against the Jews. He said that his Empire was always open as a refuge for Jews. I said, 'When Professor Vambery told me Your Majesty would receive me, I thought of the old story of Androcles and the Lion. Your Majesty is the Lion. Perhaps I am Androcles. Perhaps there is a thorn to be drawn out. I consider the public debt to be that thorn. If this could be removed, Turkey would once more blossom in all her strength.' The debt had accumulated under his Majesty's predecessors and it had not been possible to get rid of it. If I could be helpful, it would be most gratifying. The Sultan smiled, shook his head yes and no, and made no comment. He gave the impression of crafty solemnity."

Herzl left the audience and touched many hands stretched out to him in the vestibule. He distributed gold pieces. The next day Herzl received a diamond stick pin. That was all he ever received from the Sultan. The Turkish debt was taken over by the French. When the time came for him to return to England, it was in fact the last available station on the zigzag march begun in 1895. The English offer of Uganda was the only definite proposal Herzl was ever able to bring to his people.

It was the summation of his life. It was a distorted climax and a mockery. He was being detoured to East Africa. The Movement would be called upon to cease reference to the Return. It would lose contact with tradition and history. Zion would become a receding memory. The Russian Zionists for whom the "haven of refuge" was intended rejected it with grief and dismay. They said Zionism was the breath of their life and they could not stop breathing. Life could not be halted as a part of a political maneuver. Although the majority was with Herzl for the acceptance of Uganda, he knew from the start that the battle was lost. He went into the caucus of the Russian Zionists and saw them mourn over the betrayal of their hope, and realized for the first time how deeply rooted was the mystic relation of the Chosen People and the Promised Land. He was driven by the power of Jewish memory to abandon the uncertain territory of his first thought and to accept without question the Land of Israel as the objective of Jewish hope. He knew then that he was not destined to lead the Modern Exodus. He was the Forerunner. A new generation would have to be born to take over the burden.

He had come to the end of his life. For ten years he had carried on with an impaired heart. He was sustained by the provocations of the adventure, its frustrations, his superhuman obstinacy. When he launched the Movement he was a young man at the height of a brilliant literary career. At forty-three he was old and exhausted. When the proposed detour was rejected he stood where he had started: a larger following, instruments of action, a press, the beginnings of a bank, a Congress, an organization, but no nearer the political goal than when he published *The Jewish State.*) One who saw him at his last Congress said:

> The imposing figure is now stooped. The face is sallow. The eyes are darkened. The mouth is drawn in pain and wracked by passion.

His obsession had destroyed his personal life. The wife of his youth was estranged and unhappy. When she married the writer of plays, the brilliant journalist, she looked forward to a social life in the intellectual circles of Vienna. Instead she found herself in the excitement of a rude movement associated with the emotional disturbances of the Jews of Eastern Europe who invaded her well-kept home and took her husband away into the peculiar by-paths of a political struggle in which she could have no place. She resented the adventure. She was cold to its surprises, its passion. It was estranging the father from the children. There were disagreements and reconciliations. He had no time for the articles he should have written, and was too proud to receive payment for Zionist services. He preferred to borrow endlessly from his father. He left his family penniless, his children destitute and unprotected, scattered and under the guardianship of various friends. He did not pause even when his physicians advised rest again and again.

To his last day his mind was excited by alternative projects. When he passed away he was under the impression that his life had been a barren failure.

The offer of a colony in East Africa had been rejected and he seemed to have suffered a major defeat. But the ideal of the State, which had been relegated to the background by the Lovers of Zion—whose program had lost its momentum and become a tired discussion—was transformed by his death and incorporated in a Zionist Movement infused by and infected with the ideal of the Jewish State, which would never again be obscured and washed out of the corporate responsibility of the Zionist Movement.

He did not know that he had fired a revolution in Jewish life and thought. He did not know that he had created the instrument of redemption which would live on long after his departure, and would ultimately reach the goal he had missed. In the first flush of revelation he had thought freedom would come through the contributions of Jewish philanthropists, through foreign influence bought and paid for. He organized the Jewish Colonial Trust. He set in motion the Jewish National Fund. He made the Zionist Congress the international voice of the Jewish people. In the final hours of his life he knew that redemption would come from the struggle of his people, their sacrifices, their belligerency, their obstinacy. It was his historic privilege to set the Jewish people on the road that would bring them to the Promised Land—not *any* land, not Argentina, not Uganda, but the land which finally found a living place in his bruised heart.

He said that the foundation of the Jewish State was laid at the first Basle Congress. He foretold that fifty years later the Jewish State would be a growing reality. The First Congress was held in 1897. The Balfour Declaration was issued in 1917. The Jewish people proclaimed the State of Israel in May, 1948.

The personality of Herzl is best reflected in his *Diaries*. It is the record of his Zionist life. It contains everything of him—his

foibles and caprices, his human weaknesses and his resoluteness, his discoveries and inspirations. It is crammed with contradictions and deep understanding of human nature. You see
his confused mental state in the process of clearing. You see
the reflection of his hopes and disappointments with nothing
hidden or disguised. You wonder at his courage and audacity.

He lived with the shadow of death in his heart. He was
driven to move fast to avoid being overtaken. You see the
emergence in this amazing record of a personality of great
proportions, who was led by the mystic influences of a great
ideal to act as if he were really the State Builder, really the
Redeemer of an oppressed people. It shows how, in a maze
of activities extended in various directions at the same time,
he gave life to an ideal and forged an instrument that could not
be broken. He was impatient with God and aimed to achieve
in the few years of his own life what his people were unable
to achieve in two thousand years of suffering and faith.

In his last will he asked that his remains be buried in the
Jewish cemetery in Vienna near the grave of his father "to remain there until the Jewish people take my body to Palestine."
When the Russians entered Vienna in 1945, it was found that
the Nazis had overlooked the desecration of Herzl's grave. The
new State of Israel—the reality of all Herzl had striven for—
resolved to fulfill his wish. On August 17, 1949, the dust of
Herzl was gathered together and brought from Vienna and
interred in one of the hills of the Holy City of Jerusalem where
the Memorial to his historic struggle will be an everlasting
shrine.

MAX NORDAU (1849–1923)

When I went to my first Zionist Congress in 1913, it was sug-
gested by a quixotic friend of mine, Boris Katzman, that I must
see Max Nordau in advance of the Congress, for I would learn
much from the Sage of Zionism who lived in Paris. At that time
I believed in Katzman as an experienced traveler and a wise

Zionist. (Affection bound us together for many years.) He came from Russia, had studied in Vienna and France, had many friends in Berlin, was a delegate to the First Zionist Congress, and then came to us. I took his advice. I left the boat at Cherbourg, and Julius Meyer of Boston and I blundered our way to Nordau's residence, to be told by the concierge that the Sage was on vacation in Spain. At the opening of the Congress a cablegram from him was read which provoked a point of order that a political cablegram even from Max Nordau was out of order. Obviously, relations with headquarters were not good. I saw Nordau for the first time in London at the first Zionist conference held at the end of the First World War. He spoke to our American caucus and at the Albert Hall mass meeting. He was still a remarkable orator. He was critical of the Zionist leaders and of the Balfour Declaration, and did not hesitate to say so. He favored a mass migration to Palestine, which startled most of the delegates, but he went his own way and seemed to think that those who disagreed with him were lacking in foresight. His experience during the war in Spain had made him suspicious of the pious words of the English, and he believed it would be good for the Jews to change over from unqualified acceptance of the Balfour Declaration to a clamor for deeds. His audience was not sympathetic. He was not well. There was a grimness about his manner of speaking and many of the leaders resented his critical tone as not in keeping with the mood required by the moment. He had grievances against the Zionist regime which had not treated him with the dignity his historic service entitled him to. He left London and returned to Paris, recovering some of his household property and his library. He really did not feel at home in the Movement, which seemed to be satisfied with the smooth phrases of conformity and lacked the passion of the earlier days. He had come to the Movement when it was important that the world should hear its voice. He brought with him an incisive mind, a sweeping imagination, and his words raised the spirits and hopes of all Jews sensitive to drama and emotion. With the Balfour Declaration a new message was required. You had to speak of funds, you had to speak of rights, you had to speak with familiarity of the Land as well as of the Promise. The voice of the author of Degeneration *and* Conventional Lies *seemed wholly out of place.* Nordau *must have felt that in the quiet moments of his privacy. All his comrades-in-arms seemed to have passed away. They left him alone with the thoughts of the incredible effect his voice must have made in those early days when he was the central personality of the Movement.*

Max Nordau was one of the first and the most powerful supporters of Theodor Herzl. He was born in Pest, Hungary, in 1849. He was eleven years older than Theodor Herzl. When Herzl came to see him in 1895 with the manuscript of *The Jewish State*, he was an established man of letters. He was the author of *Conventional Lies*, published in 1884. He had written *Paradoxes* in 1885 and *Degeneration* in 1893. He was the author of a number of provocative plays and novels. He was on terms of personal friendship with the leading writers of many lands. He was a striking figure in the highest intellectual circles of Paris. He had arrived as a thought-provoking journalist whose field was the civilized world, and he was fairly prosperous.

At fourteen, one of Nordau's sketches was published in a local newspaper and paid for. At sixteen, he already had a fair income from his writings and at eighteen, was a regular contributor to the *Pester Lloyd*, the leading Hungarian newspaper. He paid his own way through the university and graduated at the age of twenty-two. He was sent on two transcontinental journeys by the *Pester Lloyd*, which made his name known to the readers of that journal and resulted in the publication of two travel books which had quite a success. In 1879, he left Pest for Paris, where he practiced medicine as a psychiatrist. To be financially more secure he continued to write, however, and never for long devoted himself exclusively to the practice of medicine. From the start his books aroused an enormous interest. His *Conventional Lies* established his reputation as a fearless and original thinker. It provoked the thinking of friends and foes; it was banned in Russia and Austria and denounced by the Pope. *Degeneration* elaborated on the theories of Krafft-Ebing and Lombroso and served as the spearhead of a general attack on the decadent tendencies of the day. He hated the so-called "decadents" uncompromisingly. He was one of the most sensational writers in European literature.

Nordau was more conscious of his Jewish background than Herzl. He had a smattering of Hebrew and could speak Yiddish and possessed an intimate knowledge of the Jewish way of life. His father was a Hebrew teacher who was highly respected as a Hebrew grammarian and a poet, and had a marked influence upon his son's character. When he entered the university and began the study of medicine, he freed himself from the authority of religion and tradition. He was an emancipated Jew. His intellectual life had passed out of the Jewish environment. He rid himself of provincial conceptions and became a man of the world. He was an analyst, a critic, a moralist. He diagnosed all social ills and challenged all standards. Society was strapped to his operating table and he reported, without fear or favor, on whatever disease his scalpel revealed. He was essentially a physician and scientist. He was proud of his calling and paid homage to no authority but his own conscience.

Nordau's friendly reception of Herzl was therefore most unusual and indeed surprising. The keen analyst should have seen through him. He should have paid attention to Herzl's excitement, his exaltations and depressions, his self-depreciation and doubt. He should have appraised him as a patient, and everything said and how it was said should have been taken as material by the psychiatrist. But nothing of the sort happened. The two men talked for three days in succession! Nordau gave Herzl, as Herzl reported, "a lightning-like understanding." The older man had a strange paternal feeling toward the younger man who was struggling with an inner revolution. When the talks were over Nordau said: "You may be mad, but if you are, I am as mad as you."

Nordau gave a brief account of his "regeneration" in a letter he wrote to Reuben Brainin, the Hebrew journalist, in 1896, some time after he had met Herzl. He said:

My father was extremely pious, sternly Orthodox, and observant of all the rules and regulations pertaining to the Jewish religion. He did his best to bring me up in the same spirit so that I might heed all the Jewish commandments and become a pious Jew.

When I turned my fifteenth year, I abandoned all the Jewish rules and the Jewish code of behavior, and from then on Judaism and Jewry became for me nothing more than a memory, but a pleasant memory, be it said.

Thus you will see that from my sixteenth year until my fortieth my way of life and my relationships were entirely alien to all things Jewish. By conviction, by emotion, and by philosophic conception, I was German through and through. My Jewish feelings slept in me; I believed that they had died completely and that all that had been Jewish was now completely destroyed, leaving not a trace behind.

Anti-Semitism opened my eyes and turned me back to the Jewishness which I had forgotten. The hatred of others for us taught me to love our people. And from year to year my enthusiasm and love of my people grew greater and greater, and my pride in my Jewishness grows ever stronger. Now I know that I am a brother of all Jews, a son of my people.

It may be that his encounter with Herzl, coming at a time of public excitement over the Dreyfus Case, made Nordau more sensitive to Herzl's psychic disturbances, released the impulses of his own youth to which he refers. The critic may have seen in Herzl the burning zeal of the martyred prophet and was dazzled by its incandescence.

From that day on Nordau became Herzl's most loyal and serviceable friend. He had received the gift of a new faith. As Nordau said later, Zionism gave his own life "its aim and content." He was no longer the emancipated man of letters. He was no longer alien to the hopes and aspirations of his own people. He was the captive of Herzl's mission. No matter what differences arose between him and Herzl—and there were many—Nordau was always tolerant and forbearing, often aiding in spite of disagreement, always loyal and affectionate. He was never part of the organizational structure of Zionism, preferring to maintain his personal independence. But he was the ablest and most belligerent interpreter of Herzlian Zionism, appearing as its advocate in Zionist Congresses and on the platform, fighting off the influence of the "practical Zionists" many years after Herzl passed away.

It was Nordau's opposition to a conference of notables which Herzl proposed to call that led Herzl to call the Zionist Congress in Basle. Nordau was the chairman of the committee which formulated the Basle Program. He proposed an inventory of Jewish resources as preliminary to planning the Jewish State. He emphasized the physical training of Jewish youth and thus was the inspirer of the youth movement in Zionist life. He wrote some of the more important memoranda of Herzl. He introduced Herzl to many of the leading men of the day—writers and statesmen and philanthropists. He was the most effective propagandist of Zionism during the formative years of the Movement. He carried on the Herzlian tradition with audacity, even in the days after the Balfour Declaration was issued.

Herzl was the incarnation of the leadership of the Zionist Movement. Nordau was the resonant voice of the Zionist Congress. At ten Zionist Congresses in succession—the last at Basle in 1911—Nordau spoke for the Movement. In these addresses he spoke for all Zionists. His were the first public addresses in which the renascent Jewish people set forth its cause in all its nuances, with form and color and passion. They were addressed to and heard by a world audience and evoked world interest. They thrilled all Jews with a common emotion and hope. They set the Zionist Movement on its difficult way.

When he called attention to the blindness of Jews and their indifference to the call of destiny, the theme was novel and daring and never before uttered with such eloquence and directness and dignity. There was no pulling of punches, no conventional diagnosis. He showed the emptiness of the French Revolution, so far as Jews were concerned, in that adoption of the formula of equality did not change the fact of anti-Semit-

ism, which at that time showed itself in its crassest manifestation in the Dreyfus Case. Read those addresses today and you
will marvel at their clarity and daring, their dignity and wisdom. Time has not washed away the glow of his words.

Many leading Jews had emancipated themselves. They were
to be found in London, in Paris, in Vienna, in Berlin, in St.
Petersburg. They left the masses of Jews behind in their varied
ghettos and made the pretense that *their* emancipation would
soon be shared by all other Jews. But full emancipation for the
Jewish people was not coming anywhere. There were social
and political and economic discrimination and persecutions,
cold and hot pogroms and general disdain. Here was an emancipated Jew in the person of Nordau—a defender of modern
civilization, a bitter critic of its derangements, who was part
of that world—declaring that only through freedom in their
own land as a people would they be restored to equality
among the nations.

By all standards Nordau was an amazing orator. He spoke
freely from notes without manuscript. There was nothing
theatrical about his appearance. He was short and stocky. He
had a massive head and a patriarchal beard which hid his features. But his words cut through sham and circumlocution.
Words came hurriedly at his bidding. When he spoke (his
gray eyes flashing, his arms upraised, every now and then rising in a gust of passion, sharp anger or sarcasm), it seemed as
if he were conscious that he was speaking to the whole world,
that he wanted them to understand what he meant—to feel
the depth of his indignation and the heat of his truth.

I heard him in London at Albert Hall in July, 1920. Those who
were there then saw him at seventy-two, still retaining his intellectual vigor, majestic in appearance, still capable of deep
insight into the realities of the political situation. There was
drama in his appearance on that platform, for he was the only
untarnished relic of the days that had produced Herzlian Zionism. His faith and confidence were amazing. He said at that
time with a total disregard of the practical situation, the views
of his colleagues, and the official atmosphere in which he
spoke:

Only political Zionism has a simple and clear doctrine of sal-
vation: We need Palestine, not disinterestedly but effectually;
and not a Palestine occupied by individual owners. We need
it for the people, that we may establish there those millions of
our brethren who are being threatened with massacre or rapine
in the Ukraine, whom Poland is trying to strangle slowly but
inexorably by means of economic boycott, and whom Austria,
Hungary and Germany want to push back into the ignominy
of the Ghetto.

"It is not possible, there are no houses to live in!" No houses?
They will live in tents to begin with. Rather that, than to have
one's throat cut in pogroms. "They will have nothing to eat!"
We will feed them until the first crop. During the four years
of the war twenty-two million troops, who neither sowed nor
reaped, were fed. "It will cost billions!" No, but many millions
—and they must be found. The Jewish people will give the
required money when they will know for certain that it is to
be used in a manner that will produce lasting results.

We claim Crown lands in Palestine. We want to establish our
fellow-Jews on it; first hundreds of thousands of them, later
millions, not in fifty or a hundred years, but quickly, to save
them from the assassins and to make them a valiant vigorous
Jewish nation, rejuvenated, planting deep their roots into the
nourishing holy soil; realizing the moral ideals, the ideal of
justice and brotherly love, as preached by the Prophets of
Israel; giving to the world, for the first time, the example of
complete man, cultivating the earth, and at the same time,
their minds, handling the plow and the book, producing
material values, living intensely the full intellectual life of their
times, forming a vast elite of work and thought.

That is the program of political Zionism as Herzl and his
collaborators always understood it.

There are not several, there are not two, there is only one
single method of overcoming this difficulty; we must by all
means and with the utmost speed see to it that our numbers
are equal to those of the Arabs in Palestine, and that we out-
number them as far as possible, however large the difference
may be at first.

Nordau's audacity in the expression of his views, regardless of
the climate of public affairs at the time, wholly unaware of the

practical difficulties, can be appreciated by the fact that he spoke
in the presence of Arthur Balfour and other English statesmen.
He spoke with the same freedom that characterized his first
Zionist Congress addresses. He spoke as Herzl had spoken in
1897. His body was broken, he knew what war meant now;
but his backbone was as stiff as when he denounced the "de-
generates" of his younger days and he was no respecter of persons and disdained formalities.

The First World War was a personal tragedy for Nordau from
which he never recovered. He had lived in Paris since 1879
but remained a national of Austro-Hungary. He never acquired
French citizenship. The French Government regarded him as
an enemy alien, a journalist working for an alien journal, and
confiscated all his property. He was first imprisoned and then
allowed to go to Spain, where he spent the war years in Ma-
drid under great difficulties. When the war was over, permission was obtained for him to go to England. He came to London
in 1919, and found himself in an atmosphere not to his liking. In
his view, the Balfour Declaration was inadequate for the creation of a Jewish State; it should have been more explicit. In
addition, he found himself in a circle in which none of his old
friends, except Joseph Cowen, played a part, and the leadership was in the hands of men who in prewar times he regarded
as being merely "practical Zionists." Generally speaking, Nordau always resisted, consciously and subconsciously, the eager
desire of the "practicals" to proceed with the colonization of
Palestine regardless of the political conditions. He was irked
by an inadequate practicality. He wanted action even on the
Balfour Declaration to be held up for further elucidation. Nor
was Nordau's advice sought on many important problems under discussion. He felt himself slighted. He had no part in the
planning of the future. He could find no adequate place for
himself at 77 Great Russell Street (headquarters of World
Zionist Organization). The movement seemed to have passed
him by. Being a proud man, he never raised the personal issues
and suffered in silence.

He advocated the settlement in Palestine, without delay, of

600,000 Jews taken out of the Ukraine, Poland and Rumania. He was in deadly earnest about it. He spoke of it on a number of occasions, but his views were not accepted. Nordau felt a great mistake was being made. The redemption was being delayed for a hundred years, if not forever. In disappointment he returned to Paris in 1921. He was old and quite ill. He would not accept Zionist assistance and tried to resume his literary labors and practice his profession. His devoted wife and daughter Maxa did their best to make his life easy. So did a number of friends like Joseph Cowen and Jean Fischer. He worked as best he could almost to the end, and died in 1923.

He was never personally concerned with the building of the Jewish National Home. He left that to the practical men. It was his business to analyze the Jewish problem and suggest the remedy. He remained true to the old line of the Charter and to the grand, moving ideals of Theodor Herzl. He challenged the trend of history that seemed to be passing the great moment of liberation. He never saw *Eretz Yisrael* with his mortal eyes. His remains rest side by side with Ahad Ha-am and Bialik in the old cemetery of Tel Aviv.

DAVID WOLFFSOHN (1856 or 1858–1914)

The last Congress David Wolffsohn attended was held in Vienna in 1913. He looked well but it was rumored that he had suffered recurrent heart attacks which made him an invalid for periods of time. At the Congress, however, he was vigorously aggressive and at his best in the give and take of debate. He came to the Congress, he said, to protect the financial institutions of the Movement, which had the effect of angering his opponents to the point of frenzy. Was he needed to protect the finances of Zionism against Otto Warburg, Julius Simon, or Dr. Arthur Hantke? He had no great orators on his side. The old guard—men like Nordau and Alexander Marmorek—were not present. The last of Herzl's disciples were not an impressive group on a platform. I remember Jacobus Kann of The Hague. He was a tall, thin man, a dry, matter-of-fact speaker, incapable of using his imagination or of giving anything to an audience or drawing anything out of it. There was Jean Fischer of Belgium, who had a way of shrieking in falsetto and making German sound like a strange jargon which could not be understood by the Germans or by those delegates who had come to know Congress German. Wolffsohn was himself the best advocate of his cause. He had been elected chairman of the Congress as a result of a quarrel between Ussishkin and the Zionist Executive. He won the American delegation because he seemed to be talking good sense. He was also cordial, witty and passionate in his pleas for segregating the Zionists' funds from the control of the Zionist Executive, the same Executive marked for reelection. Elect them, he advised the Congress, but don't give them the keys to the safe. This seemed irrational but sounded sensible to most of the delegates for they had acquired a deep affection for Wolffsohn in spite of the propaganda conducted against him. We Americans left Vienna with the feeling that Wolffsohn, ill as he was, his days being numbered, was the strongest man in the Congress. He had followed Herzl loyally and with pride. He had reluctantly taken on the leadership, knowing that he had few years to live and that he lacked the experience to lead the Movement. He was not equipped by education or training for leadership. He was not a writer or experienced orator. But he accepted the Mantle worn by Herzl and died in the service, if not in the leadership. He had no children. He provided as best he could for Herzl's orphans and left all his possessions to Jewish institutions in Palestine.

David Wolffsohn was never at ease as the successor of Theodor Herzl. His admiration for the great leader never waned nor was he able to rid himself of the specter of his influence. He thought of himself as the guardian of the Herzlian heritage. When he came to see him in Vienna for the first time, he was surprised to learn that Herzl had never heard of nor read Pinsker or Moses Hess, that he knew nothing at all of the Chovevei Zion Movement in Russia. And yet, so impressed was he by Herzl's majestic presence, his self-confidence and the daring of his program that without hesitation he said: "All that I am and all I have is yours without condition." He never lost that glow of discipleship. He lived in Herzl's shadow. Others have followed Herzl when they thought he was right, but Wolffsohn followed him—as he wrote—even when he was convinced Herzl was wrong.

He lost his guide and mentor when Herzl died. He did not feel fit for leadership. He was not a general; he was not a speaker or writer or politician; he was a rough man of affairs, plain, simple-minded, without experience or special talents, but he was capable of unbounded devotion. He urged Max Nordau to accept the leadership. But that astute individualist was obstinate and said again and again, "Thou art the man." Escape was impossible. Wolffsohn was bound to the servitude of Zionist leadership.

The death of Herzl was the finish of an exciting decade of Zionist history. The political opportunity had passed. The Sultan of Turkey turned away from Herzl and made terms with France. The offer of Great Britain had been rejected by the Zionist Congress. The Leader had fallen on the battlefield and his partisans had retreated in disorder. A new procedure, a new orientation or a new inspiration was called for. The Russian Zionists pressed forward to take "power" and Herzl's disciples were being overwhelmed by the life forces of the Movement which had its source in Russia and among the Yiddish-speaking Jews. The heritage of Herzl was slowly being retired to the pages of history and new forces were coming forward to fill the vacuum. There was a half-hearted defense against the clamor of the "practicals." The call for action had the right of way and petty enterprises of all sorts were being blown up to large dimensions. The questions were, what kind of action, where shall we get the funds, where do we start. Regardless of the Charter of Right, basic to Herzl's program, the Jews were to begin the slow penetration of the Promised Land. No power on earth could prevent the inevitable drift toward the fulfillment of the Basle Program. Nor was Wolffsohn himself interested in checking the drift, for he was in fact during this entire period, in spite of his veneration for Herzl, a Chovevei Zionist of the earlier days.

Strangely enough, the Russian Zionists looked aksance at David Wolffsohn because they said he was a German Jew. But he was born in Lithuania near the Prussian border. His father was a Hebrew teacher; his childhood and youth were formed by the orthodox life of the community. He knew the Bible; he had a smattering of the Talmud. His memory was filled with Biblical and Talmudic citations. His way of life in his formative years was determined by the simple habits and customs of orthodox Jews. He knew Yiddish. He was the youngest of a family of sons who, as they reached maturity, crossed the border into Prussia to evade military service. For the same reason David left Lithuania when he was fifteen and joined his brothers in Memel, which was a way-station of the underground leading to freedom for the Russian Jews. Many of the refugees remained in Prussia, many of them moved on westward to other European countries or to the United States.

Wolffsohn remained with his brothers. He had an aptitude for business. He was cordial, good-humored and quick in business transactions. He worked for a while with one of his brothers and then branched out as a salesman in Libau and then in Lyk in East Prussia. He became a lumber merchant. He made friendships with the men of standing in the community. He got to know Rabbi Isaac Ruelf, the author of a Zionist pamphlet entitled *Healing of my People,* based on Pinsker's *Auto-Emancipation.* He was intimate with David Gordon, the publisher and editor of *Hamagid,* a well-known Hebrew periodical. He overcame the hardship of being an *Ostjude,* but never lost consciousness that Yiddish was his mother-tongue. He was interested in all communal affairs and was appreciated for his good sense, his integrity and generosity. Love for Zion was a part of his Jewish education. He was interested in Hebrew literature and the organization of a Zionist group in Cologne. It was said that he never spoke German well, that he never overcame the handicap of his origin, and yet he made the impression of a substantial member of the German middle class. He was a merchant and he was proud of it.

Theodor Herzl laid the foundation of the Zionist Organiza-

tion, but it was not much of an organization. The leadership
was concentrated in his own hands. He and his friends had to
provide the funds. He was both the leader and the administrator. His office was the bureau of the Organization. There were
few checks on his leadership between Congresses. The "democratic faction" was formed to register disapproval of Herzl's
policies, but its dissents were limited largely to demonstrations
at Congresses. It was Wolffsohn who developed the Organization. He became the president of a democratic organization
and was responsible to his constituents. By this time he was a
very prosperous man in Cologne. To that city he transferred
the head office of the Zionist Organization. He enlarged the
editorial forces of *Die Welt,* adding Dr. Berthold Feiwel and
Dr. Abraham Coralnik to its staff. He built up the *Juedischer
Verlag* in Berlin of which Dr. Feiwel was made the director.
Nahum Sokolow was appointed the general secretary, and
Israel Cohen, of London, English secretary. A quaint Russian
character later known as Avadio (Davidovitch) was the con-
troller, remaining in office through the Weizmann regime as
the financial member of the Organization. Max Bodenheimer,
a young jurist, became the head of the Jewish National Fund,
taking the place of Johann Kremenetzky of Vienna. He drew
into the Zionist service Dr. Arthur Ruppin. He won the support
of Franz Oppenheimer, a leading German economist, who was
the founder of the colony Merhavia. He established a branch
of the Jewish Colonial Trust in Constantinople with Victor
Jacobson as its manager and chief of the political work in the
Turkish Empire. He ventured on diplomatic missions to Constantinople and St. Petersburg. He visited many Jewish communities, engaged in many controversies with his opponents
and in the course of time had to be accepted as the leader of
the Movement.

But he was not able to give the Movement the magic touch
of leadership, to raise it to its previous state of Messianic excitement. The mood inspired Herzl never returned. Wolffsohn may have lacked imagination, but there was nothing to
inspire him. He had no material for the building of a homeland
and saw no need to make plans which would not go beyond

the blueprint stage for lack of means and men to execute them. He had to resort in effect to the methods of the "practicals" for which Herzl's followers were being criticized by the "practicals" themselves.

He carried the weight of Zionist responsibility, like Herzl, until he fell under the burden. His heart gave way as did Herzl's. In 1911 he left office undefeated, resisting what he regarded as an attempt by his successors to use the financial resources of the Jewish Colonial Trust and the Jewish National Fund to serve wildcat party politics. He wanted to conserve the assets of the Movement, to live thriftily, honorably, with patience and faith, not to be excited by illusions, not to risk what one had for the unknown. He grew in stature with his experience. He refused to join in opposition to the new regime which succeeded him. He guarded himself against bitterness and disciplined himself to be just to his opponents. He lost interest in winning the partisan battle. He remained for the rest of his life the target of an organized propaganda conducted by the Russian Zionists. They thought they had to destroy him in order to defeat him. They wanted to show Wolffsohn as a man of ordinary education, without ability, without judgment, lacking *schwung* and leadership, who did not understand the Herzlian ideal of which he professed to be a disciple, an *Ostjude* masquerading as a *Yehudi*. This rabid propaganda extended to the United States. All our European visitors had the same story to tell about Wolffsohn to American Zionists.

The writer attended the Vienna Congress in 1913. Wolffsohn's official pictures showed him to be a tall, robust, bearded man with good-natured features. He always seemed to be wearing a Prince Albert coat. At Vienna he was not robust. Illness had given him an appearance of emaciation and fatigue. His Prince Albert coat hung loosely over his large frame, but his eyes shone with great eagerness. He seemed to be burning himself out in the course of this Congress. All our preconceptions of his personality were untrue. He appeared at the caucuses as a commanding personality, a fairly adroit debater, a good story teller, quick in repartee. Although he sat among the delegates, he was the center of the Congress. The issue was, should this ex-president of the organization be made president of the Congress? His opponents said "no," but they were divided on the issue. Finally, the Executive was defeated, Ussishkin won, and Dr. Weizmann as chairman of the permanent committee presented Wolffsohn's name as the president of the Congress.

Wolffsohn sat among the delegates while his successor, Otto Warburg, delivered the President's address. He heard the speaker outline the new policy and realized for the first time that they were dethroning Herzl and consequently himself. Warburg said that there were three periods in Zionism. In the first, all work in Palestine had to be subordinated to the great political ideal. In the second, as political difficulties arose, work in Palestine had to be regarded as a concession to the impatient. In the third, work in Palestine had become an end in itself, an integral part of policy. Wolffsohn heard Warburg praise Herzl and Perez Smolenskin, without even a formal reference to the name of his own predecessor. Wolffsohn realized his loneliness when he saw Nahum Sokolow ascend the platform to take the place of Max Nordau as the orator to describe the Jewish position in the world. He heard Shmarya Levin speak of Baron Edmond de Rothschild (whose philanthropy Herzl had proposed to destroy) as a great man, the protagonist of "a heroic method." At this, his last Congress, he found himself without a group to defend his life's work.

But in the general debate which followed, Wolffsohn scored a personal triumph with his own magnificent speech. The deterioration of his heart had reached a dangerous stage. He was fearful it would not sustain him. He certainly was not an illiterate; he certainly knew what he was talking about. He argued his case with great conviction, but he did not know how to conserve his strength. Yet his address was a masterly attack on his adversaries, moving, persuasive, passionate and with interludes of humor. He dominated the scene. He asked the leadership to consider the organization as a whole and not to act for a party, whatever its majority. He said that he took the floor to protect Herzl's legacy from being dissipated, to save "the sacred pence of the poor." He defended the integrity of the Bank in London and in Jaffa. He recalled how hard it was to get together the capital to establish the Bank, how it lacked the confidence of the banking fraternity and how it slowly acquired a certain prestige which should not be frittered away. He said that his health was poor, that he did not know how long he could continue, but he was determined to be present at the Congress, to save the Bank and to prevent it from becoming the football of party strife.

The sentiments of the Congress were with him. They forgot all that had been said by the able speakers who preceded him. They arose in applause and the session had to be adjourned. It was felt that Wolffsohn had vindicated his cause, that he had established a human relationship with the opposition, which he had never done before.

It was Wolffsohn's bad luck to be too loyal a follower of Theodor Herzl and at the same time a Zionist whose love for Zion could not be hemmed in by the formula of the Charter. It was his bad luck that he had to be loyal to Herzl, which meant to be loyal in defense of Herzl's policies, while the trend of history demanded a new orientation, the synthesis of work and political effort. It was his misfortune that he could not inspire the spirit of partisanship among his friends, that he himself was no partisan and therefore found himself standing alone as Herzl's disciple while the Movement and himself were being forced by historic circumstances to take another road.

He was a friendly, generous man. Whatever fortune remained with him at his death he left to the movement and to Palestine. He was a fatherly man, taking over the guardianship of Herzl's children and providing for them while he lived. He could not see himself as a leader in a movement in which party advantage had priority over its larger interests. He passed away before partisanship became the rule of conduct in the Organization to which he gave his best. He died as the opening guns of the First World War shattered the world in which he lived.

from Herzl to Balfour

The dynamism excited by Herzl was exhausted when he came to the Sixth Congress. The East African offer was the last card he was destined to play. He had turned from door to door, seeking in vain the Archimedean point on which to base the Movement to which he had given life. In an enigmatic figure of speech in his *Diaries* he said: "Great things need no firm foundation. An apple must be placed on a table so that it should not fall; but the Earth swims in space; the secret is to be found in movement." He may have been playing with the idea that it might be possible for Zionism to get along for a time without *terra firma;* that he need not be overtroubled about a specific land. But whatever his thought may have been, he finally arrived at what seemed to be a formal exit from the dilemma of a territory in the blind alley of East Africa.

Not for a long time were Zionists again to be quickened by the excitement of discovery. Not for a long time were they to experience the sensation of touching the fringes of the garments of the Messiah. The glamour and the excitement were on the wane. Their sights were lowered. Zionism grew in substance, in dimensions, in complexity and color; but it moved at a slow pace, with shoulders braced for a long pull. It was prepared for a dull prosaic existence and waited for the ultimate miracle which would have to come some day.

The East African project died in Herzl's stiffening hand. In due course, it was pushed off the agenda. The first Congress after Herzl's death—in 1905—pondered the report of a commission of experts sent to explore the territory. The two Jewish members rejected it as a suitable territory for Jewish colonization. The English member was of the opinion that in time and with patience it might accommodate about 20,000 settlers. That should have dismissed the subject. But the Russian Zionists were determined to extirpate every trace of the territorial heresy. They organized themselves for a long relentless siege. Their preparations for battle were excessive beyond reason. In fact, the East African offer was dead even before the discussions in the Congress were registered in a vote. The English themselves were not as keen as they appeared to be when the Foreign Office made its offer. However, the controversy within the Zionist ranks outlasted the relevance of the problem. Israel Zangwill, a fervent supporter of Herzl, made an "ideology" of territorialism and set out to win adherents. His brilliant advocacy was not successful, for he was not adept in political debate and thought more of a striking phrase than a persuasive argument. Nor did he understand how to approach his opponents. The more he talked, the more the Russians were convinced that he was indeed a *goy* trained in *pilpul,* who by accident had wandered into a Jewish movement.

The Russians won the verdict of the Seventh Congress, reaffirmed the Basle Program and rejected any form of colonization beyond Palestine and its vicinity. It brushed aside the British offer and laid it on the table indefinitely. But the issue remained a thorn in the side of the Zionist leadership for a number of years. Zangwill and his partisans seceded from the Congress and initiated an organization which continued a running fire against the Zionist Movement from a distance. The Zangwill group set forth to locate a territory for Jewish settlement anywhere in the world. They were ready to consider any reasonable offer, but they never found a suitable territory and dwindled down to a Movement in miniature and decided to send Jews for settlement in Galveston, Texas. Some of the territorialists returned to the Zionist fold. Many of them, loyal to the memory of Herzl, spent their time heckling the Zionist leadership, and used their devotion to Herzl to punish those who had not been loyal to him while he lived. They intended never to forget that sin.

The novelty of the Zionist Congress wore off and the glow of its first years could not be restored. Congress sessions became normal calendar events, occasions for stimulating the propaganda of Zionism in the Diaspora. The Zionist leaders lost their skill for the dramatic, and the formalities of parliamentary action cramped their style. The mood of looking for miracles vanished. Many Zionists who had been fascinated by the personality of Herzl lost their keen interest. They lived on the memories of Herzlian Zionism which seemed to have lost its meaning, but they had reason enough to find fault with Herzl's successors on general principles. They returned to their normal pursuits and flared up only whenever Herzl's name or ideals or slogans were mentioned. Many of them were chagrined, perhaps, because they had been taken off guard by the glamour of a dream or the fascinations of a dreamer. They were still political Zionists, but the dream was a cliché, not a definition—a manner of speaking. In fact, work in Palestine became the order of the day without a charter or legal guarantees, even without a plan or blueprint.

The pogroms in Russia Herzl feared finally came soon after his death. In the light of subsequent Jewish history, they were insignificant. They raised the immediate fears of Jews for a brief period; they stimulated Jewish charity and organization; but had no lasting effect on political events. They brought to life a Jewish reaction favorable to solidarity that had not been present before, but the Jewish question was not raised through them to the level of an international problem. Zionism had a long way to go to that end.

Of greater significance was the Turkish Revolution, which broke the empire through unseating the Sultan and placed the Goverment in the hands of the Young Turks, who undertook a revolution on modern lines. The Zionists welcomed the Young Turks and their revolution. They anticipated that the new regime would be reasonable with the nationalist aspiration of the Jews, that they would welcome peaceful infiltration of Palestine by Jews. They were mistaken. The Young Turks resisted every form of supporting Zionism and were jealous of their sovereignty. They did not intend to give freedom to any minority except under strict control. Their own native Jews were resentful of the attempt to segregate them as Jews and were opposed to the intrusion of Jewish nationalism in their domestic affairs. The Zionists took counter steps to influence the Turkish Jews. In 1908, they opened a branch of the Jewish Colonial Trust in Constantinople with Dr. Victor Jacobson in charge. Several French periodicals were subvened. At the 9th Congress in 1909 David Wolffsohn said that Zionism was compatible with loyalty to the Ottoman Empire, and gave assurances that Zionist objectives would be pursued in harmony with Turkish law. This was a fatal impairment of the charter idea. Surprisingly, Dr. Nordau also shared the view that the charter idea was no longer useful or necessary or relevant. He argued that there really was no need even to amend the Basle Program, for its text had no reference to a charter. Although these explanations made no impression on the Turks, they had the effect of modifying the waning conflict between the practicals and the politicals in the Movement. In fact, all party differences on this score were apparently washed away by the realities of life. Dr. Weizmann's formula, enunciated in 1907, which was called "synthetic Zionism," was generally accepted as a statement of indisputable historical fact. It was something all Zionists could live with. Furthermore, there was nothing else in sight to absorb their interests or their loyalties. They could no longer live on verbal abstractions. They developed new party differences which were highly interesting and provocative of dialectical entertainment. They quarreled about Palestinian projects. But the earlier disputes were passed over in an agreed silence, broken only by the echoes of the old controversies.

The problem of the Jewish State perforce took a back seat; but the foundations of the organization and the beginnings of

the Jewish settlement were laid in this period which seemed
barren of political significance. David Wolffsohn did not allow
his affection for Herzl to violate the habits of a man of affairs.
He knew the value of credit at the bank. He cherished the
title of merchant. He adhered to the slogans of political Zionism after Herzl's death largely as a matter of piety, but was
drawn closer to the program of work in Palestine. It is difficult
to understand why his opponents had less prejudice against
Herzl (the alien) than against Wolffsohn (the *Litvak*). Wolffsohn was from first to last a member of middle-class society and
should naturally have been found in the ranks of Russian
Zionists. But throughout his life, the Russian Zionists carried
on a vendetta against him. From 1904 to the beginnings of the
First World War, when Wolffsohn died, they were determined
to eliminate the symbol of the Herzlian legend if possible. The
more devoted Wolffsohn became to the practical ideas connected with Palestine, the more determined they seemed to be
to give expression to their rejection of Herzl by rejecting his
successor. But they were the inevitable heirs of Wolffsohn's
practical efforts in the fields of organization and finance.
When he died, there was a substantial estate to take over
which they never acknowledged in adequate terms of appreciation.

He made the Cologne office the active headquarters of an
international organization, not a personal bureau as it was
under Herzl. Nahum Sokolow, an outstanding personality in
the Hebrew renascence, became its secretary. Dr. Berthold
Feiwel was the editor of *Die Welt* and the manager of the *Juedischer Verlag*, Dr. Max Bodenheimer, Wolffsohn's friend,
headed the Jewish National Fund. The Zionist Congress assumed the features of a permanent institution. Wolffsohn was
personally interested in the management of the Zionist funds.
He avoided sensations and dramatic appearances, political adventure and prophecy. On several occasions he ventured into
the field of political action but confined himself largely to the
obvious steps that could be taken by a sensible person to acquire economic and cultural positions in Palestine.

In this formative period, Dr. Arthur Ruppin, a German economist, was attracted to Jewish work in Palestine. He became
the administrator of colonization and industrial enterprises. He
was the planner of the Zionist work, the central directing
agency in all economic endeavors. From 1907 until his death
in 1943, Dr. Ruppin was the theorist of Zionist practical work.
He had a keen vision, a deep sense of responsibility, rare intellectual integrity and an unusual talent for interpreting the
plans he had in view for the development of the land. He was
not a partisan. Economics was his profession. When he first
went to Palestine, he was not even an avowed Zionist, but
gradually and thoroughly became the master of the facts in Palestine, which he endeavored with skill and intelligence to
shackle to the Zionist cause.

He reported in 1913 that when he first traveled through Palestine as a tourist in 1907, what depressed him most was the
lack of energy and courage in the colonies. He described the
condition as premature age. The colonies were on the average
20 years old. Those who had once as young men founded the
colonies had been worn out in hard and futile labor, and the
succeeding generation was missing, for the youth had not inherited either their parents' enthusiasm or their hope for gain
and many of them left to seek their fortunes in the towns or
in foreign lands. Many colonies looked just like homes for
the aged, Ruppin reported. He was convinced that there was
only one thing that could improve matters. The colonies would
have to be regenerated by new young enthusiastic Jews from
Europe.

Reinforcements came to Palestine in 1905 in the form of the
Second *Aliyah,* which left a permanent impression on the future of the Yishuv. These were young Jewish workers from
Eastern Europe who had lost their hope for freedom under the
Czars after the pogroms and the suppression of the first revolution. They were inspired by collective ideals. They made
"work" their religion. They wanted to recapture national traits
lost in the Diaspora. They were determined to find their future
in the Promised Land, and it was to be a future unlike the
past. They were not welcomed by the Turkish authorities. A

substantial number emigrated from Palestine. Those who remained endeavored to find work in the Jewish settlements, but
the early settlers preferred Arab labor, which was seasonal and
therefore cheaper. The newcomers contrived their own forms
of colonization and forced the Zionist organization to come to
their relief.

Dr. Ruppin centered his interests in the Palestine bureau
which began operations in Jaffa in 1908. It is surprising what
he was able to do with a meager budget. The income of the
Jewish National Fund was at his disposal, but it was always
insufficient. He established the Palestine Land Development
Company as the central land purchasing agency for all Jewish
interests. The company acquired large tracts of lands, prepared
them for cultivation, divided them into small holdings, provided water and laid the roads. Through this agency, cooperative land purchases by other Jewish concerns were regu-
lated. The company took over the management of several
colonies. It organized the founding of the city of Tel Aviv,
neighboring the old city of Jaffa. It aided in the development
of the Herzliah Gymnasium, the first modern high school in
Palestine. The Bezalel Art School was founded by Boris
Schatz, with American Zionist support.

The outlines of the Promised Land began to appear. The
Zionists became aware of the difficulties of their national task.
They had been preaching Zion and Promise and Redemption
for over a decade with a dim appreciation of the land that
had to be redeemed. For the first time they saw the people
who were to be their neighbors and felt the hatred directed
against them and prepared themselves to grapple with defense.
They saw Arabs divested of legend in the clear light of day.
They drew upon their memories of Zion from the Bible, from
the Talmud, from the modern romances written by new writers and saw that the present had no points of identity. The
propagandists and orators in the Diaspora carried the message
of rebirth to the distant lands, where ignorance of the realities
of Palestine was dense, and indulged their fancies to their
hearts' content, fearing no contradictions. Small groups of

pioneers spread out over the land, collided with the Arab peasants, jostled them in the city streets. They had to deal with Turkish officials and learned the ways of bribery. They settled in the Jordan valleys and worked the ancient roads and began the building of villages and cities. The dedicated Jewish workman and farmer appeared. The cooperatives dug deep into the soil and clusters of green trees marked the places the Jews intended to make their homes. The Jewish *Shomer* on horseback was silhouetted against the sky, taking his chances with Arab marauders in the dark of night. Soon, oases of labor and culture became visible in Galilee and in the Sharon with the help of the Jewish National Fund. Tel Aviv grew with amazing rapidity and excelled Jaffa in every respect—in size, culture and the amenities of social life. An agricultural experimental station was established at Rehovot, supplementing the school at Mikvah Israel. The first cooperative colony founded in 1909 was Merhavia; it was initiated and directed by Franz Oppenheimer, a well-known German economist. In this colony the workmen received fixed wages. It was directed by an appointed manager with whom the workmen could not agree. Soon, however, Merhavia became a cooperative which seemed destined to become the most appropriate colonizing form of settlement for the Jews in Palestine. Franz Oppenheimer came to the United States to speak of the ideals of Merhavia and to collect funds. Then the *Moshavim* appeared and other colonies based on individual enterprises were developed. The Jewish National Fund undertook large-scale afforestation and became responsible for the planting of trees in every available section of the country. Plans for a Hebrew University were being discussed.

Under the influence of the Second *Aliyah,* the Hebraic elements in the colonies, and the pioneer work in Hebrew development of Eliezer Ben Yehuda, a network of Hebrew schools was established in these years. A technical institute was built in Haifa which became the center of a foreign language controversy, through which Hebrew was forced into the educational program, and from year to year the influence of Hebrew as a spoken language penetrated the life of the Jews in

Palestine. There were about 60,000 Jews in Palestine in 1904.
Their number was estimated at 85,000 in 1914. These were the
roots from which there grew a new political situation. It was
always Dr. Weizmann's thought that if the "things" were provided, a reflection of them would be revealed in political situations.

The Balfour Declaration was the climax of this period of
development. It was not a promise of a Jewish State. It marked
the birth of a new form of national life within a prescribed
autonomy. It gave the recognition of the Allied Powers to the
historical connection of the Jewish people and the Promised
Land. It placed a seal of approval on what seemed to be
Herzl's *end-ziel*. As the war was coming to its conclusion, it
seemed to most Zionists natural and even predestined that
England would take the initiative in a political situation in
which it could exercise effective leadership, not only because
it had sentimental and religious interests in the Return but because it looked forward to the opportunity to enter the field of
the Middle East, for which it had been preparing. The
breakup of the Turkish Empire was inevitable, and the question was who would occupy the vacuum and replace the authority of the Turks; who would take over a region largely in-
habited by Moslem Arabs? During the war, England sought to
enlarge its social and political connections in the area. The
Turks were allied with the Germans. The Arabs were not
united, and their national spirit was below par. England was
able to find only one Arab connection of value. Due to the
efforts of Lawrence of Arabia, a mysterious Englishman who
was alleged to have enormous power over the Arabs, the
friendship of the sons of Husein, the Sherif of Mecca, later
the king of the Hejaz, was won to England's side. Their military support was negligible, but the significance of their
friendship had a large influence in the Middle East. England
made liberal and even contradictory promises to both sides
as was its wont in such situations. The French were its rivals
in Lebanon and Syria and had to be eased out of the situation.

The Arabs and the Jews were both tools with which it could operate.

The friendship of Joseph Chamberlain extended to Herzl was related in a vague way to the general interest of England in the future of the Jewish people. The return to the Promised Land was a familiar theme in England's liberal and religious circles. England was the land of the Bible. *Daniel Deronda* was written in English. The Earl of Shaftesbury urged the Jewish restoration in 1840 but found no support in government circles. He returned to his hobby in 1876 and noted the growing bond of union between the Jewish people and Palestine. Herzl's first political efforts were directed to Germany. He thought of the ambitious young Kaiser; but soon realized that he was an unstable symbol of interest in the Jewish people. Herzl realized that when war would come—as was expected—England would be called upon to take the lead and would lend itself without too much persuasion to thoughts of the Promised Land. His love for and interest in England were reflected in the fact that although educated in law in an Austrian university, he insisted that the Jewish Colonial Trust and the Jewish National Fund be incorporated as English companies. He frequently used English legal phrases. In 1898 he wrote to the English Zionists:

"From the first moment I entered the Zionist Movement, my eyes were directed towards England, because I saw that by reason of the general situation it was the Archimedean point where the lever could be applied."

The knowledge that England was considering the Jewish problem also evoked an interest in Germany and its allies. The Germans thought that it would be wise to endeavor to win the good will of the *Ostjuden* and Jews in general, by promising Jewish national rights in Poland and in other lands to the east in which Jews were numerous. A Zionist committee was organized in Germany which, with the support of the Government, sent emissaries and propagandists wherever it was thought possible to reach neutral Jews. Such a propagandist found his way to the United States.

From the beginning of the war, Jews in neutral lands sympathized with the Germans because of their remembrance of Russian persecution. They did not want Russia to win. In the United States, Jews were pro-German until the negotiations with regard to the Balfour Declaration were initiated and became known. The committee in London was headed by Dr. Weizmann, who took the lead in the discussions and formed an influential committee of Zionists and non-Zionists, English and Russian Jews and some of the leading English statesmen. A neutral office had been established in Copenhagen which acted as a propaganda center for both sides of the war front. In the United States, representation of the Zionist cause was taken over by the Provisional Zionist Committee of which Louis D. Brandeis was the chairman. After a considerable amount of negotiation, formulas presented and rejected, new formulas being considered, opposition ideas being laid on the table, at long last, on November 2, 1917, the Balfour Declaration was issued in the form of a letter signed by Balfour and addressed to Lord Rothschild.

> I have much pleasure in conveying to you, on behalf of His Majesty's Government, the following declaration of sympathy with Jewish Zionist aspirations, which has been submitted to and approved by the Cabinet:
> "His Majesty's Government views with favor the establishment in Palestine of a national home of the Jewish people and will use their best endeavors to facilitate the achievement of this object, it being clearly understood that nothing shall be done which may prejudice the civil and religious rights of existing non-Jewish communities in Palestine or the rights and political status enjoyed by Jews in any other country."
> I shall be grateful to you if you would bring this Declaration to the knowledge of the Zionist Federation.

It was the first authentic political success of the Zionist Movement. It expressed sympathy with Jewish Zionist aspirations and favored the establishment in Palestine of a national home for the Jewish people. It pledged England's best endeavors to facilitate the achievement of this object.

The Declaration had a difficult road to travel before it was validated as the Mandate and issued to England by the League of Nations. By that time peace had revived old ambitions and reminded the peacemakers of old scores they had forgotten to settle. The war had just been put to sleep. The agreement made by Dr. Weizmann with Prince Feisal was soon broken, and the Arabs were engaged in civil war and especially in violent behavior toward the Jews settled in Palestine. Opposition developed in England and in the House of Lords, which rejected the declaration. As the Mandate finally emerged in 1920, it differed substantially from the terms of the Declaration. The vision of the first act was doomed by what followed. It became necessary for Lord Balfour to appeal to the Arabs not to "grudge that small notch in what are now Arab territories being given to the people who for all these hundreds of years had been separated from it." Most of the amendments to the Declaration were incorporated in commentaries on it in the Mandate and in the White Paper which was issued and bears the name of Winston Churchill. The White Paper dismissed the rumor that Palestine was to become as Jewish as England was English. It reassured the Arabs that their language and culture would not ever be subordinated to a Jewish majority. It said that it was not contemplated that Palestine as a whole should be converted into a Jewish National Home but that such a home would find a place *in* Palestine. It kept Jordan under the jurisdiction of the Mandate but excluded it from the Jewish National Home and in effect created a new Arab state under the domination of the English. Thus, a throne was provided for another son of the Sherif of Mecca.

In a conference with an Arab delegation about that time, Churchill rejected their demands to annul the principle of a Jewish National Home. He said it was right for the Jews to have a national home and reminded the Arabs that they had been freed from the Turks by British arms and that a Jewish success would be good for all the inhabitants of the land. In May 1921, after an attack by the Arabs on the Jews of Jaffa and vicinity, Jewish immigration was stopped.

Despite the mutilation of the original purpose of the Dec-

laration and the Mandate, it gave the Jewish people an opportunity to develop the National Home in Palestine under the
guardianship of England. Having guided the negotiations with
all parties concerned, Dr. Weizmann's leadership was assured.

The Mandatory Government was the first school in which
the Jewish people were prepared for statehood. They had their
struggles with High Commissioners and Administrators of Government. They acquired political acumen and experience in
dealing with the Colonial Office. They learned the art of preparing memoranda for the Mandates Commission of the League
of Nations. Their temperament was subdued by their contacts
with the British. They acquired a sense of national responsibility. Zionism in the Diaspora followed the example of their
leaders in Palestine in developing public relations with their
fellow citizens and the governments of which they were citizens. They learned how to conform to protocol and diplomatic
forms. They learned how to apply their democratic procedures
to political conversations. They learned how to build a National Home under corporate and collective responsibility.
From a scattered group of colonies they became a federation
of colonies. They recovered the soil through the National
Fund. They learned how to establish farming villages and how
to deal with the problems of economic life, how to make labor
pay, how to defend their property and their rights. They
learned how to provide the budgets which were so essential
in the building. The National Home was prepared under the
roof of the Mandatory regime, which gave it slight protection
in times of storm but was an adequate formal defense at all
times, enabling the growing organism to flex its muscles, to
use the intelligence of its citizens to enlarge the scope of its
endeavors and consistently to win with the years an ever
larger Jewish and non-Jewish support in the Diaspora. It was
the House of Refuge which was prepared to receive the refugees from Hitler's barbarism when the time came. But there
was no force on earth, Jewish or Christian, that was able or
willing to intervene to prevent the massacre of 6,000,000 Jews
which preceded the birth of the State of Israel.

their successors

IN EUROPE

CHAIM WEIZMANN (1874–1952)

From his earliest years—as a boy in Cheder—Chaim Weizmann was bemused by Zionism, the Promised Land and the Return. He lived in an environment where Jewish life was the only atmosphere in which one was free to breathe. Whenever he left home to study elsewhere he always returned, certain of finding the rich family life of his people, as if no interval of absence had intervened. He followed the growth of Zionism at first merely as a student, a debater, a critic, a member of the audience. But from the days he caught hold of the political threads in England until the day of his death, he was the only man who identified himself with the burdens of leadership and who regarded Zionism as the inescapable center of his life. He was a member of no party. He was sensitive to all the ills of Zionism like a mother to the ills of her growing child. He was perplexed and worried by its problems. He looked ahead and never saw the end of the road. His scientific training forced him to think that his tortured people had a long way to go to reach even the shadow of the goal of freedom. Who could tell how many generations? He thought of the Movement as a process of planting seeds of national life in the

*ancient homeland and in the hearts of the Jewish people in
the Diaspora. Quality was as important as quantity. Patience,
creativeness and sacrifice were of the essence. He was the
guide and protector. Ever after I crossed the ocean and saw
with wonder the new life Zionism had brought to the ancient
soil and heard the voice of Weizmann in Vienna, in London,
at Zionist Congresses through the introductions of Shmarya
Levin, he guided my life in the support I was able to give to
his struggling leadership—its successes and failures. He remained faithful no matter who was faithless. Not that what he
did was always wise, not that he always spoke with strength
when strength was required, but he was the symbol of the
struggle and the carrier of its burdens. In office or out of it he
could be relied upon to do his utmost, to do his best, to endure.
He was always true to himself and on great occasions often rose
to heights as if he were the reincarnation of the spirit of Jewish
prophesy.*

The grand tradition of Zionist leadership was restored by
Chaim Weizmann. He was not a disciple of Theodor Herzl. In
his early days he had no faith in diplomacy or the quest for a
political charter. Unlike Herzl, he did not have to return to his
people from alien ways of life. He was born in the heart of
the Galut. He was at home among his people. He knew their
languages and traditions and shared their hopes. He studied in
Jewish schools—from the *Cheder* to the Yeshivah. He was
never estranged from Jewish life. He experienced the traditional love for Zion from his earliest days. His childhood was
enriched by the memories, the legends, and the mystic hopes
associated with Jerusalem and Zion.

He was nurtured in a normal Jewish home only slightly
touched by alien culture. He was one of a brood of brothers
and sisters who left home at an early age to complete their
education abroad. He was one of the many Russian students
who departed from their homes to study in Germany and Switzerland. From his youth, he had an irresistible ambition to become a scientist. While in Switzerland he joined in the long
drawn-out debates between Mensheviks and Bolsheviks, be-

tween Jewish Bundists and Zionists. He missed being a delegate to the First Zionist Congress; but at the Second Congress
he was one of the leaders of the Democratic Faction and became known for his wit and audacity as a debater. In a mild
way he was a follower of Ahad Ha-am. He spoke of youth and
culture. He participated in literary movements but was not a
writer. He prepared a program for a Hebrew university to be
established in Palestine. He was a lieutenant in the Russian
Zionist group of which Menahem Ussishkin was the leader.
He was Jewish in gestures and manners, in his way of speaking.

His destiny led him to England, where he cultivated tact
and dignity and the value of understatement. In the course of
time he became the friend of political and intellectual leaders
in England. He was a stranger to the English way of life, but
proved an apt pupil. The Zionists of England resisted his influence for many years. They were Herzlian Zionists and regarded him as one of the group responsible for the miscarriage
of the Uganda project; the man who had crossed Herzl in the
Congresses. He made a deep impression, however, upon the
young men of England and was welcomed by the Yiddish-
speaking community and acquired a place of distinction in
Jewish and Zionist circles, where he was appreciated for his
original contribution to Zionist discussions. He became known
in Germany, in Austria, in Poland and in Rumania, and his
name was carried over to the United States.

His leadership matured when he took over Zionist affairs at
the time when the Balfour Declaration was under discussion.
He was spurred to action by the imminence of Israel's recognition in an international covenant; when it became possible,
for the first time, for the Jewish people to undertake the building of their National Home. He was the leader of the Zionist
forces during the entire period of the Mandate.

I remember Dr. Weizmann at the Vienna Congress in 1913.
He gave the impression of studied indifference to what was
going on around him. He was easily bored. He was still the
promising young man who had joined in debate with Theodor

Herzl at the first Congresses and with the followers of David Wolffsohn. As chairman of a Congress sub-committee, he was called upon to settle internal disputes and to bring in a list of nominations. The writer was a member of that committee. Dr. Weizmann's rulings were a study in temperament. He was impatient with *pilpul* and sharp in procedure. He had a mordant sense of humor. He was scheduled to address the Congress on the Hebrew University. The imperious Ussishkin took the ball from his hands, announced the beginnings of a fund, and Dr. Weizmann's *referat* was a matter of academic interest. The older men dominated the caucuses. Dr. Weizmann stood in the rear of the hall, his eyes half closed, listless. He was a ready debater and liked to speak; but in Vienna there was no drive in him. He seemed to be listening and waiting. There were few intimations of the coming war. The burden af all speeches was: Get along with the work in Palestine as best you can. The last I remember of the Vienna Congress was the tired appearance of Dr. Weizmann reporting the nominations at the end of the Congress.

The First World War projected Dr. Weizmann into the political field. The Zionist leadership was scattered. Dr. Weizmann moved into the vacuum without opposition, for he was in control of the political situation in London. He had been meeting the men who were to mold the immediate future of England and of the world. He touched a sympathetic chord in the mind of Arthur James Balfour. He stirred the imagination of David Lloyd George who believed in the prophecies. He made a lasting friendship with C. P. Scott, the editor of the *Manchester Guardian.* He won the cooperation of H. L. Brailsford, a journalist who thought that England's imperial policy should include Zionism. He had acquired friends in France. Together with a group assembled in London, and with the cooperation of American Zionists led by Louis D. Brandeis, he carried through the long and tedious negotiations of the Balfour Declaration to their final issue.

By now he was a distinguished chemist who had made an important contribution to the conduct of the war. His early

years in England had been spent in privation. His reputation
as a chemist became known in England and France. His
success had freed him of financial worries. The Weizmanns
now maintained a commodious home in London where many
distinguished personalities of the political and scientific world
found hospitality. He was in a position to absorb himself completely in Zionist affairs. His public utterances in England revealed a stately approach to the Jewish problem and commanded world attention. He was conscious of standing on a
high platform. He was no longer listless and indifferent. He
had banished the trivial and spoke as if the Jewish cause were
using him as its medium. He made the impression of a man
prepared to walk a long distance.

His leadership was confirmed at an international Zionist
conference held in London in 1920. The democratic structure
of the organization was revived and revised there. It was a re-
union of the survivors of the war. Max Nordau, the majestic
voice of the early Congresses, came from his exile in Spain.
Otto Warburg, no longer the affluent member of a great family, came from Berlin. The Russians did not know where they
belonged in Soviet Russia, or in Palestine, or in the limbo
of any country that would receive them. They were represented by Ussishkin, the Goldbergs, Naiditch and Zlatopolsky.
Yechiel Ischlenow died there. Nehemiah de Lieme represented
the Dutch Zionists. There were Stricker and Boehm from
Austria. There were about forty Americans led by Louis D.
Brandeis.

England was prepared to accept the Mandate, but the building of the Jewish National Home was to be the responsibility
of the Movement. The miracle of propaganda was to be followed by the even greater miracle of securing the manpower
and gathering the material resources for the task of creating
the National Home. The funds of the Jewish Colonial Trust
could not be used for hazardous enterprises. The meager resources of the Jewish National Fund were limited to the
redemption of the land. There were no reserves. In London,
the Keren Hayesod was founded. An appeal was issued to

world Jewry. The level of giving was raised. The era of fund collecting set in. A tremendous wave of popular excitement passed over all Jewish communities. The funds raised, however, were always inadequate. There were chronic deficits and strange bookkeeping procedures. Dr. Weizmann had to devote himself to the continuous grind of collecting funds in every part of the world. He became the most effective of all Zionist propagandists.

American oratory has its own standards. Foreigners do not appreciate it. It stems from the rough and ready West. Its dependence upon sound suggests the open spaces. Dr. Weizmann did not qualify as an American orator. His voice was not resonant. He had few gestures. He used no groping introductions or exalted perorations. He hated the impersonation of emotion. He had no ear for the rhythmic phrase. He acquired the English gift for understatement. He did not propagandize himself as a person. He was not made for stage effects.

In spite of these limitations, no Jewish speaker ever made the same deep and lasting impression—even in the United States. Dr. Weizmann spoke as if his words were the issue of suffering. He made the impression of a murky flame that had to be fanned to give heat. Shmarya Levin had burning passion; Sokolow was a master of brilliant narrative and analysis and of sly humor; Ussishkin took his audience by storm with sledge-hammer blows; Bialik spun exciting ideas and fascinated his listeners with figures of speech that did not require form to make them live. Dr. Weizmann had none of these qualities. He established an identification of himself with what his words were trying to convey. He seemed to be able to capture the wisdom of Jewish life. He drew his thoughts out of an invisible responsibility. There was prophetic significance in his phrases—a mystery striving to explain itself. There was a stateliness in his speech which was unique. He seemed to speak ex-cathedra for the silent Jewish people. He was their interpreter and advocate. A cause had found a voice for a people emerging from the clouded past and demanding justice from the modern world.

He grew with his responsibilities. His personality acquired
stature. It was formed by his intimacy with Jews the world
over, as well as by his adjustments to the non-Jewish world.
He sensed difficulties before they appeared. He was over-
cautious. He never took refuge in formulas or programs. He
coined many formulas but threw them away with great uncon-
cern. The return to Zion was indeed a vision of redemption,
but it had to be worked out in the terms of hard reality. It
was the longing of a people scattered in exile to be free and
to be Jews in their own land. Whither these longings would
lead them could not be foreseen or foreshadowed. The road
would be hard and the directives never clear. It was the business of the leader to avoid the dogmatic phrase and not to
allow illusions to lead action. All slogans had to bend as the
strategy of the movement demanded. To be controlled by
definitions and clichés and nostalgic sentiment would be fatal.
Time was not of the essence; growth was.

One of the most dramatic episodes in his life—and histori-
cally of the greatest importance—was the American conflict.
Zionist opinion in the United States was divided in its support
of the Keren Hayesod (Palestine Foundation Fund), upon
which the Jewish agency depended for the initiation of the
new tasks offered under the Mandate. No Zionist agency could
operate without funds. Dr. Weizmann had no reserves. The
future of the Movement was tied up with the American conflict. It involved the authority of leadership, the traditions
of the organization and the possibility of meeting a budget for
the work in Palestine. Dr. Weizmann was called upon to carry
the issue to the United States for settlement in public discussion. He was a man of compromise and peace. Yet, his
credentials as leader had to be vindicated and established in
an area of open dispute and controversy.

When Dr. Weizmann entered the waters of New York Bay
in the spring of 1921 to launch the Palestine Foundation
Fund, the controversy was in full bloom. The breach with
Mr. Brandeis, scarcely apparent in London, had been widened.

A bulky record of misunderstandings had been piled up. There were letters and memoranda, and messengers going to London and returning with grim reports. Eventually, the two sides seemed to be speaking different languages. The issue was forced when Dr. Levin initiated a Keren Hayesod campaign without the approval of the American leadership, who believed that by holding the purse strings of the largest Jewish community in the world—which they thought they could control—their views should be taken into account regardless of votes at congresses or conferences.

But the masses of American Jews were not controlled by such views. In fact, they were prepared to meet Dr. Weizmann as the victor in a movement which had brought recognition of the age-long Jewish hope. He had helped to make the dream of Herzl a political reality. They gathered at the Battery and awaited the moment when he touched American soil. They cheered him on his way to his hotel, lingering in the lobby for him to appear. The largest mass demonstration ever held in New York greeted him when he was given a public reception by a national committee. These audiences were not impressed by the debate. They were impressed by the historic facts Dr. Weizmann symbolized.

When he spoke to them he saw before him not a fractional part of Jewish life but a microcosm of all Jewries. He saw more Jews from his home town than he had ever seen in Motele or Pinsk. These were the relatives of the Jews of Vilna, of Warsaw, of Bucharest, of Krakow and of Vienna. They were waiting for him to speak and they would rise and greet the historic opportunity he would describe. They were thirsting for his words. A leadership that could not speak to them in the language they understood, that persisted in going its own way without considering their feelings, prejudices and ideals, would not be able to lead them in the great period of building. These Jews declined to raise any barriers between Zionists in America and Zionists in Europe. They were not aware of any double loyalties. They had become Zionists through the passion of their leaders in Russia, in Poland and in Rumania. They had not been separated from other Jews

by time and distance. They were not the lost tribes of Israel.
They were kinsmen who had wandered from home and who
had found freedom in a new land, but they remembered their
origins.

Dr. Weizmann might have accepted compromise and let
time settle the issues, but Palestine could not wait. The
Americans wanted to negotiate and Dr. Weizmann felt that
he had no authority to negotiate. He was dealing with a
challenge to the organization maintained intact from Herzl's
day as the corporate responsibility of the Zionist Movement.
To have departed from that line would have created two
Zionist centers, two Zionist authorities, two Zionist funds,
and thus would have made the task of the Jewish Agency
impossible.

There were peacemakers who sought to adjust differences.
There were turbulent conferences. At times it looked as if
Dr. Weizmann was about to yield, but his resistance was
stiffened by pressures from London and Jerusalem and by his
colleagues in New York. He was faced by a man who had
great qualities of endurance, who had fought a powerful
railroad group with amazing tenacity, who had evolved his
own idea of how Palestine should be rebuilt, and who would
not easily be deflected from his course. Mr. Brandeis seemed
unable to appreciate what the democracy of the Zionist Movement meant in terms of economic resources. He seemed to
have in mind a planned economy for a people not yet organized, for whom a land had to be prepared, who did not
have to be consulted as to what kind of a home should be
built for them. His hand was not being forced by time and
need.

In the last analysis, American Zionists did not go along
with him. They were not impressed by his American experience. By an overwhelming majority they repudiated the position taken by Mr. Brandeis and his friends and elected a new
leadership. Following an un-American tradition, the defeated
party retired from the organization, abandoned the struggle
and awaited the time when their cause would be vindicated.
It never was.

In the course of years, with great patience and skill, Dr. Weizmann led some of the dissidents of 1921 back to active Zionist service. But his aim was the winning of the philanthropists and assimilationists. Mr. Brandeis had won a number of such converts, but they were not in the leadership of Jewish communal life. The American Jews could be reached only through their responsible organizations, which were growing in influence and resources. Their leaders, however, maintained the traditional opposition of the Reform movement. The implications of Zionist ideology alarmed them. However, when President Wilson gave his approval of the Balfour Declaration and a joint resolution of the American Congress accepted it, the same desire to be loyal to the United States led them to greet the Declaration and to approve of Palestine as the Jewish National Home. Tremendous popular excitement prevailed. There were parades and mass meetings. The Balfour Declaration was regarded as a great historical event. The prejudices of the past—especially against Zion—were softened, but the Zionists were by-passed. The ideal was ignored but the fact was accepted. The armor of many non-Zionist reform rabbis was pierced and their hearts were touched. They now became friends of the Land. Nathan Straus, the big-hearted humanitarian, was interested in several Palestine projects. Samuel Untermeyer, the corporation lawyer, became the head of the American Keren Hayesod. The aging Jacob H. Schiff, the militant, outspoken opponent of Zionism, publicly reversed himself and expressed his faith in Palestine as a Holy Land, the center of Jewish religion.

The new trend toward Palestine gave Dr. Weizmann the opportunity to push forward with his proposal for an enlarged Jewish Agency. He found a powerful friend in a man of strong convictions who was regarded as the leader of the non-Zionist group. Louis Marshall was a distinguished American, but unlike Mr. Brandeis, was deeply involved in Jewish communal affairs. He was the chairman of the American Jewish Committee and an officer of the Jewish Theological

Seminary. He was stubborn and had strong prejudices; but he could be persuaded by reason. He was greatly influenced by his contact with Jewish leaders when he went to Paris as a member of the American delegation to the Versailles Peace Conference.

He was a provincial in the best sense of the word. He was born in western New York. His home town was Syracuse, where the smell of hay filled the streets and farmers came to market in the center of the city. He knew how the city lived —what its merchants, farmers and workmen were thinking of. In fact, all his life he remained uncontaminated by the large city in which he rose to eminence as a lawyer. When he was once convinced of the justice of a cause he became its partisan.

Dr. Weizmann found in him a loyal friend and a stubborn supporter, without whose influence and aid he could not have succeeded in winning non-Zionist cooperation in the Jewish Agency. Marshall was the spearhead of the Movement. He drafted most of its legal documents. He was responsible for its constitution—a rigid, unworkable instrument. He solved many of its legal difficulties. He defended the work of his hands with vigor and enthusiasm. In 1924, he said:

"It is no longer a theory but a condition that confronts us. The Balfour Declaration is no longer a mere pronouncement of one nation. It was adopted by the Peace Conference as a part of the Treaty of Versailles. It has been set in motion and effectuated by the League of Nations . . . We are no longer confronted with the question as to whether this should have been done or should not have been done. It is an achieved fact. The question is whether the Jews of America who are not Zionists should remain indifferent to the situation which exists, the continuance of which is guaranteed by the action of the Great Powers, and which has the endorsement of the Congress of the United States. We have no right to be indifferent . . ."

Dr. Weizmann brought the non-Zionist delegates to Zurich in 1929, when the extended Jewish Agency was formally established. That was a scene without parallel in Jewish history. The leaders of the Jewries of the world were present on its platform. It awakened high interest through the world. The Zionists met in their Congress and—with difficulty—ratified the constitution of the Agency. Then the non-Zionists followed suit; the American non-Zionists uniting with non-Zionist groups from all parts of the world. Finally, both sections met, and with impressive exercises all agreements were sealed.

The year 1929 saw the beginning of a rapid deterioration in international relations so far as Palestine was concerned. The Passfield White Paper was the first of the black papers which recorded the obvious effort of England to escape its obligations under the Mandate. The Peel Commission in 1937 proposed the partition of Palestine. The failure of that proposal led to a final effort to adjust relations between Jews and Arabs at a conference held in London, and then came the act of desperation known as the White Paper of 1939.

Under these circumstances, it was impossible to develop the Jewish Agency or effectively to engage the non-Zionists in the affairs of Palestine. The riots of 1929 not only shocked the neophytes, but the death of Louis Marshall left them bereft of leadership. Felix M. Warburg, his successor, was a genial, sympathetic sentimentalist who had no inclination to lead and was embarrassed by responsibilities. Mr. Marshall might have saved the Jewish Agency. He knew how to work with men. He had the patience and intellectual skill for negotiation and adjustment. He might have solved the problems of geography involved in an international council with members scattered over three continents. Such non-Zionist leadership did not emerge in the hectic period following the 1929 riots. The extended Jewish Agency disintegrated.

The survival of any leadership through such a time would have been a miracle. Dr. Weizmann had a way of carelessly stimulating opposition. He loved to indulge in wide-range speculation. He tested his theories in formal and informal meetings. He saw the long road ahead and engaged in imagi-

native fabrication of future events. He realized that Jews had
no power to restrain a world bent on self-destruction. He saw
the beginnings of the march of Italian fascism; he saw Japan
invading its Chinese neighbor without interference; the Nazis
growing in strength, power and arrogance; he saw the
League of Nations disbanded. There were no defenders of the
right. The free world was in retreat.

How would the Jewish National Home fare? Would full
betrayal be preceded by a Palestine partitioned or by a bi-
national state? Dr. Weizmann weighed these prospects and
vacillated in his choice of one of the two evils. He thought
we would have to live through the storm and make the best
of a crumbling world. He was prepared to maintain, on the
barest minimum of national existence, the Sanctuary that had
been set aside for the fulfillment of the ancient hope. He had
faith that another day would come, no matter how dark the
night. He believed in struggling for the Return, no matter
how narrow the road to freedom would become, how thin
the line would be worn down to, for Justice would triumph in
the end. You had to live through the night.

But this was not the temper of the Movement. It did not
want to be reconciled to what seemed to be the inevitable. It
felt that its frustrations and despairs should be registered in
its leadership. Unable itself to act in the arena of public
life, it wanted its leader to be vocal above the din of conflict.
It was willing to take out in sound and fury what it could not
give expression to in action. It was exasperated by immobi-
lized faith. It refused to make terms with reality. It rejected
the peace of supineness. It began to develop its underground
fighters. The thoughts of youth were turned to violence and
vengeance. The leadership became the scapegoat of this dilemma and thus, in Zurich, in 1931—two years after the
establishment of the Jewish Agency—Dr. Weizmann was
forced to retire from office.

The futility of his retirement was reflected in the fact that
Nahum Sokolow, Dr. Weizmann's close associate during the
entire period of the Mandate, was named as his successor.
Morally as well as politically, however, Dr. Weizmann was

the leader during the four years he was not President of the
Organization. He retained his office, his desk and his secretary
at 77 Great Russell Street. He went to South Africa for the
Keren Hayesod. He became the head of the *Aliyah* of German refugees. He appeared at the World's Fair in Chicago.
He absented himself from the Prague Congress in 1933. In
1935, the organization had no alternative but to recall him to
leadership.

His return meant the acceptance of the crown of martyrdom. It revealed the unseverable roots that bound him to the
destiny of his people. The Movement was the heart of his life.
He knew that a hopeless situation faced him. The lights
were going out in the world. It was to be a war, total in its
effects. Engaged in that war would be the fighters at the front
and the civilians at home. All the rules of what used to be
called war would be ignored. The aggressor would risk everything on the gamble of the winner taking all. In such a war,
fought under such conditions, the Jews would not find friends,
or protection, or even a semblance of security. They would
be the first to be sacrificed. Their rights would be the last to
be considered, for the free world was engrossed in the problems of its own survival.

Dr. Weizmann resumed his difficult journey. He made his
memorable address to the Royal Commission and received the
proposal for the partition of Palestine. He saw the failure of
the Arab-Jewish discussion at the St. James Conference. He received the White Paper of 1939. He endured the intolerable
administration of a High Commissioner who had determined,
in spite of the tragic circumstances of Jewish life, to enforce
the White Paper. He saw English officials turn Jewish victims
of the war away from the welcoming shores of the Promised
Land to perish in the sea. He saw the failure of every political
mission he undertook. He was called upon to witness the destruction of his people and the disinclination of all professing
friends to come to their rescue. He knew that he was waiting
in the anteroom of history, that the door might not even be

opened. He was unable to hear the conversations that were being held in camera, and did not even know that the fate of Israel was deliberately being bypassed.

He clung to the Rock of his Faith. The validity of that Faith was revealed in what Jews had achieved in Palestine during the years of the struggle in connection with the Mandate. He had always felt that freedom would come through self-liberation, and that the masters of the world would be asked to contribute only free passage to freedom. Here was the great demonstration:

Along the narrow path of a shrinking Mandate the National Home had become visible, potent, colorful and exciting. Its 85,000 in 1914 became 600,000 in 1944. The malaria-ridden pioneers had produced a generation of youth that had gone out on the battlefield to die for the honor of the Jewish name. Dead cities had been given new life, new forms, new hope. The eastern shores of the Mediterranean were dotted with night lights that carried a message of resurrection to all parts of Europe and Africa. The dead soil had been fertilized by the sweat and blood of thousands of Jewish pioneers. A great university had been established on Mt. Scopus, a center of a network of Jewish high schools, technical institutes, agricultural schools, elementary schools and kindergartens. The Hebrew language had come to life, singing the songs of Rebirth. When the war came, these victims of a cruel world had become the builders of an arsenal of great resources which they placed at the disposal of the Allies. They even had to fight for the right to fight under their own flag, but nevertheless fought bravely on every battlefield.

At the age of 70, clear of mind, vision dimmed, but firm of body, he waited to see his faith in statesmanship justified or sealed in frustration for decades to come. England, which had made the Promise, had plunged into a state of utter forgetfulness of its greatness; giving way to the pressure of evil spirits; fearful of arousing its youth to the inevitable arbitrament of force; conniving with the chicanery of diplomats; and almost wholly forfeiting its place in world affairs. He lived to see the bankrupt leadership of Neville Chamberlain supplanted by the personality of Winston Churchill, in whom England renewed its strength, recovered its hold on its heritage; and summoning all kindred forces of earth to rally against the enemy, finally drove that enemy into the shambles of defeat and dishonor. Dr. Weizmann had suffered for his faith in England. He was derided for it. He was humiliated when England was contemned. Now, his hope was that through Churchill a new England would emerge from the silenced battlefield.

Dr. Weizmann could not rid himself of his tradition and his habit of relying upon England, but again his hope was wrecked by the government which took power in England after the war. It was not headed by Churchill. The leaders of the Labor Party, however, were committed to the hilt to the cause of the Jewish people. They were fellow-travelers of Zionism for two decades. They had spoken of their friendship and written of their friendship, but within a few days of taking office it was evident that their purpose was to continue the White Paper of 1939 to its bitter conclusion. They did not have the moral courage to support their convictions and their pledges. Ernest Bevin was the symbol of their perfidy. He was an unfeeling man, a brutal opportunist, discreditable not only to the English Government but to the honor of that England which had given life to the Balfour Declaration.

Thus ended Dr. Weizmann's faith in England. He gave up his British citizenship, his home in London, his friends in England, and settled in Rehovot, finding escape in the great work of the institute which bore his name. He left the Zionist leadership at the Congress of 1946. He appeared as a witness at the Anglo-American Commission hearings in Jerusalem. He participated in the deliberations at the United Nations. He completed his memoirs. The State of Israel was proclaimed in May, 1948. He became its first President. He last visited the United States in the spring of 1949. He was an invalid in the last years of his life and died in 1952.

The Jews pouring into the free State of Israel vindicated his faith in Zion. The Zionists had rejected his leadership of peace and patience and restraint. They had refused to wait on good-will and brotherhood and took up arms to meet arms, violence to meet violence, brutality to meet brutality. Weizmann was the builder of the Homeland, but they won its freedom with blood and sacrifice, and made the emergence of the State inevitable. They raised the flag of Zion over the New Jerusalem their hands had built and their arms had defended. They defeated their enemies in battle and forced the acceptance of an armistice. They began the building of the State and opened its doors to the hordes of refugees from Europe and Africa and Asia.

In the long fitful reveries of his sickbed Dr. Weizmann saw a free generation of Jews, their roots deep in the soil, their arms at attention, prepared to go forward valiantly with the redemption of Israel, down the long and difficult road of national rebirth. The dream of his youth was being fulfilled in his own age. He never really expected that to happen. He was not pleased with the national trend. He was frightened by the speed of its growth. He never thought that his eyes ever would see the reality of the Jewish State—but there it was. He could see it (when his eyes were good) from the window of his home in Rehovot.

By his own choice, he was buried, not in Jerusalem, but in Rehovot, the child of his Vision, which he had designed as the creative center of Israel's future.

NAHUM SOKOLOW (1860–1936)

Nahum Sokolow was a pioneer in Hebrew literature and equally prolific in Yiddish, Polish and German; but he maintained an attitude of aloofness toward the Zionist Movement which made the early Zionists suspicious of his sincerity. At one time he contributed to Polish as well as Hebrew journals; in his Polish work he wrote little of Zionism, and with his usual graceful style in the Hebrew press but avoiding commit-

ments. *He was the one Zionist in all Poland who carried off the illusion that he might be a Polish nobleman. His manners were impeccable. He spoke Yiddish with a Polish accent and seemed to have no genuine interest in Jews as a mass, but only in such Jews who achieved the credentials of Hebrew learning or social prestige or wealth. He was in effect a perfect specimen of a diplomat, bordering close to the type of the familiar* Shtadlon. *He was older than Dr. Weizmann and had a recognized position in the world of letters when Herzl first came to the Jews. But he hesitated too much and too long in deciding whether he should go along with Herzl or with the Russians. He always found it difficult to land his thinking on a firm decision. He had a low opinion of the reliability of the Russian Zionists—he, who could talk for hours and entertainingly, thought the Russians impractical because they talked too much. He regarded Dr. Weizmann as a talented young man, but was never reconciled to the idea that his colleague could conduct a proper diplomatic conversation with statesmen. Dr. Weizmann was always too young for him, and he was sure he could never overcome the handicap. Before the Balfour Declaration, it was Sokolow who talked to the French and Italians and had an official conversation with the Pope, which was also done by Herzl. He never got over the disappointment that Dr. Weizmann—and not he—should have gotten close to important English statesmen who sponsored the Jewish National Home. He could not imagine how Dr. Weizmann was able to do this. Nevertheless, Dr. Weizmann was always the president and he was always the chairman of the Executive Committee. His lingering ambition was satisfied when he succeeded Dr. Weizmann as president in 1931, but his victory came too late and lasted too briefly. He costumed his activities in the conventional garb of diplomats and never missed a point of propriety or protocol. He enjoyed life best when he moved in an atmosphere of diplomatic deportment. He was capable of serving Zionism in many fields, but made the mistake of wanting to keep too many fires actually burning at the same time, with the result that he missed greatness in any one field.*

Nahum Sokolow was in the Zionist leadership for many years, but always gave the impression of being a "fellow traveler." He spent the larger part of his early life in Warsaw and from his youth, as an infant prodigy, he was an integral part of its domestic affairs. He was a prolific Hebrew journalist and wrote equally well and voluminously in the Yiddish and Polish press. He knew many Jews of diverse intellectual interests and was the center of many Jewish discussions. When Herzl appeared on the scene, Sokolow decided to go along with the Herzlian stream only after long and cautious deliberation. He went to the First Zionist Congress as a journalist and there was persuaded to become a Zionist. He was not a man to get himself excited too quickly. He had measure and calm. He seemed to lack passion. He maintained a calm demeanor to the end of his days.

When he took the plunge and became a professional Zionist, he offered his services to David Wolffsohn, the successor of Herzl, taking over the editorship of *Die Welt* and the secretaryship of the organization. He went to live in Cologne, the seat of the Zionist administration. He went with Wolffsohn to Constantinople in 1909 on a political mission. In fact, he could not be held down to a seat. He liked having a roving commission. He traveled extensively and made friends for Zionism among prominent men of letters and politics. He did not have to remain in Cologne to edit *Die Welt,* just as later he did not remain in Berlin or London to edit *Haolam,* the Hebrew organ of the movement. Although a protege of David Wolffsohn, he did not hesitate to join the Russian Zionists in overthrowing him. At that time he was the one Zionist—aside from Victor Jacobson—who could boast of some experience in political affairs. Victor Jacobson was left to concentrate his attention on Constantinople. The rest of the world seemed to belong to Sokolow.

Sokolow was one of the members of the Zionist Executive who found himself in London at the outbreak of the First World War. Other members were marooned in middle Europe. Shmarya Levin was in New York. When Dr. Weizmann began his negotiations with the British Cabinet, a committee was formed in London to consider the proposed statement of the British Government. It was inevitable that Sokolow should be a member of the group. He could name with familiarity dozens of leading European statesmen.

It is a curious fact that throughout Dr. Weizmann's long career as a political leader he was destined to have Sokolow as his partner. They were jointly representative of Zionism in the political field. This was not agreeable to either party. Dr. Weizmann disliked the double-headed leadership and the incongruous combination. He felt that Sokolow was a little too easygoing in his political conversations, that Sokolow was too much of a *raconteur;* he put too much emphasis on manner and too little on substance. On the other hand, Sokolow, who was the elder, placed no great reliance on Weizmann's skill or knowledge of history. Dr. Weizmann, in his view, was a novice in the field of politics; Sokolow had knowledge and experience. He felt that Dr. Weizmann also lacked *savoir faire.* He never would concede that Dr. Weizmann's personality, such as it was, was an important asset and that his different method had its own peculiar value. But the two men managed to get along with each other, each in his own field, each in his own manner, each with his own limitations and rare qualities. Dr. Weizmann won lasting friends in the political field. Sokolow helped to maintain friendships. The one was serviceable in the Anglo-Saxon countries; the other had his value in France and Italy.

As journalist and political representative, Sokolow was urbane, unhurried and sagacious. He never could be forced into a partisan position. He was always found in no defined position at all. In any alignment of opinion he never could be claimed by either side. He held himself in reserve and when the talk warmed up and he had time to think the matter over, he was prepared to come to the rescue of the disputants and suggest a workable compromise, thus restoring order and peace. This led to the charge that he never knew his own mind and had no convictions of his own. This was unfair, for on a number of occasions he was able to make the best defense of policies for which he had assumed responsibility. He was by nature even-tempered and judicial, and hated quarrels. In the growing party disputes which gave Zionism its colorful effects he was above the battle, not as a pretense or convenience, but with sincerity. That was why he seldom failed to find a middle course which was attractive to both sides. He once explained: Why should the partisan who hurries to a conclusion be credited with principle because his mind is easily prepared and runs fast? That was no virtue. He believed that the principle of restraint was more important and that it was better to be guided by prudence than by emotion.

He lacked temperament as a speaker. His blood pressure seldom rose when he spoke. He liked to talk in a conversational tone of voice. On the rare occasions when he lost his balance he made the impression of hollow emotion. But his addresses always had form; he had the light touch of a feuilletonist; his universal knowledge was always on tap; he was always good-humored and pleasant to listen to. He rejected rhetoric and dramatic points. Even his speeches to raise funds were sprinkled with apt historical allusion and anecdote.

He was an extensive traveler and was never discommoded by any form of transportation. He went by sea or plane or train with indifference. He was never known to be seasick on the roughest sea, and in the midst of a storm could be seen jotting down his notes for the encyclopedic dictionary he was writing the last years of his life. When over seventy, he made trips to South Africa and the United States. His home was in London where his motherly wife awaited him in spite of the fact that he was seldom there.

Sokolow visited the United States for the first time in March, 1912. He spoke at a mass meeting in Boston, at which Mr. Brandeis appeared for the first time as a Zionist. It was he at that time who tried to interest Mr. Brandeis in an investment corporation. This was, indeed, a strain on Sokolow's versatility. Mr. Brandeis thought it queer, too. When he reported on his talks with Mr. Brandeis at the Zionist Congress in Vienna that fall, some of the Socialist delegates interrupted and shouted: "This is no place for *reclamen*." He came over in 1922 with

Vladimir Jabotinsky and Dr. Alexander Goldstein to conduct the Keren Hayesod campaign. The American Zionists had introduced a joint resolution in Congress, endorsing the Balfour Declaration. The resolution was adopted and signed by President Harding. Both Sokolow and Jabotinsky frantically urged American Zionists to withdraw the resolution; they were sure it would be defeated. Such fears could be expected of Sokolow, but not of Mr. Jabotinsky. They were in good company, however, for Dr. Stephen S. Wise and Judge Julian W. Mack also condemned the American Zionists for taking such a rash step. It was indeed rash, but there were really no difficulties. The resolution of 1922 served as an important political document. In subsequent years it was pointed to as the authentic record of the Zionist policy of the American Government, which was continued with varying interest by all subsequent administrations.

When Dr. Weizmann resigned his office in 1931, having been refused a vote of confidence, Sokolow, who was his collaborator for over a decade, agreed to accept the presidency and was elected to succeed Dr. Weizmann. Sokolow found himself in a very difficult position. Dr. Weizmann had resigned, but he was still regarded by Zionists the world over as the Zionist leader, and Sokolow remained, as heretofore, one of the sagacious representatives of Zionism who was not destined to reach the height of practical leadership. Early in life, he was regarded as an Elder Statesman. These embarrassments did not faze Sokolow at all, who went along as usual, making hard trips to various lands for the Keren Hayesod, leaving the work to the secretaries, but always insisting upon all the titles which were his. He carried these titles with dignity for four years, when Dr. Weizmann was recalled to the leadership.

Sokolow was adroit and impressive and sagacious in political conversations with European statesmen with whom manner and form seemed important. He made a number of visits to the Vatican and was on good personal terms with some of the learned scholars who had influence with the Pope. He met

American presidents and secretaries of state. His memory of persons, their public achievements, their personal idiosyncrasies, was accurate and comprehensive, and full of vivacious description. He would often astonish his listeners with appreciations of off-the-record foibles of people he knew. In discussion he was not profound, but he had a light and easy touch. All history was at his command. All literature and gossip and anecdote seemed to float into his memory and stay there, and he suffused all his knowledge with a wisdom that left a lasting impression of a charming gentleman. He practiced a French style after leaving Poland and settling in London. He dressed the part he played with meticulous attention to detail and to the etiquette of social and political relations. He often wore spats and a monocle. It was his privilege often to close a Congress in full dress. At the Prague Congress, he waited in his diplomatic uniform from ten o'clock at night to nine the next morning, emerging fresh and debonair to make the closing speech.

He was a remarkable writer in many languages. His mind wandered over a wide field; his memory of the written page was amazing, and everything he thought of he put into a book. He wrote a textbook on natural geography in 1878. He wrote a history of anti-Semitism in 1882. He wrote a historical novel in 1883. He wrote a geography of Palestine in 1889. He wrote a treatise on Baruch Spinoza in 1929. He wrote a book on mass psychology in 1930. He published essays on personalities in three volumes. He wrote a two-volume history of the Zionist Movement in English, with an introduction by Arthur Balfour. He is said to have written over forty-five hundred articles and thirty books in Hebrew, Yiddish, Polish, German and English. He was the first Hebrew journalist to introduce the feuilleton. He edited *Hatzefirah* from 1884 until the First World War. He was the founding editor of *Haolam* in 1907, which was continued and concluded in Jerusalem by Moses Kleinman. Bialik, the Hebrew poet, once said that if you gathered together all the books Sokolow had written, it would take three hundred camels to carry them away.

He grew old with grace. The man who wrote volumes upon

volumes and was known everywhere as a scholar and an author of political history, in the last years of his life accepted a degree of Doctor of Hebrew Letters from the Jewish Institute of Religion in New York and ever after insisted that he be called Doctor Sokolow. He was proud of being president of the Jewish Agency and also president of the Palestine Foundation Fund. He insisted on occupying the best suite of rooms in the hotels he visited, not because of personal comfort or ostentation, he said, but anything less than the best was a derogation of his official position. He had to radiate affluence in order not to put the Jewish Agency to shame. For years he suffered from diabetes and had to be taken care of by his devoted daughter and companion Selena, who was a physician. He died in London on May 17, 1936. After a long delay—the State of Israel had passed its eighth anniversary—he was buried in the Promised Land.

Sokolow contributed to the Zionist Movement a clear understanding of its ideals, with the ability of communicating them to non-Jews. He had an encyclopedic mind and an ease of manner which had a soothing effect upon all those whom he tried to persuade to accept Zionism during its more hectic days. He maintained his dignity and prestige until the day of his death, a remarkable product of the Hebrew renascence and the modern Zionist Movement. It was aptly said of him that he was born an *Illui*, but never became a *Gaon*.

MENAHEM USSISHKIN (1863–1941)

Ussishkin always had the reputation of being a "man of iron will." He usually came forward as the last participant in a debate, when his views stood up against the whole assembly. He was also noted for strong and enduring antipathies. He had far-reaching ambitions which were invariably frustrated because of his rough disregard of the views of others, thus creating for himself walls of opposition that had nothing to do with his theories. He had a great reverence for Jerusalem and looked down upon Tel Aviv as a reflection of an upstart polyglot Galut creation. He was fanatically Hebraic but seldom quali-

fied in the taste of the elite either as a writer or speaker of Hebrew. He was chock-full of grammatical errors in every language he knew. At first he suspected the motives of Herzl and rejected his leadership; he resisted Herzl's influence with implacable energy; but he was soon reconciled to Herzl's leadership when he learned of his devotion, his lofty vision and his unseverable attachment to Israel's hopes. In spite of the limping languages he used, however, his presence in a debate dominated the discussion and what he said—not how he said it— made the deepest impression. By nature he was a tyrant, but off the stage he was a man of simple tastes, and with a thrifty sort of friendship. He seldom was able to get rid of prejudices of a personal nature. This was true not only of Herzl but also of Tschlenow, who was his rival in Russia, and, who, to his last day, was the object of Ussishkin's antipathy. He thought that Weizmann was too easygoing, too loose in language and prone to compromise. Strange to say, he had a genuine affection for Jabotinsky. He was an outstanding figure in the Zionist Congresses. He was the dominant personality in Russian Zionism. He made a slight impression in the United States when he came here with Weizmann in 1921. He was not a theoretician of Zionism. He was, however, one of the strongest pillars of Zionism on occasions of conflict or controversy. He was the head of the Jewish National Fund in his later years and lived in Jerusalem, where his home attracted all those who esteemed and respected him for his great services to the cause and for his obstinacy in defending his views.

Menahem Ussishkin was a Russian of the old school. He looked like a rugged Cossack and behaved like a medieval boyar—a challenger of czars. There were many obstinate Zionists in the early days but none had his arrogance. He was rude and despotic, paternal and sentimental; and humor never touched him. He liked to throw a bombshell of blunt dissent into a debate and defied the majority to overcome his vote. What opponents did or said never disturbed him in the security of his own views.

Ussishkin settled in Palestine when the Bolshevik Revolution overwhelmed the bourgeoisie. He would have been at ease with the Czar or with Kerensky, but he could not abide the Communist dictatorship nor would they have been pleased with him once they got into their dictatorial stride. He left before they had screwed up their courage to undertake wholesale purges. He came to Palestine as the head of the Zionist Commission (1920). Had he been asked he would have said he could not stomach the Arabs or the English. He ignored them both as long as possible.

To his way of thinking the English had no business to be in Palestine at all. God had made a promise to the Jews and there was no need for the English to endorse the promise or help to fulfill it. The Arabs were the Ishmaelites; obviously they had no share in the covenant, and they should be made to know their place. When he was asked in those primitive days to wink an eye at the softening of the petty Arab politicians in Jerusalem with coffee and cake in the cafes—as the primitive beginnings of Arab-Jewish relations—he turned down the suggestion with hot indignation. He dismissed the young corrupters of Arab morals from his office and told them never to darken his door again. That they never did. They were his enemies for life. As far as he was concerned he would have no truck with the British at all. He tolerated them. He wanted the whole of Palestine, on both sides of the Jordan, and nothing less. He would never agree to a bi-national or federated state in Palestine. He wanted the Land of Israel as established in Jewish tradition and would make no compromise with that sacred dogma.

But he managed to live through all these difficulties in spite of his prejudices. He lived in his own world of tradition and was never disturbed by the clash between his austere views and the realities of the life he had to lead in Jerusalem. Herzl may have thought of Haifa as the great international center of the future Jewish State. Ahad Ha-am, Bialik and Shmarya Levin preferred Tel Aviv. But Ussishkin planned his future in Jerusalem and became the dogmatic partisan of the primacy of the Holy City. His eyes flashed anger when anybody mentioned any other Jewish center as comparable to Jerusalem.

He resented the pretenses of Tel Aviv, the upstart city built on sand. There was nothing holy about Haifa. His sanctuary and his fortress was Jerusalem where he lived until he died in 1941.

This man of granite seemed made to rule. That was what he thought, too. He had the nature of a czar whose opinions issued in the form of edicts. He was deadsure that he was always right and no one else could be as right as he. But he found no kingdom at hand to rule. He had his Zionist origin in the slow-paced days of *Chovevei Zion* in Russia. Pinsker was its ideologist and leader, and Ussishkin was the heir-apparent, who never took over the succession. He was a follower as late as 1906. He greeted Herzl with doubts and reluctant admiration. He could not be expected to welcome Herzl with open arms, for how could a man so alien to the Jewish way of life lead the Return? He had no faith in any *Daniel Deronada*. Grudgingly he came with the Russian Zionists to the First Congress and challenged Herzl from the start. They heckled him month after month, year after year; Herzl had a trying time with him all his Zionist days. Ussishkin was the chairman of the Charkov Conference in December, 1903, which threatened a revolt unless Herzl undertook "in writing" to abandon the East African scheme and confine himself exclusively to Palestine. They struggled for a voice in the affairs of the Vienna Committee. They attacked Herzl's *Altneuland* for its views on Hebrew, for its misunderstanding of the quality of their Zionism, for not perceiving that the new Zion must witness a Jewish rebirth; not a Zion on a German base. But when Herzl at the Uganda Congress vowed never to forget Jerusalem, Ussishkin forgave all his mistakes and paid him tribute in a gracious speech. But he never overcame the feeling that Herzl was not exactly the anticipated leader. He suspected that he himself might have filled the bill with better results, but that history had passed him by. That was his fate.

Ussishkin also resented the leadership of David Wolffsohn, who was a Lithuanian Jew and knew Yiddish and Hebrew, and the Jewish way of life. Wolffsohn was suspected because he had transferred his allegiance from the Russian Jewish world to the German. Wolffsohn was too much the businessman, although Ussishkin was somewhat of a merchant himself. Wolffsohn was not a fanatic about Hebrew or nationalism or Zion. It is true Wolffsohn made one of the first gifts to the Hebrew University and was always mindful of his responsibilities toward Hebrew literature. Subconsciously, however, Ussishkin felt that there was something about Wolffsohn which invalidated his leadership. He was too much political and too little practical.

The same pattern of relationship may be discovered in Ussishkin's attitude toward Yechiel Tschlenow, his Russian rival. Tschlenow also stood in Ussishkin's way; he was the soft, persuasive, friendly man, devoted to any task he assumed, modest and humble. Ussishkin was no conciliator, no hand-shaker. In a pinch the choice was always Tschlenow in preference to Ussishkin. When Wolffsohn finally retired, the political combination produced Tschlenow in the Executive—not Ussishkin—and it was Tschlenow who was present in London when the Balfour Declaration was under discussion.

That historic moment found in Chaim Weizmann, the young chemist, the leader to take over Herzl's heritage in what appeared then to be the consummation of Zionism. In Ussishkin's eyes Weizmann was a novice, too easygoing, not firm enough, too eager to make friends with the English, too diplomatic and not aggressive enough. The curse of the situation was the English language, which Weizmann knew and which remained a secret code to Ussishkin all his life. He nursed a grudge against Weizmann, which only his honesty and integrity forced him to modify on many occasions. He came with Weizmann to the United States in 1921 and aided in the struggle for the recognition of the Keren Hayesod. He was a member of the Zionist Executive for a while and finally passed over to the chairmanship of the Jewish National Fund, which became the main Zionist front he defended for the rest of his life with an amazing concentration of purpose and possessive-

ness. For there he was, for the first time, the undisputed master
of a situation. He was the defender of the *Land* of Israel.

He wanted to be known—in those days—as the Redeemer of
the Soil. Dr. Arthur Ruppin and Joshua Chankin, the pioneers of the National Fund, were shifted into the background
and Ussishkin stood out after all his years of service, after the
death of all his political ambition, as the man who did the
most to acquire the land of Israel as the everlasting possession
of the Jewish people.

He was all of one piece, in private and on public view. On the
platform or in committee he was dogmatic, thrifty with words,
hard to alter once his views were expressed, and lacking in the
social graces, unable to turn a corner with good humor, nursing
grudges with great consistency and fervor.

Ussishkin spoke Russian, Yiddish and Hebrew, and a sort of
German, but in none of them did he stick to syntax or to the use
of words in their proper relations. Nevertheless, he was capable of great passion in speech and often touched heights of
classic oratory excelled by none of his contemporaries. In his
home he was the lord and master but capable of deep affections, always thoughtful of the interests of his family. He was
generous and considerate of others but his prejudices were
formidable. His love for Zion was unshakable. It was the obsession of his life.

He was still the head of the Jewish National Fund when the
Second World War came. Weizmann had offered Zionist
cooperation to the British in spite of the White Paper of 1939.
Palestine was being threatened by Rommel from the west. The
Arabs had laid down their arms before the war began. They
defended none of their cities. They waited for the conqueror
to enter, ready to receive him with open arms. They had all
their flags ready to be unfurled the moment Rommel entered.
Ussishkin could not oppose the offer of Weizmann to help defend Palestine. He had to admit that Hitler must be fought
with all available allies.

The whole of Palestine was in a state of excitement, con-

scious of revolutionary changes, anxious about what the revolution would bring and eager to put themselves in the vanguard
of those changes even if they and their children would die in
defense of their rights. The larger number cooperated with the
British. A group of determined Irgunists fought the British.
They all feared civil war with the Arabs who, in frustration,
might have turned against the Jews, but Ussishkin was no
longer physically able to participate in that struggle. He had
spoken for the last time at the Zionist Congress in Geneva in
1939. He died before the State was proclaimed. Had he lived he
might have raised his voice against the partition of Palestine.
He would have stood alone with God against that sacrilege.

SHMARYA LEVIN (1867–1935)

*The profile of Shmarya Levin which follows is inadequate. It
does not reflect, as I recall, the personal side of his influence
upon a generation of American Zionists. The larger part of his
life was spent with us, when he was mature and we were groping youngsters. He was a Messenger of Emancipation—equally
known in Russia, in Germany, and all of Eastern Europe—but
we had the impression that he was most at home with us. His
whole life, it seemed, was an endless tour except for the years
he gave to us in his last years and in Palestine. His first appearance was connected with his career when a member of
the Duma, which we made the most of. But he was the catalyst
of Zionism in many segments of our society, even among those
who protested that they were our opponents. He was on close
terms of friendship with Julius Rosenwald, visiting him in
Chicago as his guest at his place of residence, which was called
Tel Aviv. He was a companion of the professors at the Hebrew
Union College and the Jewish Theological Seminary. His passionate, colorful speeches and conversations fascinated many
who rejected the dynamism of his ideas. He was one of the
earliest advocates of the leadership of Chaim Weizmann, for
whom he had a special affection he never disguised and never
lost. He often spoke of himself as Weizmann's forerunner. He
was with us when the war erupted and it was our good fortune*

*that the ship on which he left for Europe was turned back and
he had to spend the war years with us. His authority as a member of the Zionist Executive was utilized to call the Provisional
Zionist Committee into being, and he had the privilege of
traveling with Mr. Brandeis on his first speaking tour. Dr.
Levin often wondered at the intuitions of the great man of
American Law who had missed being born in a Jewish environment. With Dr. Levin, I escorted Bialik on his first trip to the
United States. The poet was sick all the way over. Shmarya
rushed about the decks looking for a chess partner and marveled at Bialik's amazing resources in curse words garnered
from Hebrew literature. Shmarya was never an orator at Congresses. He was often discounted as a Maggid, but on his own
platform, with his own audience, he had no peer. He did not
like controversial political talk and avoided it. He played chess
not as one seeking perfect moves or games. He played to while
away the time, and insisted on playing fast, and was impatient
when any player mooned over the board as if the best move
was of any importance. He was a sick man many years before
he left for Palestine. He had to speak often while in great pain,
and he was impatient with friends and guests on such occasions. He knew he was going home to Zion to die and was prepared to spend the rest of his days near Bialik, playing chess
with General Wauchope—kibitzing his way along. But his
work was cut out only for the Diaspora. In fact he was always
on vacation in Zion and felt that he had nothing to do there.
He brought his daughter Anna with him to the United States
on several occasions. She resembled him in many ways. She
was married and died in Palestine at an early age. His son,
Boris, is a practicing chemist in Israel. It was Shmarya who persuaded me to leave the editorship of the* American Hebrew
*forty years ago to enlist in the Zionist Movement. I shall al-
ways remember him for that with gratitude.*

Shmarya Levin was one of the great preachers of modern
Zionism. He was a pre-Herzlian Zionist of the Pinsker school.
He carried Zionist thought to many parts of the world. His
public career began in Russia where he was one of the pioneers

of the Jewish renascence. He spent many years in Germany and developed a school of intellectual and political disciples who were the leaders of Zionism in Germany and Austria. He came to the United States soon after the Kishinev pogroms and was the inspirer of a whole generation of American Zionists. He ,was not merely a propagandist; he was a teacher of great ability who drilled his ideas into the minds of his audiences with eloquence and force, with wit and humor. He was a vigorous writer in Yiddish and Hebrew, but he loved speaking best. Nor was his speaking confined to the public meeting. He practiced his art with extraordinary vivacity in the drawing room and in cafes, where he drew eager listeners to his conversation.

He was born in Russia in 1867 and received his early education in Jewish schools and in a secular school. He studied at the Universities of Heidelberg and Berlin and after receiving his doctor's degree, returned to Russia where, from 1896 to 1906, he was a "government rabbi" at Grodno, Ekaterinoslav and Vilna. He was elected a deputy to the first Russian Duma and was a member of the liberal Cadet Party. His powerful addresses in the Duma made him known to all Jews who read the Yiddish and Hebrew press. He was one of the signers of the Viborg Manifesto, protesting against the Czar's dissolution of the Duma, which made it necessary for him to leave Russia for good. He established his home in Berlin. He won the support of the *Hilfsverein der Deutschen Juden* in 1908 for the Haifa Technical Institute in Palestine and then became the leader in the language controversy when the German organization wanted to use the Haifa Technical Institute for the promotion of the German language. It was as a deputy of the Duma that Levin first came to the United States.

Levin became a member of the Zionist Executive in 1911. It was as one of the leaders of the Zionist Movement that Levin came again to the United States in 1913. He was marooned in the United States during the period of the First World War. He initiated the organization of the Provisional Zionist Committee of which Louis D. Brandeis was the chairman. When the war was over, Levin returned to Berlin but visited the United

States repeatedly in the interests of the Keren Hayesod. Levin
was responsible for launching the first Keren Hayesod campaign in the United States. He was a member of the Weizmann
delegation to the United States in 1921. He induced Bialik,
the Hebrew poet, to visit the United States with him in 1923.
He was always talking of Zion, but his work and his interests
kept him in the *Galut*.

He was the teacher of a whole generation of Jewish educators and Zionist officials. His schoolroom was the lecture
platform. He had no textbooks or charts but delivered his message in impassioned, illuminating addresses on all the Zionist problems of the day. He was able to make what he said
glow with fire and passion. He was a master of invective and
sardonic humor. He was remarkable in castigating his own
people for their lack of vision, their disinterest in organized
action. He was savage and relentless in his indictments. He
was capable of terrible anger. He excited his audiences with
his descriptions of what was being done in Zion—it was not
much then—and how it was transforming the Jewish personality. No other Zionist propagandist gave as much as Levin to
the spirit and intellectual life of American Zionism.

He was not noted for his addresses at Zionist Congresses or
meetings of the Actions Committee. He spent most of his time
at Congresses in the lobbies or coffee houses. He was disparag-
ingly referred to as a *Maggid;* and that he was. But he surpassed many a Congress orator in his ability to excite the
mind and spirit of his listeners and to persuade them that what
he was saying was an echo of what they would find in their
own hearts if they would only search for it.

He had none of the tricks of oratory. When he came to
the end of what he had to say he stepped back off the platform.
He would start his discourses with a stray observation and
slowly find his way to his central theme, rushing along at top
speed to drive home the idea which had burst into expression.
He was like a spraying fire reverting to old thoughts and
finding a new form for them, giving them forth as a new

revelation. Old thoughts and old stories always were given new life in his repeated addresses. Whatever he said sounded as if it had just been thought of.

He was an agitator in a literal sense. He provoked thoughts and feelings against the will of his listeners. He was angry with Jewish life, and like Bialik, felt humiliated by Jewish indifference and lack of self-assertion. He was a panegyrist of Zion and spoke glowingly of the sprigs of new life that had appeared. He exalted the work of the pioneers, but glowered upon those who clung to the fleshpots of Egypt. He made the few green spots in Zion look like the beginnings of great forests; but did the Jews of *Galut* really deserve those green spots? He brought with him a nostalgia for all things Jewish. He was able to find Jewish quality in many things gathered under the moss of *Galut*. Zionism was the preserver and protector; it was the builder of the Temple of the Jewish future. The world had covered Jewish life with indignities and humiliations; the emancipation would drive Jews into assimilation and extinction; Zionism was the destined liberator.

He came into our American life to burn out the unclean. His voice would break through formalities and tear apart the pretenses and shams of the contented, the indifferent, the short-visioned, the ignorant. He was always a wanderer, never at home, but only contented in spirit when he found in far-off places kindred souls who shared his vision. One felt that he came from an ancient shrine filled with unforgotten traditions and that he was inviting the whole Jewish people to worship at that shrine. He lived in strange hotels, underwent the cruellest physical hardships, spoke when every word was pain; but one felt that all of this pain was being self-inflicted in order to earn the right to return home and there to find rest.

Many American Zionist conventions were made memorable by his closing addresses. He would stand alone on the platform, the hour would be late, and the delegates would be fatigued; but when he began to talk, with his hands in his pockets, he created an electrifying interest. They remembered him as he stood there, looking remarkably like Lenin, the communist revolutionary. They remembered the lather of excitement in

which he was immersed. They remembered the tone of exaltation which rang in his voice, the sarcasm, the rebuke. He appeared like a Mephisto in reverse, speaking like an angry
Prophet of God.

Levin was older than Weizmann and Bialik, but among the
three men there existed a deep personal affection, based on
a fraternal relationship which did not exist in other Zionist
groups. Levin was a political disciple of Weizmann. He never
pretended to the possession of political qualities. He lacked patience and understanding of political conflicts. He was led by
Weizmann. In 1910 he let people know that he thought Weizmann was the coming political leader. He told it to American
and German Zionists as if he had found the new Leader.
Levin had the greatest reverence for Bialik's genius and
humility. Only in the presence of Bialik did Levin retire to
the position of a listener. Bialik was an incomparable story-
teller and if you wanted an identification of any literary
reference, Bialik could give it with remarkable accuracy, but
he was always shy about his resources. He had to be coaxed
to reveal himself. Levin treated the poet with great tenderness.

He was an inveterate chess player and played with a vindictive desire to win. Not that he was a good chess player; he
never concentrated strongly enough; but he played for intellectual exercise, to pass the time and in order to overcome an
adversary. He loved the play of skill. If he lost he became ill-
humored; when he won his vanity was childishly jubilant.
When he crossed the ocean—before there were planes—he was
never affected by storms, but ran about the decks incessantly,
looking for someone to talk to, or for someone to play chess
with. He would get terribly cross with a chess player who
played patiently and slowly to win. Facing such an unreasona-
ble adversary, he would prod him with sharp urgings to move,
reminding him that life was short, that chess should not be
taken too seriously. He was always restless.

Although Levin was one of the Russian group who overturned David Wolffsohn, he had no appetite for the party
struggle in Zionist affairs. In his later years, he retired from the

political field altogether and was devoted to the promotion of Hebrew literature. He was one of Bialik's colleagues in the organization of the Dvir Publishing Company, to the affairs of which Bialik and he gave a great deal of personal attention while serving the Keren Hayesod. Levin always had his own favored campaign, his own extra-curricular interests for which he was a remarkably persistent and successful solicitor of funds. He specialized in discovering patrons of Hebrew literature.

He was a writer of talent, an essayist, a publicist. He was editor of a number of Hebrew and Yiddish journals. He founded the Yiddish *Volk* in Vilna. His articles appeared in *Hashiloach, Hamelitz, Der Fraind* and other important publications. He shared in organizing the Hebrew monthly publication *Hatoren* in the United States and was a frequent contributor to the *Day* in New York. He gathered the best of his articles into three volumes which served as his autobiography. They were admirably translated into English by Maurice Samuel. His style of writing resembled his speaking in many ways. He was terse, direct, cruel to the irrelevant, and knew when his work was finished. Nor did he ever overstay his time on the platform.

He was always reserved in personal relations. His wife lived a retired life in Berlin. There were two children, Boris and Anna. Anna died in Palestine at an early age. Boris became a scientist in the Hebrew University and later an industrial chemist. The greater part of his life was spent away from home. His children grew up in his absence. He knew them when they were adults. His wife died in Berlin before Hitler came.

Levin returned to Palestine suffering from a serious chronic illness. His home was a rendezvous for visitors from the *Galut*. Dr. Weizmann never failed to visit him when in the country. Friends from the United States and Canada and Germany knew where to find him.

They found him a restless prisoner in Zion. He could do nothing to help in the building. His thoughts reverted to the *Galut*—his many great moments in Russia, in the United States, in Germany. His future was where he had spent his past. His historic task was to awaken the *Galut;* now he was an invalid in

Zion. Around him a new life was being built, but he had no personal relation to it. Life did not feel good. Hitler was on the march. Incredible dangers threatened the *Galut*, but the Land was not prepared, the political situation was unfavorable. He was impatient and bitter. His occupation was gone and living was painful and empty. Henrietta Szold saw him ten days before his death, "speaking with the same bubbling fullness as always." He passed away in 1935 on the Carmel, topping Haifa, surviving Bialik by about one year.

LEO MOTZKIN (1867–1933)

It was said of Motzkin that as a young man he was a mathematical wonder, but that legend faded away as he settled down to the status of an "everlasting" student, always studying but never getting anywhere. After the Kishinev pogroms he was asked to compile a historical account of those tragedies, which he did after several years of laborious concentration. It was the heaviest task he ever undertook. The rest of his life was spent as a public figure in Jewish affairs. In the founding of the Committee of Jewish Delegations, he played an important part and then drifted into the position of being representative of the Committee at Geneva. But he spent most of his time in Paris, from which he refused to be dislodged. Whenever required, he went to Geneva, where he hobnobbed with representatives of other crippled minorities, and then returned to Paris. In fact, he was more influential in helping the Goyish minorities than the Jewish. His name was associated with the Delegation for the rest of his life, but being a transient, so to speak, he was open for Zionist service when and as required. In the course of time he became known as the chairman of the Committee of Jewish Delegates, the chairman of the Zionist Actions Committee, the chairman of the Presidium of the Zionist Congress, to which he finally attached himself as the master of the gavel. In that chair his imagination rested and was exercised on occasion. He was a routine speaker, had no fire in him, but was an interesting raconteur; in the cafes and lobbies he was a colorful and arresting personality. He was ingenious, resourceful and

*witty as a chairman and could be relied upon to prolong dis-
cussions instead of curtailing them. Thus, he was popular with
all debaters, past and present. He enjoyed life best when he
sat in the chair and ordered the procedures of discussion.*

Leo Motzkin never could be hurried. He preferred to stroll
through life. He loved the warmth of meetings. He always
expected to be tagged to take the chair. So he was often made
the *Vorsitzer,* for he sat so well and looked so wise and genial.
In a real sense, he was a moderator—turning to the right or left,
and eventually, after a great deal of fumbling, finding a true
balance somewhere in the middle. The center was where he
fitted—in the Russian Revolution and in the Zionist movement.

Russian by birth and education, he came to Berlin when he
was fifteen. He aimed to be a mathematician. The legend was
that he abandoned his career to follow the light of Zionism.
The certainties of mathematics would have suited his temperament, but he was too weak to resist the temptations of Zionism and to run away from its blandishments. Thus it was always said that mathematics was one of his lost illusions, which
was due to the magic of Zionism. (His son was to follow in
his footsteps and become a professor of mathematics in the
Hebrew University of Jerusalem.)

Zionism captured his mind at an early age. He was a Zionist long before Herzl sounded his trumpet. He was a member
of a youthful group in Berlin which published its manifesto to
students in 1888, calling for a Congress to formulate the aims
of "Pan-Jewish" Zionism. The manifesto criticized the slow-
paced Lovers of Zion. Even at that time these young men
said: "Give flaming youth the right of way!" Motzkin was then
sixteen.

He was proud of his mastery of German and loved the
German way of life. That was when educated Russian Jewry
opened their windows to "enlightenment," looking longingly
to German philosophy, science and worldly knowledge. Many
became devotees of Russian culture, but more turned to Berlin
and Vienna and the Swiss universities. Motzkin addressed
Zionist Congresses in German. The delegates were *meine*

Herren und Damen. Much later he was able to call them *Rabatai.* Of course, he knew Yiddish well. It suited his purpose, however, to pose as a German professor, and he always seemed dressed for the part in a careless way. He liked German cigars.

He was one of the first to respond to Herzl's call. He was impressed by the dignity of Herzl's bearing, the beauty of his German and his success in journalism. But he was not one of his disciples. He was a leader of the "democratic faction" in the earliest Congresses. He believed that if a Congress had no opposition, an opposition would have to be created, for uniformity would be fatal. The "democratic faction" was small, but it had audacity which it kept within bounds. It had no intention of refusing Herzl a vote of confidence or of forcing his resignation by its behavior. It used its right as a group to heckle the great leader, to challenge the procedure, to embarrass Herzl in order to show him how correctly and courageously these talented young men conducted their opposition.

With the defeat of the Uganda proposal and Herzl's death, the "democratic faction" lost itself among the "general" Zionists, who never could be charged with having a program or an ideology. Nevertheless, the "general" Zionists were to lead the Movement for a number of decades, maintain its financial solvency, and, through Dr. Weizmann, carry it to the edge of the liquidation of the Mandate. In the course of time, the Party Zionists waxed strong. In 1909 the Labor Party finally joined the Jewish Agency; the Mizrachi ceased being the religious party and assumed a role of "clericals." The "general" Zionists in self-defense were driven to organize a quasi-party, whose chief trouble in later years was to find a reason for its being. Personally, Motzkin raised his head proudly above and beyond party, always.

Motzkin's specialty developed with a gradualness almost invisible. Following the Kishinev pogroms, he was asked to write a book about them. Looking back to that startling episode, one wonders at the violent emotions raised by what, in the light of subsequent events, seemed to have been a minor incident. Those pogroms took the lives of less than 100 Jews. The property destroyed was not impressive. But the fact that it was possible for such murders to take place at all, just as Jews were expecting more liberty (not less), made Jews feel that civilization was reversing itself.

The Russian pogroms followed the revision of the Dreyfus Case. The French outburst of anti-Semitism found Jews spectators of an old tragedy, but themselves inactive. The pogroms aroused Jews to action. Protest meetings were held in all Western countries. The pogroms were the signal for the awakening of slumbering Jewish communities the world over. More money was collected for relief than could be used. Jews in democratic lands turned their heads to look backward with apprehension, wondering whether they were really on the verge of universal emancipation.

Motzkin tackled the task of gathering material for his report with great energy and spread himself without reserve and produced two heavy volumes in German. He gave five years of his life to the project. On the basis of that performance he was regarded as a professional, as a political analyst and an authority on political affairs. He read a lot of books and reviewed Jewish current events from an international podium. He criticized statesmen, foretold political developments, and came to conclusions with solemn precision. He pontificated with delightful self-assurance as if he were a judge of a high court.

Motzkin did not indulge in rhetoric or lyricism. He was not an orator. He was not a sentimentalist. He could not rhapsodize about Zion. He was too reserved to get himself into a lather about the historic monuments of the Promised Land. He was in no sense a propagandist. He refused to ghettoize Zionism. Like Herzl, he thought of the Movement in international terms. He saw the Jewish world as a whole. He wanted Jews to build a homeland with their own hands, but he also saw Jews scattered the world over, denied their rights, suffering persecution. He saw Zion as a hill; the Diaspora Jews as in a dark valley; sometimes trailing clouds of glory, sometimes dragging their glory in the mud of poverty and persecution, but all bound together in the same destiny. He believed in one God, one Torah, one People; but not dwelling in only one land. He thought that the Zionist Movement should face both ways—towards Zion and towards the Diaspora—and should maintain a balance. Unfortunately, Motzkin did not live long enough to see the State of Israel and to tackle the realities of this fantastic conception. Diaspora nationalism split Motzkin's personality as it did a number of other leading Zionists'.

Thus, never able to connect his life with Palestine, he got to occupy two chairs—one at the Committee of Jewish Delegations, the other at Zionist Congresses. He was absorbed in the problem of Jewish disabilities, the political state of the Jews in Russia and Poland, in Rumania and Hungary, in the Oriental lands; and incidentally, as it were, in the political affairs of the Jews with regard to Palestine.

When the First World War overwhelmed Europe, Motzkin was sympathetic to the Allies and had to leave Berlin. He went to neutral Copenhagen to take charge of the Zionist office. He shared responsibility with Victor Jacobson. They made Copenhagen an important Jewish center for relations with Jews of all lands during the war. They were in touch with Arthur Ruppin, who had been removed by the Turks to Constantinople. The Bureau was visited on occasion by Zionists coming from Berlin. Emissaries of the American Zionists maintained relations with Copenhagen. Correspondents from all parts of the world flocked to the Danish capital, which became a buzzing center of all sorts of political information and intrigue. Motzkin's political horizon was broadened by his experience in Denmark. He acquired a universal outlook and aped the manners of diplomats. He learned how to dress as befitted his station, but he was guilty of many lapses. He was never like Victor Jacobson who was a diplomat to the manner born, but he was a patient student of protocol and learned a great deal from the Germans, the Swiss and to some extent from the French.

After the First World War, the scattered Zionist authorities assembled in London. Sokolow and Motzkin were appointed to organize the Committee of Jewish Delegations, which was formed to speak for the European Jewish communities. Sokolow took his assignment in his usual Olympian manner, but Motzkin was a *Litvak* who took his work seriously. He put his mind to the study of the problems of minorities. He gathered around him leaders of many Jewish communities. In fact, before the League of Nations was liquidated, he was the leader of all the minority group representatives in Geneva. He was the symbol of a portfolio which he proceeded to fill with briefs and drafts of speeches and correspondence. The Committee of Jewish Delegations went along with the League of Nations to Geneva, but Motzkin hovered between Paris and Geneva and London and did not know where he should hang his hat permanently. In 1920 he organized the first international conference, which became a front for relief, but had no money in its treasury. When the Joint Distribution Committee was about to discontinue its work on the ground that there was no further need for relief, Motzkin came to the United States and threatened an independent relief campaign. The threat caused the Joint Distribution Committee to change its mind and to continue its work until the Nazi terror gave new life to Jewish relief and to all other forms of Jewish endeavor.

Motzkin could not settle down, however. He was unable to go back to postwar Berlin. He could not acclimatize himself in London. He got to like Paris best of all. There he had his restaurants and cafes and he could speak a modicum of French. There he could meet Jews of all lands. If you sat at the Cafe de la Paix any afternoon, you would see a panorama of Jewish life pass by. He was beginning to adjust himself to French ways—its language, its climate, its restaurants, its boulevards. He seemed to have lost his affection for the Germans and their culture. But his duties required him to be in Geneva, and even when the Committee of Jewish Delegations, dominated by the American Jewish Congress, voted that the headquarters of the Committee must be in Geneva, Motzkin remained in Paris defying the Americans.

In appearance Motzkin was not glamorous or imposing.

He lacked platform personality. At public meetings in the United States his addresses were too professional to stir the audience. He was a stout little man with a rasping voice and a tangled beard. His features suggested Emile Zola. When he was not pompous he had a merry twinkle in his eyes as if warning one not to take his dignity too seriously. When he got to Paris his beard was trimmed but it always got out of hand and helped to muffle his voice. He spent more time drinking tea than at his desk. He loved good company and was a good listener. He read heavy literature and nothing light and easy ever crossed his eyes. He never seemed to have time for home life and could be relied upon to pack a grip and on a moment's notice go to London or Vienna or New York—wherever a Jewish cause beckoned. He disliked quarrels and partisanship. He was never at a loss for alternatives in an argument ("on the one hand" against "the other hand"). He was rather complicated in making his own points clear, but he worked hard to do so.

It was as a presiding officer that Motzkin became a legend. He was the "Master of the Gavel." His career as a chairman may be said to have started with Carlsbad in 1921. It should not be inferred that he was a brilliant parliamentarian. He had a peculiar talent which Americans and Englishmen would not appreciate in a chairman. He was the master of the agenda, he was the moderator, he was the logician and analyst of *antragen*. He had a genius for reconciling contradictions. His wit was labored, but no matter how muddy a parliamentary situation became he was able finally to emerge holding the most general *antrag* between his two fingers, prepared to put whatever remained of the idea to a vote. He did not function like Sokolow, who could preside at meetings large or small and never breach the amenities or allow disorder to get the best of him. Sokolow was brilliant at committee meetings. He would sit like a sphinx, listen to all the speakers, take no notes, and at the end of the debate was able to summarize everything said with meticulous accuracy and summarize unerringly the consensus of opinion and then suggest the common-sense action which was in most cases accepted.

Nor was Motzkin like Weizmann as a chairman. Weizmann presided in the Anglo-Saxon way; he kept the debate down to essentials. He did not hesitate to call a man to order and to put the motion to a vote with clarity and precision, undisturbed by heckling; in fact, disorder was abashed by Weizmann's disdainful attitude toward repetition and foolish talk. He was not fitted to preside, however, in moments of great heat or controversy. That was the specialty of Motzkin.

He was a Master in the sense that he gave a good performance. He intruded with his own shrewd observations. He was guilty of facetious remarks. He was loved for his casuistry. He directed the meetings with a keen eye for logical order and the general impression of the debate. He was like the leader of an orchestra who every now and then played some music of his own. He never gave the members of the presidium a chance to develop their talents. He monopolized the chair even when another occupied it, for he persisted in guiding the novice and suggesting ways out of difficulties which could not be refused. He always took the chair at an important moment in the Congress. He acted as if he were the president of the faculty and dispensed favors to his colleagues on the presidium. He was jealous of the status of his office and did not hesitate to join debate on issues of procedure beyond his authority. He had a slow way of talking, but he was quick at seeing a point. He was tenacious in the order and phrasing of a sentence until he got it just right.

At the Prague Congress of 1933 he got into a ludicrous conflict with himself. He was the chairman of the Actions Committee and was also to be the chairman of the Congress. As usual, the expiring Actions Committee held its final meeting before the opening of the Congress. A fierce controversy had arisen with the Revisionists over the Arlosoroff murder case, in which one of the Revisionists had been charged with the murder of the political officer of the Jewish Agency. For reasons difficult to reconstruct, Motzkin was of the opinion that certain questions were involved which came within the jurisdiction of the Actions Committee. As a rule, this committee had well-defined constitutional functions at its final session. It had to approve the agenda and nominate the president of the Congress. With the opening of the Congress its standing committees took over jurisdiction of all Congress affairs. Motzkin got the Actions Committee entangled in jurisdictional questions, and insisted that it should pass on certain aspects of the Arlosoroff case and prolonged the debate by raising new refinements of the issue and releasing all control of the debate. He seemed to be delighted with his own casuistry. He hypnotized hardened members of the Committee with his brilliant disintegration of the issues and their reformulation. The members allowed themselves in their helplessness to be led from one dead end to another and were persuaded that they had a right to meet even after the Congress opened. It was a fuzzy, bewildered Actions Committee that emerged, wondering how they could allow themselves to follow the music of Motzkin's harsh voice. That incident established Motzkin as a legend.

As he grew older, his views became rigid and it was hard for him to change. He went along with his destiny. His double-barreled Jewish views—on Zion and Diaspora—tangled, alternated in importance, and finally he himself could not disentangle them. He used to say the Committee of Jewish Delegations he led was only a *provisorium;* it was the forerunner of the democratic parliament of the Jews of the Diaspora. The Zionists had their Congress. The Jews of the Diaspora should also have their Congress. Strange as it may seem, however, the closer the World Jewish Congress came to realization, the more hesitant Motzkin was about going forward with it. He did not relish the idea of having his personal life interfered with. He dreaded the impact of American Jews, *i.e.,* the American Jewish Congress, upon the enterprise he had made his own. The Americans were beginning to invade Europe and also Geneva. They would certainly wrest control from Motzkin's arthritic hands, or at best, subordinate him to their superficial and barbaric notions. Of course, he believed that the World Jewish Congress had to come to life, but it might be better to delay its coming for a while. He postponed its birth by various delaying actions, but time was working against him. The League of Nations was losing its vitality; it was being badgered by the Italians; the Nazis were pressuring on all fronts. He saw the court where he was speaking for Jewish rights dying on its feet, with none to mourn its demise except —at that time—the Russians.

Motzkin suffered a stroke and died in 1934. The World Jewish Congress was formed in 1936 in Geneva. When the State of Israel was proclaimed years later, Joseph Sprinzak, the first Speaker of the Knesset, took over the gavel Motzkin had wielded in the Zionist Congresses with skill, warm humor, and sagacity. Motzkin was not forgotten in the Knesset. Indeed, he was a tradition in the Knesset when it was born.

VICTOR JACOBSON (1869–1935)

Victor Jacobson was the most inarticulate diplomat I ever knew, but in the early days of the Movement he was a very useful man. His first assignment was to Constantinople where he went ostensibly to represent the Anglo-Palestine Company, but really to make Zionist propaganda among the Turkish Jews. He worked his way into the confidence of many diplomats, subvened several French journals, and established social relations with a number of prominent Turkish Jews. For these tasks he was well qualified. He was sensitive to art and was a good musician. He became the center of a circle of friends who were impressed with his conversation. Later, he was sent to Geneva in the period of the League of Nations and became, in effect, the Jewish ambassador. He was a delightful companion, guileless, courteous, and incapable of harsh anger. He was Russian born and bred but was familiar with French and German literature. His first wife was related to Ussishkin; the divorce which followed earned for him the eternal resentment of Ussishkin. Jacobson lived through that crisis in his life and became the father of two gifted daughters who inherited his talent in the arts. Jacobson's participation in Zionist Congresses was a time of unhappiness, for he had strong political views but was unable to communicate what he thought to others and was condemned to listen while he suffered the agonies of the inarticulate, for he knew the answers but could not express them. I once sat with him for days at an Actions Committee meeting in Jerusalem. I was immune to the boredom of Zionist discussions in various languages I did not understand, but loved to listen and guess what the speakers were driving at. But Jacobson was helpless; he muttered to himself, fidgeted, frowned, looked down and up, turned around, expressed anger, impatience, and knew very well that when he finally got the floor there would be nothing left for him to say, for by that time he would have worked out his frustrations and be completely exhausted. He had a small circle of intimate friends with whom he could discuss problems that escaped him at public meetings. He was an utterly selfless man whose friendship we enjoyed at Congresses, at Zionist meetings in London and finally in Jerusalem.

Victor Jacobson was the first Zionist who aspired to be not a Zionist leader but a "career" diplomat. Nurtured in an atmosphere of assimilation and revolutionary agitation in Russia, he manifested keen interest in the revival of the Jewish nationality at an early age. He organized clubs and wrote about Zionism in Russian Jewish newspapers. With Motzkin, Weizmann and Shmarya Levin, he was one of a group who plunged into university life in Switzerland when it was a hotbed of revolutionary movements. It was there he sharpened the edge of his Zionist sword in combat with Social Democrats, Bundists, and Universalists of all kinds, and emerged chastened for work in the larger Jewish world and specifically for the promotion of the Zionist cause. He was not a brilliant debater, but had a thorough knowledge of international political relations.

In the early days of the Zionist Movement, he was sent to Constantinople, then a frail center of political attention. He had the manners and the equipment. He was placed in charge of a bank established in the Turkish capital by the Anglo-Palestine Company. He soon acquired a large circle of friends and invaluable experience in diplomatic affairs, for he had a pleasant personality and was experienced in the ways of the Levantine world. With the retirement of David Wolffsohn as head of the Zionist Organization, Jacobson became a member of the Zionist Executive headed by Otto Warburg. This was the first functioning Executive elected by a Zionist Congress. It had a policy and a program. It was not a leader and his cabinet, but a group of men sharing collective responsibility. It was a homogeneous body and not overawed by a dominant personality. It was then possible to speak of leaders, without offending the notion that the Zionist Movement had to have an individual leader, around whom the organization revolved, and to whom Zionists bowed the knee.

In this new administration which represented the victory of the "practical" over the "political" Zionists, Jacobson devoted himself to diplomacy and politics, a portfolio he shared with Nahum Sokolow. During the war, he left Berlin for Copenhagen, then one of the few refuges of neutrality; and after the war continued his work in France, Italy and other countries in which German or French was the dominant language. He acquired personal friendships with many of the leading statesmen of Europe. When Dr. Weizmann became the Zionist leader and the League of Nations was organized, Dr. Jacobson was largely responsible for building up, in Geneva, those precedents of Jewish right to participate in international institutions, around which the Committee of Jewish Delegations operated, and which was the source of an ever-widening influence. At the Prague Congress in 1933, having been theretofore merely a diplomatic agent of the Executive, he was elected a member of the governing body, but pursued his habitual course with the same modesty which characterized his entire career.

He was at first practically only a "shtadlon" and propagandist. I remember him in the last pre-war Vienna Congress, how excited and proud he and Sokolow were when they were given an opportunity to confer in person, without *baksheesh* or subterfuge, with the Turkish Consul in Vienna; maybe it was the Turkish Minister to Austria, but it really did not matter at that time. They revealed their success in secret, cautiously; it was the event of the Congress when it became known.

But he emerged from the chrysalis stage of diplomacy as the volume of his experience grew. He mastered international law and procedure. He came to appreciate that mere diplomacy was not politics, and acquired a boldness of thought and action that was entirely foreign to his former habits. He often reverted to the practical aspects of the conception of a Jewish State, wondering at the remarkable progress of the Movement from the time when the Young Turk revolution was regarded as the end of Zionist striving. In the last years of his life he believed in the possibility of building up the conception of a Jewish State in practical forms of preparation. I recall when traveling with him to Palestine in the spring of 1929 how eager he was to find an echo for his hidden thoughts of "empire"; and how avidly he absorbed the suggestion that the political situation could readily be influenced by mobilizing our economic resources for the support of a six- or seven-year plan to develop the National Home. As a diplomat, he never spoke of a Jewish State. As a Zionist, however, "daring" plans absorbed his mind, whenever they were placed on the agenda. The fact is that discretion and understatement in Zionist diplomacy were never as important as Jacobson thought they were.

He was a man of unusual talents. He loved music passionately, and was a fairly competent performer on the piano. He was sensitive to poetry. He had the refinement of one who lives in the exaltation that comes from the contemplation of the intellectual beauty of life and is not afraid of sentiment or ideals. He was a fastidious lover of books, and spent his leisure time hunting for out-of-print volumes and rare editions. He was a soft-spoken man, with a diffident smile, rare sensitiveness and modesty. He shunned the heat of controversy and the brawling of parties. Never a speaker in a real sense, what he said always had form, and he could be relied upon to speak the moderating word without prejudice or rancor and often contributed to the solution of vexatious problems. He loved quiet talk and quiet argument and was devastated by the later noises of the Movement. He loved to express his thoughts in a sort of reverie, waiting to hear the soft echoes of his words. He was always a poor man.

He was the pioneer of Jewish political representation, acting not in his own name, but as an emissary of his people. Under the Turkish regime he had to use the Levantine method, building up political connections through social contacts; always avoiding the sharpness of a direct issue; and waiting in patient oriental fashion for the insidious seed of propaganda to fructify. That was the era of the direct and indirect bribe and the contact man. You dealt not with national policies but with the whim or self-interest of a ruling oligarchy. After the First World War the methods had to be altered. You had to meet the interests of nationalities, their diplomatic representatives being their attorneys and advocates. There were briefs that had to be controverted. There was press propaganda that had to be met by stronger counter-propaganda. There were ideas to be implanted, facts to be communicated. The tactics and the maneuvers of the budding Jewish nationality had to be organized and directed.

In this new world into which Jacobson was thrown, he labored with the delicacy and concentration of an artist, not of a partisan or fanatic, not of a man interested in immediate sensation, but working persistently and with vision to build up an interest in the cause. He had to win sympathy as well as conviction. He was an unusually careful man, knowing full well that he carried a heavy responsibility and could not afford to be isolated by his manner or by his over-intensity, which so easily becomes the cause of irritation and revulsion of feeling and which logic and reason very often cannot overcome. To that growing body of political precedent in which Jews appeared for the first time in all the seeming garments of a political entity, Victor Jacobson was an important contributor.

He was at all times intensely interested in the development of Jewish national culture, but he was not in any sense a *Maskil;* most of his intellectual interests were derived from the non-Jewish world. His youth had been formed in the Russian pre-war revolutionary period—the period that expressed itself in the form of constitution, parliament, liberalism. He was engrossed in the literature of the Romance languages, and after the war acquired an easy fluency in English. Only in later years did he approach the Hebraic world and the culture of his own people. It was with difficulty that he spoke Hebrew. He stuttered and stammered his way through its intricacies. It was only in his last years that he established personal contact with Palestine. He was in all practical matters a gentleman of continental quality and interests.

In the last few years of his life one could observe an eagerness to integrate his life with the new life in Palestine. At one of the meetings of the Actions Committee held in Jerusalem, he sat next to me for days and listened intently to all the discussions in Hebrew. There was a pathetic eagerness in his eyes to follow what was said and to appreciate the mood and the emphasis of the discussion.

At that time I felt the great power of the national revival. It had taken this youth from a strongly assimilated environment, ripped him out of Russian culture, thrown him in middle age in an atmosphere of oriental deceit and shallow manners, carried him over to France and its brittle logic, then to England with its sober forms and traditions, to place him finally in a land built up by his own people speaking their own language, recovering their own aboriginal personality—making a valiant stab at it, anyway. And although he could not so easily feel at home there, the sense of loneliness, the resurgent nostalgia of a man a long time away from home, gave him the authentic feeling of a return and a recovery. In the warm embrace of that return he spent his last tired years. He died soon after the Prague Congress at about the same time that the Jewish world lost Leo Motzkin, Bialik and Shmarya Levin.

VLADIMIR (ZEV) JABOTINSKY (1880–1940)

Vladimir Jabotinsky was a remarkable performer on any stage, at a Congress or mass meeting. He was not at his best in a private meeting or conference. He was easily led astray by procedures. He could attract large audiences in Berlin, Warsaw or New York, but in the organization of his party or in the techniques of politics, he lacked understanding of the psychology of his opponents and was lost in skirmishes with them. His inferiority in this area led to his adopting dictatorial habits. His disciples seemed to know his weakness and practiced upon him the tactics he inflicted upon the Revisionist Party. He was doubtless influenced by his admiration for Mussolini, not as a political theorist but as a performer. In fact his opponents were personally greatly attracted to him. At one time, even Dr. Weizmann established cordial relations with him on a social level. The same was true of David Ben-Gurion, who on several occasions was on the verge of making peace with him, but was held back by his own party. Dr. Stephen S. Wise enjoyed himself for some time as a defender of Jabotinsky's plans, and then one day, without notice, switched over to a vigorous attack on the Revisionist Party, to which, as I remember, Jabotinsky made no serious reply. There were too many leaders in his entourage, and in the course of time, his ideas had a wide circulation and his party grew, but his leadership dwindled. He didn't know how to take care of himself in the struggles of politics, but pursued his perilous course bravely, blind to the dangers in his path. When he left the Congress with a dramatic gesture, he left the stage where he had won universal distinction. He had always concentrated on Zionism. He was not greatly concerned in the Galut Movements of the Committee of Jewish Delegations, and lived his life among the Jewish people as a Zionist leader. He would have distinguished himself and his party, had he lived to the days when the Yishuv rose in conflict with the Mandatory regime, and the power of the Revisionist Party was taken over by the Irgun. Without his presence, the Irgun was able to shatter the influence of the Revisionist Party and transform it into a bundle of splinters, shooting at the enemy in many directions at the same time.

Vladimir Jabotinsky was cast in the role of opposition in the Zionist Movement from his first to his last appearance. I remember him as a writer as far back as 1900, when I used sev-

eral articles he had written in Russian in the early numbers of
The Maccabean, of which I was then the managing editor.
Being young and uninformed, I thought that all European
Zionist writers must be older settled men, bearded patriarchs;
for they wrote with such erudition, assurance and dogmatic
conclusiveness. Especially was this so in the case of Jabotinsky, whose name had appeared frequently in the Zionist press.
Later I learned that he was at that time only about twenty
years old. Behind the seeming maturity in Jabotinsky's
writings, there lurked traces of that youthfulness which he
never lost. He seemed always filled with the daring of youth,
its vigor and cocksureness. He refused to let age master him.

In the early days, Russian Zionism lived within its own
confines. It reluctantly joined the Herzlian movement. The Russian Zionists had their own controversies and their own programs and their own ambitious leaders. They were the formu-
lators of Zionist ideology. They had their own views on *Galut*
politics. They were involved in Russian political issues. They
developed the renascence of Hebrew and lived in a circle of
their own, slightly influenced by what Herzl and his Actions
Committee were doing in Vienna. Their talent for criticism
and non-conformity was given abundant exercise in their own
conferences and then at Zionist Congresses, where they were
often at odds with the "western" Zionist leaders. They were
Herzl's "opposition" as well as his admirers. They wondered
how a *Yehudi* could have ideas of his own on matters which
they believed came within their jurisdiction. To a large extent, their language was Russian. I attended the Vienna Zionist Congress in 1913 and strolled into the caucus of the Russian delegates. There were over four hundred men present,
and I remember Tiomkin holding forth in Russian, at great
length. Ahad Ha-am was present, but I did not hear him speak
at all. He sat on one of the wall benches. He was capable of
long silences.

It was in this Russian world—liberal, not revolutionary—
that young Jabotinsky lived, and from which he was recalled
to his people. He was not a product of the Yeshiva or of a
Hebraic environment. He passed as a youth straight into Rus-

sian life, swimming with ease in its literature, sharing its hopes
and ideals. He did not return from this brief adventure empty-
handed. He had the equipment of an educated, liberal Russian. He proceeded to apply his intellectual experiences to
Zionism, and looked upon the achievements of the Zionist
Movement with Russian eyes. He was always an "outsider"
looking in. They said that he had a *goyish* head, and they were
right.

He was a child of emancipation, and saw in Zionism the
reflection of an awakened *Galut* seeking national freedom,
but using the old methods of the *Galut* to pave the way for
the *Geulah*. He hated the chains of *Galut,* and hoped that
through Zionism the Jewish people would throw off the spirit
of submissiveness, inferiority, opportunism, and that Jewish
life would become bold, proud and aggressive. He also hated
the isolation of Jews and their refusal to be like the *goyim*
on the battlefield, in the athletic world. To him Zionism
meant revolution in earnest. It meant freedom not through
grant, but through self-emancipation, and for that emancipation Jews must profit by the example of other peoples who had
won their freedom. He had found his intellectual freedom
through the culture of another people. Jews could learn from
other people how to liberate themselves and how to maintain
their freedom in self-government.

Jabotinsky was not born to be domesticated. He was always
restless, inquisitive, longing for change. He loved adventure,
movement. He began to move about the world at an early age.
After he had become saturated with Russian culture, he
moved on to Italy, where he studied for a number of years. He
admired Dante, Alfieri and d'Annunzio in literature; Mazzini
and Garibaldi as creators of Italian unity. The liveliness and
grace of the Italians impressed and influenced him in many
ways. He was a good speaker in Russia; in Italy he became a
brilliant dramatic orator, with a flair for the theatrical.
Under the Italian skies, stirred by the vivacity of its people,
his style of oratory changed and the Italian influence was rec-
ognizable in his speech and abided with him for a long

time, no matter what language he used. He had learned how
Italians had forged their democratic unity on the field of
battle; he had studied the teachings of Mazzini and found
much the Zionist Movement could learn from him. Later he
was impressed and influenced by Mussolini. He was slow in
seeing that the Fascist leader was a hollow, theatrical imitation
of the great revolutionary leaders of Italy.

During the First World War he went to England. All Russian Zionists were attracted to England as the land destined
to be of help in the realization of Zionist aims, and also as the
mother of parliamentary government. Jabotinsky learned English rapidly and made many friends in London. They were
not among the upper classes; they were of the restless, protesting middle class—dissatisfied army officers, politicians of
the minority, liberal journalists and artists. These friends he
enlisted in the work for a Jewish Legion. He got his martial
slant in the recruiting of that first group of Jewish fighters for
the freedom of Palestine. His services in the Legion gave him
a military bearing.

It was his English fixation that made him profoundly ad-
mire the English people, and at the same time the dogged
opponent of British policy in Palestine. The authentic Englishman was a non-conformist and "agin" the government. So was
he. In England he saw the Parliament in session and learned
how parliamentary speeches should be delivered, and parlia-
ments managed, but he did not imitate the English in his
speeches or parliamentary behavior. He saw how "muddling
through" was useful in maintaining democratic balances;
and envied the English their ability to cut loose from all serious problems at intervals—for tea, for weekends, for the hunting season. He appreciated the qualities of English sportsman-
ship; he learned how to be bull-dogged; what it meant to be
an English gentleman.

The fruits of his threefold adventures—in Russia, in Italy,
in England—he laid at the feet of the Zionist Movement. It is
curious that of all Zionist leaders he owed least to German influence. But when he appeared in Zionist circles and spoke of
his adventures among the aliens, he found himself more of an

alien than ever before. He could not understand how the Movement launched by Herzl could remain bogged in middle-class achievement or in the dialectics of the German Karl Marx. He imagined that at least a suggestion of Garibaldi would find its way into the Zionist Movement. He thought that Zionists would act something like Englishmen, once they became partners of the Empire in the Mandate.

To his profound disappointment he found that it was not easy to persuade Jews to accept alien methods and manners. Jewish freedom would have to come in a Jewish way. The other nations had had a long history of struggle for freedom on their own soil. The Jews had had a long history of struggle for survival through oppression, always on alien soil. The older Zionists argued that self-emancipation would have to come through an inner revolution, new conditions producing different national traits. They saw Zionism as evolution which at the end of the road would be seen as a cycle of a completed revolution. You could talk to them of the English but they were not Englishmen; you could talk to them of Mazzini and Garibaldi but they were not Italians. Nor was the Promised Land on the fringe of the Arabian desert comparable to England or Italy. They would have to learn through their own experience how to govern themselves. They would have to learn the arts of war only when war became an essential requisite for national survival. They could not become like other nations in the spirit of imitation. They would become like other nations only when driven to it by their own destiny.

But Jabotinsky was simple and direct. Personally he was a shy man, but in expression he was audacious and belligerent. He saw the idea but overlooked its practical implications. What was lacking in the picture of the Jewish State he pieced together from his study of history. Plant the seed; a flower would emerge. Set the idea in motion and its realization would inevitably come. A Jewish Army—small, one battalion, one company, a flag, a bugle—you needn't worry about the National Army. A Jewish State on both sides of the Jordan—demand it, declare it, act as if you had it—and one day a trumpet would be blown and the full structure of an integrated

State would be visible for all eyes to see, a few ships at first, then fleets; a few sailors, then a navy. Make the beginning and the seeds would multiply. He stood for Jewish national rights in Russia long before it had the slightest chance to be regarded as a practical issue. He believed in a large-scale immigration to Palestine; then became an advocate of the unsystematic, sporadic, illegal immigration.

He was a stormy petrel. He disturbed minds. He disturbed the bureaucracy of responsibility. He disturbed the leadership of the corporate obligations of the Zionist Movement. He had a personality of charm but not of persuasion. He provoked but did not soothe. When he stood up in the Vienna Congress of 1925 and launched into a grand criticism of Zionist policy —satiric, courteous, denunciatory—he was like the angry conscience of the Movement. He poured acid on open wounds. He reminded us of the goal and made us ashamed of the results.

I remember what Jabotinsky said in Philadelphia in 1923 about the Shekel. He used the illustration of the water-carrier of Warsaw. He painted a picture of a ragged, starved, un-identifiable victim of the *Galut.* The water-carrier was anonymous; he did not count; he suffered in silence. But when the Zionist Movement awakened him to the consciousness of belonging to a living people, with a destiny of their own, with national burdens of their own, that man stood up and bought a Shekel, conscious of the fact that he had a place in the State that was "in the process of becoming." It was that same Shekel which Jabotinsky many years later, angry and disappointed, tore in shreds on the floor of the Zionist Congress when he left the organization.

Even when he was at peace within the Zionist Organization, he was at war with himself. He entered the door of the Executive, signed the Churchill White Paper, and walked out in a hurry. He could not for long remain a member of the majority. It irked him beyond words to be bound in the responsibilities of the Zionist Executive. Just as he broke Zionist discipline, so he broke Revisionist discipline. He was a man who

played best as a soloist, as a lyricist; he did not fit into any
ensemble and was at his best when he spoke his own mind
devoid of any collective responsibility. For he never lived in
the regular time of day. He had his own time. While we Zionists saw the clock at six, he saw it at twelve. He did not know
what was meant by premature; whatever was true was timely.
He saw the cycle of Jewish emancipation as a thing complete
and was blind to reality.

The last years of his life were days of disillusionment. He
saw the trampling underfoot of all Jewish rights, and had to
abandon emancipation for evacuation. He had fought against
the Mandatory Power for many years and was compelled to
become an advocate of helping England defend itself against
Germany. He came to the United States when it was frozen in
the spirit of isolation, and died before American isolation became defense and aid for England. He preached to his last
days for a Jewish army and Jewish flag (Jews as allies of the
fighters against Hitler), but he did not live to see the fulfillment of that hope.

He was dazzled by a Light. He saw his people once more
like other peoples of earth, at home in freedom, the masters
of their own land, no longer suppliants and pariahs, no longer
enduring inferiority, but bravely and courageously fighting for
their freedom. That Light never got out of his eyes. Even when
closed in death they seemed to see the coming of the day. He
was a bold, imaginative, brave man. Practically alone, he
marched ahead. He was sure the army would follow him some
day.

CHAIM NACHMAN BIALIK (1873–1934)

*I got to know Yiddish fairly well by living with it, but had
only a remote familiarity with Hebrew, because there was no
way to get close to it. Bialik was the most colorful personality
in the Hebrew renaissance, but I knew him chiefly through his
delightful use of Yiddish, which was his best language. He
loved it even more than Hebrew. His Yiddish had a heavy
background of Hebrew and he could put into Yiddish ideas and*

descriptions with such idiomatic twists and allusions, as to make it sound like Hebrew but more than that, for the Hebrew helped him to find what actually fitted the Jewish tongue. He was the friendliest Zionist whom I ever knew. His stories poured from his mouth with a perfection of form and phrase and sound that made his conversations exhilarating, as if one were taking part in the creation of a poem in prose. Many a trip I made with him among the Jewish communities—big and little—and marveled at his resourcefulness and patience in explaining complex ideas to miscellaneous audiences with such good humor and keen enjoyment, with quotations from the Bible and Talmud, with stories from his childhood and tales retold of his memories of his grandfather. But, like Levin, he seldom participated in Zionist Congresses and was content to move around in the lobbies looking for a congenial friend with whom to pass a few hours in conversation. He was a meticulous editor and publisher, and was known so thoroughly to have corrected many a manuscript that often its own authors were unable to recognize it. He had style not only in prose and poetry, but also in editing manuscripts and compiling anthologies and talking at length, never tiring, never losing his form or misusing a word and never even forgetting the proper punctuation or style of type to be used. His love letters to his wife, who survived him, are remarkable for their tenderness and deep affection. He had moods in poetry. There were long periods when he neglected poetry and took refuge in editing the works of others and in speaking on Saturday afternoons to large audiences in Tel Aviv. He had the temperament of a poet, but he could be just as temperamental in berating an author or a typesetter when his wrath was provoked. He was gentle with ignorance that was cloaked in modesty, but he could not abide ignorance panoplied in arrogance or conceit. He loved the company of the humble, for he, too, notwithstanding his genius, was also humble.

Chaim Nachman Bialik was the poet-laureate of the Jewish renaissance. The Hebrew language was not his master; he mastered it to serve every need of his mind and spirit. He molded it to express light and shadow, sound and color. Nor was he disloyal to Yiddish, his mother-tongue; he used Yiddish whenever he felt the need for something to be said in simple, homely form. He loved Jewish humor, Jewish folkways, Jewish wisdom, Jewish books—even the feel of them—and marveled at the beauty of Jewish children. (He had none of his own.) No other poet in Israel was accorded such universal esteem and affection.

He was born in Volhynia in 1873, one of many children. His father died at an early age and the orphans were distributed by his mother among a number of relatives. It was his good fortune to be placed with his grandfather, an erudite Talmudist and a lover of books, who had a deep and lasting influence upon Bialik's life. While with his grandfather, young Bialik was left free to roam in the nearby forests and to discover for himself the mysteries of nature; to read books of secular knowledge found in his grandfather's library.

At the proper age he was sent to the Yeshivah at Voloshin and remained there until his grandfather died, when he went to Odessa and became a Hebrew teacher. In that active Zionist center he made friendships with Ahad Ha-am, Lilienblum and Rawnitzki, who at once recognized his talent as a poet. He published his first book of poems in 1901. He married and went to live with his wife's family. In 1905 he organized the Moriah Publishing Company which issued several Hebrew classics and a series of textbooks. To the surprise and dismay of his large circle of friends, his desire to write poetry congealed in 1908 after he had written a passionate lamentation on the Kishinev pogrom. He was devastated by the pogroms. His descriptions of the massacre of Jews have seldom been surpassed in Jewish poetry for their unrestrained and savage denunciation of the brutality of the attacks and the scorn he felt for the Jews who were the unresisting victims. The pogroms left him speechless. He turned to translations and the editing of Hebrew classics. He translated *Don Quixote* and Schiller's *Wilhelm Tell*. He edited three volumes of Ibn Gabirol's poems and one volume of the poems of Moses Ibn Ezra.

He was still in Russia when the Bolsheviks succeeded in wresting the government from the Kerensky regime. At that time Russia still had some sort of freedom and Bialik intervened in public statements against the persecution of Hebrew, the Jewish religion and anti-Zionist propaganda. His freedom and his life were in danger. Through the influence of Maxim Gorky, he and other Hebrew writers were given permission to leave Russia in 1921. He went to Berlin, organized a publishing company, and in 1924 reached Tel Aviv, which was his home for the rest of his life.

Bialik came to the United States in 1923 as a speaker to aid in a fund-raising campaign. Scores of American communities got to know him. He endeared himself to a generation of Zionists who were never aware of the deep sources of Hebrew tradition and had never seen or heard a personality of such varied Jewish quality. At that time they knew Levin, Sokolow, Ben Zion Mossinsohn and Chaim Weizmann. But Bialik was unique in every way. He was good-humored, unconventional and without pretensions. He did not look like a poet. He was more like a peasant. He seemed at that time to be most at ease speaking Yiddish, probably because his listeners were far removed from an understanding of Hebrew. He was not a master of Sephardic Hebrew; and referred to modern Hebrew as a *sabra*-mangled language. To him speaking Yiddish was like coming home and taking your shoes off and unloosening your tie. He loved a Jewish anecdote, but only one that came out of the ground covered with the dirt of plain living and simple thinking. He would engage in flights of fancy that led him far into the future, but he never lost track of the road along which his imagination had come.

With Shmarya Levin, the writer crossed the ocean with him and remembers his stupefying seasickness which led him to give vent to imprecations of lurid phrases drawn from the Book of Jonah. He was sick from beginning to end and only when the ship was docked in its berth was he able to rise and walk into the Land of Freedom.

When he settled down in Ramat Gan he persuaded Mr.

S. Bloom, an American Jew—a manufacturer of artificial
teeth—to dedicate a building for use as a meeting place,
where he instituted Oneg Shabbat lectures and discussions in
Tel Aviv. He was the leader of the exercises. I came to one of
his lectures with Jacob Fishman on a hot Saturday afternoon.
The place was jammed. At the far end, at the center of a long
table, stood Bialik speaking in a conversational tone. It was
pleasant to listen to him. Twilight was near and as he went on
with his rambling discourse, his voice rising and falling with
soft cadences, a few slivers of light came through a side door
left open for air to relieve the closeness of the summer heat.
A faint light fell on his bald head. All eyes were turned to him.
They could have listened to him far into the night.

Bialik had none of the pretensions of a poet; he was unconventional in manner and dress; he loved wholesome things;
he loved Jews with a strange affection. He knew their memories and traditions, the cut and turn of their minds, their ap-
petites and inhibitions, what was genuinely their own and
what was pilfered from others, their ruthless desire to destroy
false gods, their seeking in pain and struggle to make manifest
the Oneness of God and His world.

He had the ardor of an artist who lives and creates with an
intense desire to communicate his excitement to others, to
have them share his emotions, his vision. He was no recluse
consuming himself in isolation and refusing to open windows
through which others should be able to see what his eyes
beheld. And he was modest and humble and shy. He had to be
persuaded to reveal himself and when he emerged from his
privacy his conversation created a great and lasting excitement. His closest friend, Shmarya Levin, could hold one fascinated by his conversation, but his hearers had no room to
move about. Bialik opened the doors wide and invited all
to follow him. He led one into the open fields of thought and
provoked self-expression. Thought and image and color and
reminiscence *sprudled* through his conversation. Discussion
was raised to a higher level, exciting but not disturbing; bringing light but none of the dazzling effects of pyrotechnics in discussion. He made Jewish learning humane and homely and

simple, and gave it a touch of nostalgic sentiment, freed from verbal complexities. The sacred and profane were mingled in him in even balance.

In his voice there were tones of an endless exile, of a struggle against an unhappy fate. God was close to us in our exile, sharing it. In his words—Yiddish or Hebrew—you heard the curses and the prayers of the slaves in Egypt; the revolt in the desert before the Promised Land was revealed; you heard the despair of the Shepherd King for his sins, his reconciliation with God after prayer and confession; you heard the harsh castigation of the Prophets. His muse was a harp that gathered echoes of the long past and mingled them with the tears of today and leavened them with the hopes of tomorrow. The Jews of Spain suffered the agonies of the Inquisition only yesterday. Through his soul and mind you heard the mystic songs of the Chassidim, the sharp dialectics of the Yeshibot, and the songs and sanctifications of the Ghetto.

He was born in a Jewish world that was narrow and confined, straining against the walls that encircled it. It was a world beginning to pour itself out into alien capitals, seeking free expression. He turned the *Haskalah* back again into the ancestral groove by reviving the things that seemed to be dead and quickened the spirit wherever it gave promise of a future. When he died the Jewish world was large enough and strong enough to hold in its grip all forces seeking freedom.

He was a peasant hewn out of the granite of Zion. He could not rid himself of the clouds of memory pouring into his mind out of the genesis of his race. He had a prophetic austerity and a rare sensitiveness. He was close to all Jews in brotherly love and at home with all Jews in the dust and dirt of everyday life. He brought light and warmth and hope into thousands of Jewish homes. He was a tree with widespread branches, roots that forked their way back into the ancestral soil, fed by hidden springs.

He should have lived to a good old age but he died early in Vienna in 1934. The surgical operation went unexpectedly wrong. Ramat Gan and Tel Aviv and Jerusalem were orphaned. Jews all over the world mourned. They would no longer feel the warmth and comfort and security that came from his life. Those who had the privilege of touching merely the fringe of his being rejoiced that this luminous personality lived his mortal life in their time and that they too knew him. They were built up through knowing him and were strengthened through his strength.

AHAD HA-AM (1856–1927)

Ahad Ha-am was the founder of a school, the representative of a philosophy of Jewish life, and a personality of great intellectual strength and integrity. This frail old man, in whom the vital spark was with superhuman effort retained for many years in a tortured body, stood out as one of the most impressive of all the figures of the Jewish renascence. With Theodor Herzl and Max Nordau, Leo Pinsker and A. D. Gordon, he was the molder of modern Zionist thought. He was the most austere of all Zionist philosophers. From the beginnings of the *Chovevei Zion* Movement down to the latest phase of Zionist development, his sage words attended every Zionist act with warnings, analysis and appreciation. The quality that distinguished him was his intellectual sobriety and conscientiousness. From his early youth he disdained the temporary advantage of rhetoric, fine writing and casuistry. He was a perfectionist in thought and form.

Meticulously seeking the truth, unwilling to be deflected even if it seemed to contradict what the whole world thought, he developed into a personality with a strange stoic strain, calm and unyielding, reiterating in various forms, with marvelous restraint, the basic thought which has become associated with his philosophy. His style reflected the austerity of his intellectual methods. The truth with him was the product of knowledge, meditation, of cool reasoning. It was the postulate of intellectual experience, and therefore could not so easily be harmonized with the new truth which Jewish life, awakened, was in the process of creating through the Zionist movement. He did not believe in taking risks; he had no sympathy with adventure. He could not endure loose thinking, the easy invention of the *Batlon* mind. He was often inflamed with prophetic anger against attempts at building, which were doomed, according to his keen analysis, to topple over. He refused to go the way of mere enthusiasm or aspiration. He was no sentimentalist. In the intellectual realm he was capable of originality and of daring, but in the things that had to be done in this world he had an intensely practical and conservative mind. Even in planning the future he wanted firm ground under his feet. Curiously enough, he was associated for many years with the tea business of the Wissotkis in Odessa. He was not harassed by the element of time, for the Jewish people to him were an eternal people. He wanted Jews to exemplify in their national action the restraints and the wisdom of ancient times. He would have liked to have them revert to their Hebraic personality.

Naturally his methods led him to a conscious and subconscious opposition to the idealism of Herzl. For Herzl was the remaker of truth in the world of reality. He was the breaker of precedent. He was the daring adventurer. With all his practicality, Herzl dealt with dream, fantasy, drama, sentiment. What was not in existence, he aimed to create. He was willing to take a chance and to force the game. A rhetorical call would gather the scattered remnants of the Jewish people. Would they respond? (Reason was against it. *That* was not the way.) A Congress was to create a body to assume responsibility for the Jewish future. Would a Congress, lacking unity of speech, lacking common customs, with disparate cultures, endure? (Reason was against it. *That* was not the way.) Herzl placed reliance upon the fiats of governments, negotiations, interviews with potentates, the granting of charters. Would the fiat of governments bring the Jewish people to life—a depressed, scattered, hopeless people? (Reason was against it. *That* was not the way.) Herzl wanted to create an atmosphere of legal approval and sanction—then the vessel to hold and carry the physical body of the Jewish people—and out of this revolution he hoped that a new Jewish life would emerge. What Jews had neglected to do was no criterion of what they would do if the right conditions were created. Herzl depended largely upon inspiration and improvisation, without estimate of strength or resources, relying upon Providence or historical combinations plus the Jewish people in whom he had faith, to meet any emergency or to take advantage of any opportunity. He was the statesman, not the philosopher; the actor, not the commentator.

Ahad Ha-am was shy in speaking. He spoke through his writings. I remember him at the Vienna Congress of 1913. He sat with the Russians at their caucus. He was silent throughout, listening, with his head bowed over his cane, a medium-sized lean man with a light beard, absorbing the Russian words of his disciples, and indicating no immediate reaction.

To his contemplative, sober mind, the Herzlian maneuvers were distressing. Clay was not gold and could not possess the functions and qualities of gold. The redemption of Zion must be preceded by the regeneration of the Jewish people. The emphasis must be placed upon spirit and culture and the creation of a Jewish soul capable of visualizing and desiring the transformation of the conditions of life. All premature action would prove fatal. The foundations must be laid securely. And so Ahad Ha-am, throughout Herzl's career, held to a critical, neutral attitude, granting a point here, reserving judgment there, feeling entirely at a loss how to bring the new truth that was developing within the range of his own reflections. He was greatly disturbed when Herzl wrote *Altneuland* and exposed Herzl's lack of depth in understanding Jewish life by a merciless criticism of the book. It was the Cultur-Zionism of Ahad Ha-am that weakened the foundations of the political Zionism of Herzl.

The First World War overturned all prophecies. It radically affected all systems of thinking, and had a tremendous influence upon the Zionist Movement. Out of that maelstrom came the Balfour Declaration, in the making of which Ahad Ha-am, then residing in London, was an interested and valuable influence; and with the Balfour Declaration came the opportunity and the pressure of life to push forward in the conquest of the land. The door of Zion was opened. Not

now the time to hesitate. The charter that seemed a visionary
thing in 1900 had become an act of the Allied Governments.
The recognition of the Jewish right to Palestine was sanc-
tioned by the League of Nations. The whole structure of
thought, involving an evolutionary development of a Jewish
cultural center—to some extent separate and apart from the
establishment of the Jewish National Home—was disturbed.
What the Jewish world saw was an opportunity to bring consolation and amelioration to a race that had suffered terrible
injuries during the period of the War. Involuntarily, persuaded not so much by his intellect as by his Jewish intuitions
(for essentially, he was "one of the people"), Ahad Ha-am
found himself for the first time in harmony with Zionist action,
swept into it by the force of Jewish life, becoming a party to
its difficulties and successes, becoming involved in the welter
of self-criticism in which the Jews of Palestine were immersed,
and out of which new life was being created.

Ahad Ha-am settled in Palestine, and at once established a
position there which enhanced the services he had rendered to
the Jewish people in the first Zionist decade. He was the Sage
of Tel Aviv, witnessing with his own eyes a physical regeneration progressing on parallel lines with the spiritual rebirth.
What he had posited as the essential emphasis was swept away
by the force of human needs and by the need of taking
prompt advantage, with all strength possible, of every opportunity. His teachings became the classical approach. In the
actual rebuilding of Palestine, which he witnessed for a number of years, he found reconciliation with that mightier stream
of Zionist thought which was represented by Herzl. He always
had a fondness for Chaim Weizmann who was the exponent of
synthetic Zionism and with whom he had a natural kinship. He came to see the great beauty of spirit which animated the new Aliyah, combining spiritual ideals with devotion to hard physical labor. He came to see how simultaneously the face of the earth might be transformed by the will of
the pioneers. He saw simultaneously the conquest of the Emek
and the founding of the Hebrew University. His last days in
Palestine made him feel the greatness of the Jewish people,

which overturned all precedent, made necessary revision of all estimates, built the roof before the foundation, and yet, through persistence and endurance, was able to mold a harmony which was representative of the unity of the Jewish spirit. Endeared to all, regardless of party, respected as sage and teacher, his body weakening day by day, although his mind was ever alert, he was privileged to witness the flowering of a new Jewish life which owes much to his teachings and which progressed from the Jewish National Home to the State of Israel.

ROBERT STRICKER (1879–1944)

The martyrdom of Robert Stricker softened the harsh impression of the earlier Zionist who was the breaker of parliamentary china and loved nothing better than a scandal on the floor. He liked to be in opposition and expressed his dissents in denunciation, from the hurling of verbal insults to general disorderly behavior. As a matter of principle, he refused to pay attention to the amenities of debate. He enjoyed nothing better than to be called to order by an exasperated chairman and to resist the order to his last breath. He sometimes sided with Gruenbaum's splinter party; then he marched along with Jabotinsky for a time; then he was a primitive free-lance Zionist. His greatest delight was to be on the lookout for an opportunity to attack Dr. Weizmann which he would do with relish and keen satisfaction. I remember only a brief interlude when he spoke affably to Dr. Weizmann, but he soon repented that softness of spirit. He had no fundamental doctrines except to rise to the defense of Herzl or Nordau, to praise Wolffsohn when he was attacked, and to take the side of any minority simply because it was a minority. He was a well-built man whose black beard fanned out from his face, then was clipped short and trimmed, and his voice was loud and raucous. But he was a powerful orator, capable of reaching heights of amazing denunciation. Once, in Berlin, at an Actions Committee meeting, he pounced upon an interview thoughtlessly

given by Dr. Weizmann to the Jewish Telegraphic Agency on
the problem of a bi-national state. Stricker tore the statement
to shreds and proposed the impeachment of Dr. Weizmann.
He raised his audience to a pitch of such excitement that they
were unable to appreciate what it was all about after the thun-
der of Stricker's voice had subsided. Personally, he was wholly
unlike his public impersonations. He had all the good manners
of a Viennese; but he loved the boisterous and unruly. He had
a quiet sense of humor, and whenever he talked with a certain
sharpness of expression it was only because he felt himself
perpetually in the midst of a debate. He acted with great no-
bility in the concentration camp where he and his wife lost
their lives.

In his middle age Robert Stricker was a Vienna cafe politician and free-lance journalist. You thought of him as a heckler
at public meetings, as the leader of a crowd, as the rude in-
truder in communal meetings and as the shrill opposition at
Zionist Congresses. You thought of him—mindless of the time
of day—sitting at a table in a cafe surrounded by motley characters, talking volubly about foreign affairs, about the quarrels of newspapers, what was going on in the theater, and about
the politics of the Jewish community. In the hurly-burly of
free conversation Stricker's strident, ringing voice could be
heard above them all. He sat there long hours, eating his
meals, drinking his tea or beer, writing his editorials and articles, smoking his cigarettes, looking out at the world from the
center of European civilization which was then Vienna, soon
to be rubbed out.

Then came the terrible days of the First World War and its
aftermath of misery and want. Vienna was stricken and bankrupt. Stricker added Jewish communal affairs to his agenda,
again took up his crusade against Jewish assimilation and became a frequent delegate to the Zionist Congresses where he
held the flag of Herzl high.

He was a true Viennese, rude and gracious, but squandered
his amazing talents on the Jewish community and the Zionist
Movement. He should have delivered his impassioned protests

in a parliament, but he lived his life in the affairs of a stuffy
kehillah, in the Zionist Actions Committee and the Congresses.
He had the audacity of a Danton but played his part in the
Zionist Congresses as an unruly member of a small opposition party. He poured out his heart in Jewish journals where
he blazoned the word *Jude* defiantly in the city of the *Haken-
kreutzer*. He never concentrated on a major issue. He was
taken up with the details of life.

He was interested only when he could declaim against the
majority. He felt at ease speaking for himself. When chance
maneuvered him into a formal position as a member of a
group, he was embarrassed. He was brilliant in attack, sharp
of tongue, often vulgar and defiant of law and order. It was
then he enjoyed himself most. He loved public life as an exercise in the technique of discussion.

He was young when Herzl came and was swept off his feet
by the grace and dignity of the leader, and followed him without reserve. He was always proud of being a *Herzlianer* and
thought of himself as the last of the tribe of Herzl's loyal
and unquestioning disciples. To him, a man's Zionism depended upon his loyalty to Herzl. When the leader died, he
reverted to his natural status of freedom, and although protesting his loyalty to Herzl's legacy, he made temporary alli-
ances for tactical advantage but always retained his freedom
—an improviser of dramatic surprises in discussions, never
adhering to any party line or any order of business.

When parties began to emerge in Zionism, and the "party
key" determined one's right to speak, Stricker had to find a
party to which to attach himself. Standing alone he had no
status. He joined Isaac Gruenbaum's radical group which was
a party of leaders—Gruenbaum, Margulis, Nahum Goldmann,
Moshe Kleinbaum (now Moshe Sneh). When Gruenbaum
crossed the line and struck a truce with Weizmann, Stricker
said goodbye to him and joined the Revisionists led by Jabotinsky. When Jabotinsky walked out of the Zionist Congress,
Stricker remained with the remnant led by Meir Grossman,
where World War Two found him.

Stricker was an engineer by profession. He was born in Moravia in 1879 and graduated from the German Technical High School, and entered the service of the Austrian State Railways. There he was regarded as an efficient engineer and was transferred to Vienna, reaching the status of a Surveyor of Railroads. He remained in the service of the state until his retirement on a pension, when he was free to devote himself exclusively to his Zionist avocations.

He made his first appearance as a speaker at 18. He called Zionism, in 1897, *Makkabaertum*. He adhered to his political faith, as then enunciated, for the rest of his life. He underwent few basic changes. He used Herzl's doctrines to test any new proposal and fought any change in Herzl's dogma with the tenacity of a fanatic. He was proud of being a Jew and called the first publication he edited a *Judenblatt*. On one occasion when he was a delegate to the Austrian Parliament, he addressed his colleagues as *"meine Herrn-Antisemiten!"* His Zionism included the fulfillment of Herzl's injunction to conquer the communities. He helped greatly to conquer the Viennese community and never let up heckling the assimilationists. He did this through the newspapers he edited, the public meetings where he expressed his views, and at the Cafe Astoria where he maintained his table for many years. He wrote in a popular style, vigorously and with precision, and had a common, even vulgar, vocabulary. He spoke with dramatic gestures and voice and often startled his audiences with the audacity of his ideas and the rudeness of his suggestions. He introduced himself to the Austrian Parliament with the words, "I am a Jew." He had violent clashes with the Christian Socialists and the Social Democrats.

He was one of the most persistent and effective of the opponents of Weizmann whom he supported for only a brief period. He was opposed to Weizmann's defense of the Mandatory Government. He rejected the Weizmann proposal for the inclusion of non-Zionists in the Jewish Agency. He was the leader of the attack when Weizmann expounded his theory of bi-nationalism, which brought about Weizmann's retirement in 1931. He became an ardent supporter of the World Jewish

Congress, but internationalism did not seem to attract him. He was too much of a provincial Viennese.

He and his wife died in Theresienstadt. That was the last mile on the long road the poor man and his wife had to travel after Hitler came. He could have saved his life. He was urged at Paris before the *Anschluss* not to return to Vienna. But he insisted that his place was with his family and his community. On the day the German Army marched into Vienna he could have saved his life again and friends begged him to leave the country. He said that his place was with the poor Jews of Austria; that as a private man he could have left, but as a leader he had to remain.

His life was ennobled by the three years he spent in concentration camps where he and his wife finally passed away. Though his health had already been impaired when he arrived in Theresienstadt—at Dachau and Buchenwald—he brought comfort and consolation to all whom he met in that tragic situation. The Strickers gave away their spare linen and clothing. They shared the gifts which they received from the outside. Stricker delivered lectures to small groups. On Saturday afternoons old friends met in their one small room. Stricker spoke of the past and the hope for the future of the Jewish people. It was amazing how clearly he foresaw the turn of events. He was positive that a Jewish state would become a reality and soon.

The Vienna free-lance journalist, the fiery speaker at Congresses, the intrepid defender of Jewish rights shared the fate of six million of his brethren with dignity, integrity and faith.

ELIEZER KAPLAN (1891–1952)

Eliezer Kaplan came out of Russia before its revolution had settled down firmly in its totalitarian forms, and came to Palestine in 1923. He was immersed at an early age in Zionism and associated with the leaders of young Zionist labor groups. His father was an active Zionist. The revolution made Eliezer realize that he would have to hurry to Palestine to save his life and the ideals which had become part of it.

From the start he made the economic aspects of the Movement his special interest. He had an aptitude for financial problems. He was a pioneer in the organization of labor. He worked his way up from the economic areas of the labor movement to the Treasuryship of the Jewish Agency, and, finally, to the Ministry of Finance in the State of Israel. Twenty-five years of consecration to his self-imposed mission made him the outstanding personality in the economic life of Israel.

He was not an orator or politician. He made few contributions to Zionist theory or ideology and seldom ventured from the field of his special interests. But when he spoke or wrote on what was generally taken to be a dull, prosaic subject, he made you see the human factors involved in the budget he analyzed, in the financial problem he wanted you to know about and understand. To him, the figures of the accountant were the reflection of life itself. He talked of finances and economics with a strange animation, as if here was the heart of the cause. The problems tormenting him, however, were never merely the financial statements, but the tortured body of the state he was helping to create. He knew that no mystic word could give life to the state. He knew that freedom had to be won through hard work. It had to be buttressed by economic resources, production, material security, credit and prestige. He was impatient with the easy calculators who would inflate a budget figure and then want him to make the budget work.

He was a man of simple tastes, and lived frugally and was capable of deep and loyal friendships. He clung to his views with tenacity regardless of who opposed them. He was a bold critic of his own party. But when discussion was ended and action was called for, his resistance relaxed and he moved along the middle course of uncharted economic and financial practices, making the best of the pressures that were forcing his decision. He was a partisan within limits. He fought valiantly for the place of labor in the Homeland, but orthodox socialism was not his guide. He realized that only with a healthy, thriving, self-sufficient labor force could the Zion of our hopes, based on the social justice of the prophets, be reborn. But he was tolerant and imaginative; worried a great deal; had few moments of relaxation; and possessed a provincial sense of humor which often revealed itself even in the heat of controversy. He had none of the arrogance of leadership that looks for self-vindication at the expense of the public welfare. He was seldom the victim of his partisanship.

In the first decade of his life in Palestine, he was passionately absorbed in the labor movement. His aptitudes for economics and management were recognized at once. He was one of the Directors of the Solel Boneh—at first a school for the training of workers, and later the most powerful economic agency of the labor movement. He was one of the organizers of the Histadrut and a member of the first central committee of Mapai when it was organized in 1930. He was elected Treasurer of the Jewish Agency at the Prague Congress in 1933, when Mapai for the first time assumed a direct official responsibility in the Zionist Administration.

The tasks that confronted him as the Jewish Agency Treasurer were formidable. The effects of Nazi persecutions in Germany were penetrating Palestine's economy, and new problems of great magnitude demanded study. The political waywardness of the Mandatory and the growing Arab intransigence were becoming intolerable. And the hope that the Agency budget would increase with its enlargement was not being realized. It was the beginning of the revolutionary period in Zionism. The Mandate was losing its authority.

Kaplan created the Agency treasury. He made the funds the springboard of financial reorganization. All the resources of the Homeland were coordinated within the authority of his office. The reports of the Treasurer for the first time disclosed the total resources of the National Home. He learned how to operate without adequate resources, with deficits falling over his ears; and maintained poise and sobriety and firmness of purpose, as well as solvency, through many threatened catastrophes.

He won the confidence of the *Yishuv* in his integrity, in his reliability as a man of affairs. He raised the prestige of the Agency in banking circles in England and with the fund-raising agencies in every part of the Jewish world, especially in the United States. The structure of the financial administration he created was the foundation upon which the State of Israel was able to begin its life.

The startling change of Homeland to State found Eliezer Kaplan inevitably the Finance Minister. He was the only outstanding man of financial experience who was at the same time a leader of a powerful political party. By now his health was seriously impaired. But nothing in the world could restrain him from immolating himself in the grinding machinery of the new State. There were the means of defense to be provided. The return of the exiles was forcing the gates and presented enormous bills that had to be met. There were the hundred and one needs of the State structure which had to be established. He learned the ways of State finance in the hectic confusion of unpredictable new demands. He had to train himself to quick decisions and the assumption of heavy burdens, depending upon the miracles which had thus far sustained the national struggle. He was responsible for price controls, controls of exports and imports and austerity programs. He was forced to make and revise policies to suit recurring emergencies. He was the target of popular disapproval time and again, but undeterred and undismayed made his way laboriously through one difficulty after another with amazing skill and audacity.

He gave himself no rest. He wanted to live through the crisis and to see Israel emerging out of the storm into calm waters—strong and unafraid. That was what kept him alive. He was like one obsessed by his responsibilities.

I remember his excited appearance at a conference in London after the Arab riots in 1929. He came hurriedly from Palestine to report on the outbreaks to an emergency meeting at 77 Great Russell Street. Many Americans were still there, lingering after the Congress. Some of the leading non-Zionists were present. Kaplan looked as if he were being pursued by horrible memories he could not shake off. His vivid description of brutal destruction and murder, told in staccato sentences, gasping to catch his breath, aroused such a spirit of protest and defense as was never before manifested at an official Zionist meeting.

Death took Eliezer Kaplan before his mission in life was completed. He would not accept the summons. With great difficulty he was persuaded by his friends to leave his harassed desk and rest for a while in a quiet retreat in Switzerland. At the end of the journey, as he was about to disembark, his heart refused to carry him further. He did not die on a battlefield, but in a real sense he was a casualty in the struggle of the Jewish people for their national freedom.

PINCHAS RUTENBERG (1879–1942)

Pinchas Rutenberg came to us from an alien world. His personality had matured in the Russian Revolution. He was a solid mass of rebellion, with absolute convictions. We were never certain of the part he had played in the Revolution or what present mission he might be pursuing. There were many other crypto-rebels coming to the United States at the time for refreshment, for renewal of vision, for propaganda, or for funds which they gathered from sympathetic Jews. They spoke for a bewildering chain of related parties. Rutenberg's pockets seemed to be stuffed with secret communications, plans and orders. He walked the streets of New York furtively, glancing over his shoulder to see whether spies were following him. In company he stood by in long silence; but in intimate circles he would dilate in the commanding tones of a sergeant-major on wide-ranging plans, and speak of world-encircling strategy in which his listeners were invited to help turn the world upside down. But such outbursts would simmer down to a flat breathless silence; for far from the field of action—in New York—not knowing where or when or by whom the floods of revolution were to be released—Rutenberg was as helpless as a sailor lost in a foreign port.

He was born in a village in the Ukraine, where he attended Cheder until he was twelve. He was then admitted to the nearby secondary school, and at seventeen passed an examination which gave him a place in the St. Petersburg Technological School. He was one of the few Jews who made the grade that year. Here he immediately joined the underground revolution, and as soon as that fact was disclosed by the authorities he was summarily expelled. He went to Ekaterinoslav where he secured employment as a workman in a metallurgical plant. He returned to St. Petersburg a year later and was reinstated in the Institute. When he graduated in due course he entered the Putilov armaments plant and was given a responsible position. But his revolutionary zeal burned hot and he cast his lot with the workers in the plant and became one of their leaders. He was active in the first flare-up of the revolution in 1905. He had cut away from his own people and enlisted for the duration with his Russian comrades. As far as could be seen, he was a Jew with a Russian soul. When he first arrived in the United States he was credited with having liquidated the notorious Father Gapon who led a popular revolt in 1905 and was unmasked as a government agent. Rutenberg never admitted or denied his connection with the incident, but it provided him with credentials which served well among the American radicals who welcomed him. It was after the Father Gapon incident and the pogroms that Rutenberg reaffirmed his identity as a Jew. He organized a Jewish group in Zurich known as *Pro Causa Hebraica,* wrote a pamphlet in Russian which was translated into Yiddish, and not only confessed the error of his ways but gave expression to a positive creed and berated all Jews who did not admit the truth as he saw it. He had believed that Jewish freedom would come as part of the freedom of the Russian proletariat, but overlooked the incident of pogroms. When the pogroms came, his *Weltanschauung* was shattered and he returned to the Jews angry with himself, with those who did not follow him,

and disappointed with the revolution. He could not understand why his Jewish comrades were so obstinate. He was as
arrogant and intolerant a Jewish nationalist as he had been
when he was fighting the Czar. He insisted that the Jews were
a people, that they should have a land of their own, and that
they should stand up and fight for their rights in the new
world which the revolution was about to give birth to. But he
never looked back to his previous doctrine or discussed it. It
seemed to have been washed out of his mind. He settled
in Italy where he devoted his time to the study of bridge-
and dam-building, and became proficient in that field. He returned to Russia, however, when the ultimate revolution at
the end of the first war destroyed Czarism and Kerensky became the head of the shaky government.

Half his life Rutenberg spent in the revolution. The rest
of his life he lived out in the Land of Israel. He returned as a
prodigal but his life was at its creative beginning. He brought
to the Promised Land the great gift of light and power for
which he was prepared. But his work was not only that of an
engineer. He had to acquire the franchise and the capital. He
came to the United States on several occasions seeking a fund
for "harnessing the waters of the Jordan," as his prospectus
had it. He had to seek the favor of the Mandatory Government.
He was aided by Dr. Weizmann, Alfred Mond and Rufus
Isaacs. The Mandatory Government forced him to share his
franchise for Jerusalem light and power with an Englishman
who claimed a prior concession from the Turks. Rutenberg
overcame all the formidable obstacles. He was not only a
good engineer, but in spite of his curt manners he was also
a good negotiator and an able engineer. He built his home
in Palestine and settled down as a staid citizen of a new society, with an address of his own and a circle of friends. In the
course of time he became a man of property.

The party man of the Revolution cast off the uniform of
group discipline and found freedom in the Promised Land. He
was irritated and depressed by the excessive partisan spirit
which then prevailed in the National Home. His friends of

the Labor group seemed to be anxious to create a simple, natural, free Jewish life in which all would share equally. But by their party maneuvers they forged weapons that could be and were used to impose the will of the majority on the minority, without kindness. So far as his personal means were concerned, Rutenberg was an impartial friend, welcoming all with equal affection. He maintained an area of restraint in the expression of his personality. He did not indulge in memoirs. He wanted his privacy respected, his thoughts, his desires, his outlook on life. He wanted to live in a society of free men not chained by dogma. A man may not be a writer or speaker; he may be a plain workman, but his soul may find occult ways to communicate with others and to reveal himself. Rutenberg was that kind of a silent man. His way of life spoke for him.

At home, he seemed to have lost his interest in agitation and partisanship. He moved without resistance toward the quiet years of his life. He was at times at odds with Dr. Weizmann whose political methods he disparaged, but he seldom entered the field of controversy. He was regarded as a man above party and was held in reserve as a "dark horse" who might be saddled for a run to power, against his will, should the right time come. It never came for Rutenberg. He was in fact a middle-class man in all practical ways. After he had aided in stimulating the revolution in Russia, a mood of repentance seemed to overcome him. He could make a decision in the political field only with the greatest difficulty. He hesitated on the brink of choice. He had forgotten the vocabulary of political life. He was probably held back by memories and old habits. The blood had slackened in his veins.

Of the two prospects which changed the economic face of Palestine at that time, it was said that "mentioning Rutenberg's power and Novomeysky's potash, it would be difficult to say which encountered greater opposition in quarters which were loathe to see the country emerge from its ancient sleep."

When he died after a lengthy illness he left a will that tells more of the man than any words he ever uttered. In his last testament he wrote:

"The division of our people and communities into parties and sects has always caused disaster. Civil strife has brought us to the brink of the abyss. If it does not cease, ruin confronts us. Therefore, it is my desire and will that the Yishuv and the Jewish youth growing up in its midst should always remember that it is not this or that Jewish sect or party which is persecuted or downtrodden, but the Jewish people as a whole. Whether we want it or not, we are all brethren in distress. Let us realize this and be brethren in life, in creative effort, and in action. Our youth are our hope and future. Its proper education is the guarantee of our existence."

He left his estate, which was not inconsiderable, to an endowment fund, the proceeds of which were to be devoted to the education of Jewish youth. He urged that no collections should be made to perpetuate the endowment, and that no forests or villages be named for him. He asked that he be buried on the Mount of Olives "among the graves of humble workers and tillers," that his funeral be held in accordance with Jewish tradition without flowers or speeches, and that his nephews say Kaddish at his grave.

That was a strange homecoming and ending indeed when one remembers that Rutenberg as Kerensky's military chief in Petersburg threatened to arrest and imprison Lenin when the leader of the Bolsheviks returned to Russia in April, 1917. Rutenberg was not there when Lenin arrived.

ELIEZER BEN YEHUDA (1857–1922)

Eliezer Ben Yehuda gave his life to the task of resurrecting Hebrew as the vernacular of his people. From early youth he was a prolific Hebrew writer. In 1870 he pleaded not only for the return of Jews to Palestine but also for the revival of Hebrew as a living tongue. Born in Lithuania in 1857, he left for Paris in 1879 to study medicine, but fell a victim to tuberculosis. He was advised to seek healing in the warm climate of Algeria, but in 1881 went to Jerusalem as his cure-place. There he fell under the spell of the thought that he, by his example and his writings, would transform Hebrew into a language Jews should speak, not merely a language struggling to express ideas in the traditional forms, avoiding as sinful its awakening for everyday use but as a living form of expression. He was not greatly interested in the Zionist Movement and stubbornly concentrated on his self-imposed task. During the First World War he had to leave Palestine with his family under Turkish pressure and lived in the United States for a number of years. When the war came to an end he returned to Palestine, concentrated on the writing of his Encyclopedia of ancient and modern Hebrew, and died in Jerusalem in 1922.

To his zeal, to his intolerant, forceful and controversial propaganda, to his exalted feelings of national pride and faith in the renaissance of his people, and also to his natural genius for the language—is due in largest measure the re-entrance of Hebrew among modern languages and its adoption by a new generation of Jews as their everyday speech for all purposes. He stood almost alone. There were others who cultivated the written Hebrew word, but they were dealing with the dry bones of a retarded language, browsing among the antiquities of their people, looking back with reverence to what it used to be and refusing willingly to accept the invitation to make it the servant of the New Day. They were fed by the Torah and its commentaries; its restraints and its pieties; bound by its archaic forms. They venerated and served a Holy Language. Ben Yehuda was determined to make that language secular, fitted for the new world where Jews were called to live and to be reborn; and to have it express the thoughts and desires, the hopes and tragedies of men of this generation, engaged in a desperate struggle to maintain and develop their identity. Without perceiving the vastness of the world that would have to be integrated in the living Hebrew, the prodigious task involved in giving the stiff, old language a flexible body, a living vocal expression to include what the world had created since Hebrew stopped growing, Ben Yehuda dedicated himself to its rebirth in spite of his physical frailty, in spite of the rejection of his mission by those for whose benefit it was to be reborn; and made his mission the sole obsession of his life.

He was a superb fanatic with a fixed idea burning in his heart like a hot coal. He conceived of spoken Hebrew as the soul of a living people, without which it could not live. It was the essence of the Jewish renaissance. Without a language capable of expressing all the nuances of life, ancient and modern; capable of free intercourse in its own idiom, in all areas of human expression; the Redemption was a grotesque and meaningless anachronism, especially in the light of a growing, colorful Zionist Movement both in the Diaspora and in Palestine. He derided the contention of the older generation of Hebraists that you could find all the Hebrew you needed in the ancient writings, in the archeological remains of what had once been the vessel of speech of the prophets and the lawgivers. Disregarding technicalities, law and order—the stiffness of the language, the rigidity of its joints, the hardness of its roots—overcoming the barriers of time and place—he poured his life with amazing recklessness and physical and material interest into the great task of the renaissance of Hebrew. He was the living symbol of the revival. He was the fountain from which the words came with amazing variety. Many of the words he coined were rejected as artificial at a glance; some of them were brilliant improvisations that caught on to the tongue of its living users; many of them were reflections of a genius for sensing what was the true word. He broke the hardened shells of the old roots, tore them apart, appropriated sounds from alien tongues, set them together in new formations and flung them into a new vocabulary. His scholarship and his talent for deduction enabled the Hebrew language to tread the rocky path of renaissance, adjusting itself through practice to the vast resources of written and spoken languages civilization had given birth to since Hebrew had ceased to be alive and fertile. He had to span centuries to make up for so much lost time. He had to absorb in the new language the techniques and the practices of new civilizations. He had to feed the needs of the Promised Land and its people now involved in the process of discovering their old language for new uses. He had to find the new words to express the variety and the novelty of the speech of those generations that had long since passed the point where Jewish life had started.

Jerusalem was his fortress. There he began the compilation of his all-inclusive dictionary of ancient and modern Hebrew. There in 1889 he founded the *Vaad Halashon* consisting of scholars and experts who cooperated in coining whatever new words were needed and publishing them in a quarterly journal. He lived in the center of fundamentalist orthodoxy where his innovations were regarded as heresy. He was ostracized and condemned by the pious who were under the deadening influence of the *Chalukah* and followers of immobile tradition. He felt that he was bringing freedom for his people; they thought he was undermining the foundations of religion. He thought that he was showing them the way to emancipation from the thrall of foreign speech. They preferred Yiddish to Hebrew as the vernacular in their schools. The freedom Ben Yehuda spoke of—they felt—would lead to assimilation and apostasy. It was the example of his life—forswearing the use of any other language but Hebrew, inhibiting the use of any other language by his children in his home—that evoked allegiance to Hebrew in Palestine so that it became dogma in the Jewish schools, in the colonies and in the labor movement, and ennobled the Second *Aliyah*, giving it a distinction never before achieved by any group in the Zionist Movement. It laid the foundation for the Hebrew school system which, when Palestine became Israel, was to become the national school system. Ben Yehuda had prepared the way for the language controversy in 1907 when all the schools of Palestine revolted against the hegemony of foreign languages and created their own autonomous schools.

His work was continued by his widow Hemda and his son Ittamar Ben Avi. Hemda took over the practical side of the Encyclopedia. She secured the material support for the enterprise. She was successful as a fund-gatherer in the United States. She was executrix of her husband's literary remains; engaged competent editorial assistance for the Encyclopedia and was responsible for the publication of its 15 volumes.

Only six volumes had appeared during Ben Yehuda's lifetime.

Ittamar was a fiery, colorful orator and an able polemical writer. He seemed to be driven by the same passion which inspired his father. He, however, was articulate and capable of forensic exposition and enjoyed himself greatly in controversy. No matter what language Ittamar used he always began his speech in Hebrew. He had a way of making the words of any language sound like Hebrew. He liked to show his skill in appropriating foreign speech to Hebrew expressions. Once the writer was in Tel Aviv at a public affair and made a few remarks in English. Ben Avi eagerly undertook to translate and made the few stiff English paragraphs used sound like an oration by Demosthenes.

[The language was more important to Ittamar than the content of his speech. He loved it for its own sake. He reveled in its sounds. He was born in Jerusalem in 1884, studied in Berlin and Paris and went into exile with his father during the war, collaborating in his publications and returning with him to Jerusalem when peace was made. Ittamar spent many years in the United States as a propagandist for the Jewish National Fund and died in our midst in 1943.]

Ben Yehuda struggled to free the language for use in everyday life in natural and artificial ways, and prepared for its use by the first generation born in Palestine. He removed the fear of innovation from the heart of the orthodox. He was responsible for the birth of a sturdy generation that tackled every problem of language and emerged with new words in authentic Hebrew to fit into the pattern of life. It had room in which to shelter new idioms taken from everyday life, scientific terms, words created by the intercourse of daily life. The new generation took what Ben Yehuda gave them with gratitude; then, later, with a certain disdain and arrogance; they kicked away the ladder on which they had risen. They seemed to wish to forget Ben Yehuda whose whole life—and what he had done with it—was imprisoned in his Encyclopedia where his personality is revealed to all who seek to find it.

NAPHTALI HERZ IMBER (1856–1909)

The last years of Naphtali Herz Imber, the author of Hatikvah (the Jewish National Anthem), were spent in the United
States. He was born in Galicia in 1856 and died in New York
in 1909. He might have lived to a ripe old age, but nothing
could stop him from drinking himself to death. He knew where
he was going and made a thorough job of getting there quickly.

He came to the United States in 1892. When his father died
he left Galicia and became a traveling Hebrew poet. He stayed
a while in Vienna, in Constantinople and in London. As a
youth he had charm and wit and ingratiating manners. He
knew how to flatter and serve a patron. He became a protege
of Lawrence Oliphant, the English traveler, who was interested
in the Jewish settlement of Palestine. He went with Oliphant
to Palestine and lived there for six years. He had the credentials of a Hebrew poet and made the most of his meager opportunities to live on his talent. His first poems were collected
under the title of *Barkai* and dedicated to Oliphant. In this
volume appeared "Hatikvah," which became the Zionist song,
and "Mishmar Hayarden," another poem which was more popular with the early settlers in Palestine. After Oliphant's death
Imber went to London where he lived a precarious life. He
was a burden on all lovers of Hebrew. He always thought Hebrew literature owed him a living. Israel Zangwill made a
caricature of him in the character of Melchizedek Pinchas in
The Children of the Ghetto. It was an idealized portrait of
Imber. Many stories were told of his escapades in London
which were later enlarged upon by his admirers, who in their
youth were fascinated by Imber's bizarre personality.

Wherever he appeared he told tall tales about himself, not
many of them truthful or convincing, especially those with
which he regaled whoever was willing to hear his amorous adventures. There was nothing in his appearance when we knew
him that warranted belief in the authenticity of his romances
with women for whom, he declared, he had a fatal attraction.
Before he finally settled down on the East Side he traveled all

over the United States, sometimes as a Hebrew Troubadour, sometimes disguised as a Mahatma and fortune-teller. He wrote strange articles in English on esoteric subjects. He pretended a knowledge of theosophy and Hindu and Chinese lore. For a time he published a theosophical magazine in Boston under the title of *Uriel*. A second collection of his Hebrew poems appeared in 1902, a third in 1905 after the Kishinev pogroms. It was as a Hindu fakir that he appeared in San Francisco where he married a gentile lady impressed by his mystic behavior. This legend was never verified. He wanted to be known as the Jewish François Villon but he was not the scoundrel Villon was nor did he write such good poetry. His past was always obscure just as his present always seemed to lack the substance of reality.

I first met him in 1901 in Philadelphia at a Zionist convention. He was certainly not an attractive character. He had the head of an Indian, his face was bronzed, his hair was long and his clothes were always in tatters. He was indescribably dirty and always exuded the aroma of stale whiskey. He was on the platform at the mass meeting. When they sang Hatikvah he rose unsteadily to his feet and accepted the applause as meant for him, with a grin of self-satisfaction as if to say, "It was I who laid that golden egg." A bottle of whiskey stuck out of his coat pocket. No one in the audience seemed to know him. They marveled at his grotesque behavior.

Once having identified me as an easy mark for curiosities, which I was, he made it his business not to let me off and clung to me like a leech. He would write articles in English on large foolscap sheets and come to the *American Hebrew* to sell them to me. Every visit was an emergency. He wrote about the quaintest things in a strangely alien English and was never concerned with form or continuity; he avoided the usual Jewish themes of that day. Every now and then I purchased one of these articles, re-wrote them and published them, but he never remembered how many had been purchased or when they were published. He was only interested in the fee. He would never accept an invitation for lunch; he abhorred food; but would take the money given to him and scuttle away to the nearest saloon. He preferred to drink from a bottle, not from a glass. He haunted the East Side cafes, but no one knew where he lived. He was often disorderly at public meetings. He once came to a Yiddish theater where a Zionist play was being given in which Hatikvah was sung, but he was not allowed to come into the theater. A. S. Freidus, who was in charge of the Jewish section of the New York Public Library, interested Judge Mayer Sulzberger in him. The Judge knew of Imber from Israel Zangwill and agreed to give him a meager monthly allowance to be disbursed by Freidus. He was always overdrawn before the first of the month and pestered Freidus for days to give him an advance on the next month's check.

He was really not much of a poet. When he first wrote, Hebrew poetry was still rigid and traditional; there was more interest in language than in originality. Hatikvah was made the text of a song which struck a responsive chord by reason of its sentiment and melody. He had no philosophy nor was he really a "lover of Zion." In fact, he was not interested in Palestine overmuch. He mocked the seriousness of the Zionists, their romantic ideas, their tendency to mourn over the past. When I knew him he was certainly not a man of gallantry. Poetry could be written about Zion and Jerusalem, about the *Galut,* more especially about romance. The best poems, he thought, could be written only about wine and women. He had translated—so he said—Omar Khayam into Hebrew. He made believe that Bacchus was his favorite god and that he hated Niobe for her tears. He was a sardonic jester. To those who listened to him he spoke of vines, of fig trees, of Turks, of mysterious veiled women, of the drinks of many lands, of the Jordan and Jerusalem. He knew all the clichés. He pretended to joviality, which did not become him. His laughter was horrifying. It was hard to explain why we were interested in him; he had none of the geniality of the latter-day vagabonds of the Cafe Royal. It must have been that we were interested in him only because he had written Hatikvah.

I once visited him in the summer in Vineland where he was spending an enforced vacation in the country. He was the guest of Weinblatt, the Yiddish actor, who had retired to a chicken farm in his old age. Imber certainly looked queer in the company of chickens and cows and trees. He was embarrassed. He defended his presence on a farm by poking fun at the old actor. I saw the room he slept in. All he had of his own was a collection of grotesque canes and a stack of dusty manuscripts. He had no clothes except those he wore. He could have put everything that belonged to him in a handbag. He did not know what home meant nor was he conscious of being homeless. His escape was drink. He drank to stimulate his imagination or to dull his senses. Whatever it was, he never wrote what he was thinking about, really, and never spoke of what troubled him if anything did trouble him. He was no wandering minstrel; you never heard him sing. He was the perfect vagabond. The only thing that lives after him is Hatikvah, which is now being sung as the National Anthem of a reborn people. The words are his, but the Jewish people gave the words and the music life and meaning.

IN AMERICA

HENRIETTA SZOLD (1860–1945)

The traits of her character, molded in her youth, shone clearly throughout her long life. She changed little. Once her interest was captured, her time and thought abided with it tenaciously. Her earliest memories were detailed and could be relied upon as a reflection of a living reality. When she was associated with the Jewish Publication Society, she extended her interest from the simple to the all-inclusive, so that in time she was editor and translator, proofreader and critic and the symbol of its program. To every task she undertook she brought a meticulous perception. When later, her correspondence increasing, she was prevailed upon to dictate her letters to a stenographer, she had to proofread them again and again, for she could not bear to pass even a typographical error. The same painstaking attention she gave later to the Hadassah budget, to her work in the Youth Aliyah, and to her duties in the Vaad Leumi. She was the obedient slave of her assignments. Discipline to her seemed to be a moral command, and the clearing of her desk at the end of the day a primary duty. She seldom fought to have her views prevail in the presence of authority. Every now and then, the higher morality prevailed and she joined in controversy on issues she felt deeply, and her temper, once aroused, became a flame. She could not abide orthodox casuistry, the authority of clericals, and resisted their dogmas and procedures with a deep resentment. Her piety was not going to be dominated by the dialectics of piety! Her life was a chain of habit which she was unable to break; and as her habits accumulated and became a formidable mountain, she found herself more and more trapped in the ways of life she could not, or would not change. I remember her correspondence with me in my youth, regarding a manuscript. How patiently she explained in long letters why the manuscript had not been accepted, why this member of the publications committee, or that member, had refused to be influenced in its favor! She certainly spent an

*excess of her precious time to explain a situation, which, so far
as I was concerned, was so simple and comprehensible. That
was a fine excess of a great virtue; she had to be kind. She
could not be persuaded to rest awhile in her old age, but
worked on according to schedule close to the last days of her
life. Life was work! When she could not find any work for her
hands to do she folded them in her lap and found peace in
death.*

An army of American women followed Henrietta Szold; the
Jews of Palestine loved and revered her; but she was not the
conventional Zionist leader—the orator on the platform, the
ready writer on Zionist themes, a controversialist in the "general" debate. Her life was devoted to service—not on the
battlefield or in the hospital. She was the humble maid of all
work, the housewife whose work is never done, having no personal diversions, no special hobbies, very little of a life of her
own.

In her youth she had romantic dreams, but she was always
diverted by duties which her conscience would not let her pass
over. She wanted to be a teacher, a writer, an editor, a
preacher of liberal ideas. She had warm, affectionate parents
and five sisters. All the normal interests of a healthy, vivacious
young girl were reflected in her early years. She was eager to
hear learned discourses. She loved a good story. She was stirred
by good music and was a fair dancer. She was absorbed in
good literature and loved flowers inordinately. She had the
added spiritual delight of being regarded by her father as a
good substitute for the son he never was blessed with.

But her life diverted her course. Early, she was interested
in Zionism, but only as one of the items on her program of life.
What she thought would be her pleasant avocation became her
inescapable vocation. Zionism grew to be the dominant tenant
of her conscience. She thought that she would be able to subordinate it, but as the movement grew she found it to be an
unrelenting taskmaster whom she could not deny, not even
when she was over seventy and felt that she deserved a rest.

She served with humility. The burden of the Youth Aliyah

was thrust upon her shoulders when she was seventy-three. She was overwhelmed by the agonies she had to go through in the discharge of her duties. She had to see the mothers in Germany prepared to have their children go to Palestine to avoid the threatened dangers, and never to see them again. At that age she began a new chapter of service. I suggested then that the time had come for her to relinquish the terrible exactions of her new mission; that this dedicated servant of a great cause should unburden her heart of its accumulated grievances, impart her wisdom to the heavily-pressed Movement struggling with vital problems; or at least, to write her memoirs. (Who does not write them nowadays?)

This she never did. It was too late for her to change. She never violated the part she was destined to play. Habit had become too rigid. Prodigal in service, she remained humble and restrained in public speech throughout her life.

In private letters to friends or in conversations off the record she spoke her mind in bold terms. Marvin Lowenthal wrote of her life, as illustrated by letters to her sisters and to others in Hadassah; but none of them reflects her revolt against dogma and partisanship in the Movement. None of them gives evidence of the sharpness of her tongue in criticism. All her life was absorbed in the drudgery of administration, of recording and corresponding, drawing up budgets and spending them; talking to visitors; speaking at Hadassah meetings; collecting the nurses and physicians for the medical unit; working from sunrise to midnight in the affairs of Youth Aliyah. In the halls of discussion, in the councils of leadership she was rarely heard. She rejected that sort of leadership. She was a grand exemplar of consecrated service. That was her metier. For that service she was loved and respected by the citizens of the Homeland and by all Zionists the world over.

She was a Zionist before the advent of Theodor Herzl. Her love for Zion welled up from her love for things Jewish. She was an omnivorous reader. Any Jewish book, in German or English, or later in Hebrew, had an irresistible attraction. She was an ardent and wondering admirer of Emma Lazarus, the young American girl of Sephardic parentage who wrote impassioned Zionist poetry long before the days of Herzl. When she taught English in an evening school for immigrants in Baltimore she met *Chovevei Zionists* who sat at her feet in the classroom and repaid her in full measure for her friendship with their loyalty and devotion to Zionism. The Messiah and the Redemption were an integral part of her Jewish faith. Her intellectual life was guided by the noble example of her father, a Zionist of the old school, a man of wide learning, a personality of great integrity.

She moved out of her normal life to identification with Zionism in gradual stages. She gave voluntary aid in the founding of the Jewish Publication Society and in 1892 joined its staff as secretary and editor, and remained chained to its service until 1915. Through her hands passed some of the most important early publications of the Society. She was the translator of a large part of Graetz's monumental *History of the Jews*. She translated and edited several volumes of Louis Ginzberg's *Legends of the Jews;* Moritz Lazarus' *Ethics of the Fathers;* Nahum Slouschz's *Hebrew Renaissance*. She was more than translator and editor; she selected the paper and the type; she read the proofs; she "sold" many of the manuscripts to the conservative board of editors of the Society. She was one of the first to aid in publications for Zionist propaganda. She wrote and translated articles for the old *Maccabean* founded in 1900. She edited or translated a number of pamphlets issued by the Federation of American Zionists. She drew together a small circle of young women and founded a study circle out of which emerged the Hadassah.

She came to Zionist public meetings and attended several Zionist conventions. She finally was persuaded to take on the duties of the secretary of the Federation after Dr. Judah L. Magnes had retired from the office. Dr. Magnes was responsible for his immediate successor, who was not adequate and had brought the finances of the Federation to the verge of bankruptcy. It was characteristic of Miss Szold that when she was told of the financial disorder, she agreed to become the secretary on a voluntary basis and for a limited period. She was determined to bring the finances back to normal and was outraged by the fact that the receipt of contributions to the Jewish National Fund had not been acknowledged. Night after night, for eight months, she was absorbed in digging out the names and addresses of contributors, sending them proper receipts and adjusting matters with the head office of the Jewish National Fund in The Hague. She spent long evenings at the musty Zionist office on East Broadway and finally had the satisfaction of knowing that every contributor had been identified, given a receipt, and his account closed. That duty being performed, Miss Szold returned to her normal pursuits. But she was finally won over completely to Zionism at the beginning of the First World War when the Provisional Zionist Committee was organized under the chairmanship of Louis D. Brandeis and she was asked to serve as director of its Education Department.

When she severed her relations with the Jewish Publication Society in 1916, her Zionist work filled her whole life. She was the inspiration of the first group of Hadassah women. She prepared and equipped the first two Hadassah nurses who went to Palestine. Her assignment to the field of education of the Provisional Zionist Committee became a major operation. She organized a group of educators to assist her and at one time threatened to absorb in her bureau a full program of educational propaganda (as well as a larger part of the budget of the Provisional Committee). She had the advice and cooperation of Reuben Brainin, the Hebrew writer; Kalman Whiteman, the Hebrew pedagogue; and Emanuel Neumann, then a young man in the teaching profession. For the first time in its history the Zionist Movement was equipped with an educational apparatus that commanded respect. The work continued until 1919 when Zionist policy was diverted to accord with Mr. Brandeis' views as to the future of the organization. Education was to be directed exclusively to service of specific projects. Political propaganda was to be discontinued. There was an interval of uncertainty as to Miss Szold's future which was solved by sending her on a mission to Palestine which she had not seen since 1909. Together with Dr. Seth Hirsch and

Jacob de Haas she had organized the Hadassah medical unit.
Now she was to go to Palestine as liaison for Hadassah with
the medical unit and to share direction with Dr. Isaac Ru-
binow.

That assignment settled her course. The rest of her life was
spent shifting from Palestine to the United States and back
again. She continued her interest in the medical unit and the
growth of the Hadassah in the United States. She made a number of American speaking tours. She participated in Zionist
and Hadassah conventions. On the other end of the line she
joined the *Vaad Leumi* (Jewish National Council) in charge
of Palestine's social service. In 1927 she was elected a member of the Zionist Executive, serving with Frederick Kisch and
Harry Sacher. In 1933 she took over the Youth Aliyah which
was her last, long assignment.

The curious thing about Miss Szold was that in spite of her
deep love for Palestine, her great interest in every phase of its
development, her intimate friendships with hundreds of people in Palestine, she never could rid herself of the longing to
return home to Baltimore. Her mind and body were occupied
in Palestine, but her memories clustered with deepest affection
and sentiment around her life in Maryland—her father, her
mother, her sisters and their children. It was an incurable
nostalgia. She was always promising to return home to remain,
to spend her last days with her surviving sisters and their children, to index her father's library for shipment to Palestine
(a pious pledge she was never able to keep). She wanted to
see and smell the flowers of Maryland. But there she was in
Jerusalem, the beloved foster mother of thousands of orphaned
children, and the captive of the Cause to her last day. She died
in Jerusalem in 1945 at the age of 85.

She remains imbedded in the memories of Hadassah women.
She remains a warm and sympathetic personality in the history of the Zionist Movement in the United States. She will be
remembered in the free State of Israel for what she did for
thousands of men, women and children. She will be remembered for her great devotion, her wide sympathies and her

understanding of the difficulties of a mass of human beings, coming out of servitude to freedom; she was a mother to them all.

STEPHEN S. WISE (1874–1949)

The first period of Zionism had to win Jewish recognition of the Promise. The seeds were brought over from Eastern Europe. But Stephen S. Wise was the first American Apostle to the Gentiles. In those days he was eager to find a cause to fit his ardent nature and give him scope for advocacy. He used the platforms available for his oratory also to serve Zionism. He was a liberal in religion and in politics, but he was not a theologian or a politician. He fraternized with American leaders and got a hearing for his views, for he had a great capacity for friendships. His stay in Oregon made him well known as an orator and a reformer on the Pacific Coast. He was a leader in exposing municipal corruption and stood out with other religious leaders for the reform of municipal government. He achieved a prominent place in the Democratic Party and soon was accepted as a formidable leader. He seldom overlooked an opportunity to further Zionist interests or Jewish causes. He carried the message to far-off places and made the press in effective headlines. He was the only outstanding Zionist in that field until the advent of Louis D. Brandeis, who was also known as a leader and reformer, but in a more impersonal way. Mr. Brandeis reflected liberal ideas but he never actively co-operated in any political party. When the great lawyer became known as a Zionist, many new doors were opened for our Cause, and Dr. Wise naturally gravitated toward him and joined forces with him in the interests of Zionism. The prestige of Mr. Brandeis and the oratory of Dr. Wise led to the conversion of many in the group which was then backing Woodrow Wilson for the presidency. Dr. Wise was accepted as a Democrat in good standing, but he seldom allowed that fact to bind him when he thought Jewish interests demanded freedom of action. He had many collisions with Franklin Delano Roosevelt, but maintained an unbroken friendship with Harry

S. Truman. He grew mellow with age and began to seek peace and friendship where formerly peace was his least concern. He welcomed the State of Israel with fervid exaltation. He felt that his life had been given to the greatest Cause one could experience in Jewish life. My friendship with him had its ups and downs. I was the victim of formalism and always liked to play the game according to the rules. He was the incorrigible improvisor, and was ready, without hesitation, to follow the beckoning of opportunity, if it led to immediate startling results. He went along with Mr. Brandeis in the Keren Hayesod controversy, but soon came back to serve the Fund he had rejected. I worked with him in the American Jewish Congress during the exciting period when the menace of Hitler aroused, in gradual stages, the American Jewish Community. I stood with him in the organization of the American Jewish Conference and then of the World Jewish Congress. He lost his interest in the American Jewish Conference quickly and I was left to carry that burden until its affairs were liquidated in 1948. We were comrades-in-arms when the State of Israel was born and when Dr. Weizmann retired from the Zionist Organization. He was a generous friend and a forgiving foe and capable of magnanimous behavior. American Jewry has never had another leader of his stature and gifts.

Stephen S. Wise was one of the founders of the American Zionist organization and its best known leader for half a century. But it would be unfair to claim that his colorful personality was limited to one area of public life. He followed many lights. His was not a single-track mind. He was a leader of many causes. To Jews he was a commanding figure in and out of all parties. Wherever he took his stand, he had his own accent and was likely at any moment to breach the program and the tactics of the issue in which he was interested. He was a Reform rabbi, but seldom conformed to the dogmas and strategies of Reform Judaism. He was often at odds with Orthodox Judaism, but as he became older he had a reluctant sympathy for the old piety and old customs. He used to say that he was a "general" Zionist, but he ranged freely from one party

to another and the end of his life saw him embrace all Zionist
parties in an upsurge of sentiment, when the flag of Israel
was raised.

So too in American life. To his non-Jewish friends (and they
were legion) he was the broad-minded American rabbi who
"raised his voice" for every humanitarian cause, regardless of
creed, nationality or race. He was an admirer of Theodore
Roosevelt. He was a Wilsonian Democrat. On occasion, he
stood with the insurgents of both major parties. All his life he
fought municipal corruption under whatever banner it masked
itself; and he was relentless in opposition to Tammany Hall.
He was as ready to fight as to support the party in which he
was enrolled. He was never frightened by the bogey of consistency. He followed his own *daemon.* He waited for the spark
that ignited his spirit to free his speech. It was a sense of justice
or humanity; it was friendship or prejudice; often it was excess of indignation or temperament; and more often it was the
glimpse of an inspiring phrase which he seized with swift passion and made the most of. He could not endure shackles. He
would not walk a straight line. He had no respect for logic.
But, in the last analysis, no matter what might have been the
aberration, he was the prodigal son returning to his own people in every crisis, marching along with them wherever they
were going.

When Herzl's *Jewish State* startled the Jewish world, Wise was
a young man just out of college. He was a postgraduate
student at Columbia in the Semitics Department, studying
under Professor Richard Gottheil. His father was a learned
rabbi and wanted Stephen to follow in the family tradition and
also to become a rabbi. Through his father's influence Wise
secured his first pulpit. It was the B'nai Jeshurun Congregation
of New York. The writer was a stranger in the city at the time
and by chance heard Wise preach on a Sabbath morning. It
was a modified Orthodox service. In spite of his youth, Wise
was an impressive figure in a gown, a mitred hat and a high-
church turned collar. He was even then the master of ritual and
form and knew how to use his resonant voice. But he was not

at home there. What kind of a rabbi he was to be—whether a
rabbi at all!—was not clear to him then. He was not a graduate
of a rabbinical seminary. His father wanted him to turn his
mind to scholarly pursuits. His education did not include
more than a contact of courtesy with Hebraic or Talmudic
tradition. He was more at home with the New England Tran-
scendentalists, with the leaders of the Unitarian Church, with
the son of a rabbi—Felix Adler—who had rejected Judaism and
founded the Society for Ethical Culture. The larger part of
Wise's cultural equipment was American. He had not found
the springs of the Jewish renascence which were then effer-
vescent in Eastern Europe. He was an isolated figure looking
to the right and to the left, uncertain of the way he should go.

The Jewish community of that period—as he saw it—was
drab, parochial and unattractive. The older settlers from Germany were ridden by rabbis educated in Germany, many of
whom were still speaking German and preaching an easy unresisting assimilation and a universalism based on the prophets,
a "mission" which had no missionaries. The newcomers from
Eastern Europe were crowded into the East Side, with their
own language, their own traditions, their own press, struggling to find a place in the new world, but determined to do
that in their own way. The two groups seldom met as brethren.
Philanthropy was the only bridge that brought them together, but not as equals. They had different standards and
clashing hopes. The Hebrew Union College was graduating
young rabbis who were sent forth to Americanize their congregations. The Jewish Theological Seminary, based on conservative ideas, was in the first stage of its development. The
East Side Yeshivahs were merely inadequate replicas of their
East European models.

The call of Theodor Herzl determined Wise's destiny.
Herzl's pronouncements in the European press, the support
given his views by Max Nordau, the press agentry of Israel
Zangwill, the calling of the First Zionist Congress, the protest
of the rabbis of Munich, the attacks of the Anglo-Jewish community and of Orthodox rabbis everywhere gave Wise his
cue for action. Here was a cause which was in need of militant

advocacy. He offered his services to Richard Gottheil, who was its first official Zionist spokesman in the United States. He got to know the American rabbis whose sympathies were with Zionism, the Jastrows, the venerable Gustave Gottheil, Benjamin Szold of Baltimore, Bernard Felsenthal of Chicago. He met Herzl and other Zionists in Europe. The isolation of Wise (as well as of American Jewry) was broken by the advance of Zionism. Thus, while in a general way Wise had a cursory knowledge of Jewish theology from German sources and from his father, his Jewish masters were not theologians or rabbis. They were Theodor Herzl and Max Nordau, whose sensational utterances at Zionist Congresses inspired an ever-growing Jewish interest in the United States. That movement thus conceived became the guide of his life, colored his thinking (but did not monopolize it) and gave what he said when he spoke on Jewish subjects a tone and dignity and purpose it could have acquired from no other source.

In the issues of the *American Hebrew* of over fifty years ago will be found the contributions of Wise which were tolerated by that publication because they were official communications. Zionism was being attacked on the editorial pages of the *American Hebrew* with consistent resentment of its intrusion on the American scene. But Wise did not remain long in New York. He left in 1900 to occupy a Reform pulpit in Portland, Oregon, where he remained for six years. It was a voluntary exile, for he could have remained in the East had he chosen. In Portland, he matured as rabbi, preacher and social worker. He was now a full-fledged Reform rabbi. He was interested in labor problems and municipal reform and national political issues. His qualities as an orator became known from coast to coast. He would return to the East on brief visits. He won friends in non-Jewish as well as Jewish circles. His going to Portland was due, it seems, to his secret hope that by serving as the rabbi of a Reform congregation, he would qualify for the pulpit of Temple Emanu-El of New York—proud citadel of Jewish wealth and social exclusiveness. He had a friend at court in the person of the venerable Rabbi Gustave Gottheil, but he was opposed and rejected by most of the lay leaders of

the congregation. Fortunately for him and his people, he was
not destined to be chained to that golden chariot, to be
cribbed and cabined in thought and action. Upon the frustration of his ambition, he hit out for freedom through the Free
Synagogue.

He was never intended to be the rabbi of a parish or congregation. He was more than a minister, whose sermons were
incidental to parochial duties. He always saw himself standing
on a platform addressing a multitude, arousing them to war
against injustice, stirring the public conscience, preaching the
brotherhood of man, regarding nothing human as alien to
him. And he was determined that not only should his congregation hear what he had to say but that his words should push
their way into the press, and win the larger audiences.

The Free Synagogue was his platform for fifty years. He became the boldest, the most exciting commentator on American
and Jewish affairs. He took Felix Adler's place at Carnegie
Hall. He sponsored lost causes with the fervor and fire of
consecration. He was irrepressible and unpredictable, but always spoke his own mind. He could always be depended
upon for audacity of attack, as the master of winged words,
never to be controlled, reckless of the consequences to his
own personal career. It was from the platform of the Free
Synagogue that Wise took his stand on all the issues of the day.
He was concerned with national and state government. He
was savage in his attacks on the municipal rottenness in New
York and Philadelphia and all our large cities. He was a
leader in defending civil and religious rights, in demanding
that racial and religious discrimination cease. The suppression
of minorities anywhere in the world aroused his denunciation
and stormy protest. He associated himself with the apostles of
freedom in all lands.

But the central theme of his varied interests, the most
sacred of all causes which he served was the Zionist Movement,
in which was included not only the ideal of a Jewish State in
Palestine but the rebirth of the Jewish nation. In Zionism
was included, so far as he was concerned, Jewish rights everywhere, Jewish democracy, Jewish survival. It was the Ameri-

can Jewish Congress and the World Jewish Congress; it was
the structure of the Jewish community; it was Jewish education; it was resistance and protest all along the line against
Jewish inequality; it was Jewish pride and dignity.

The first phase of modern Zionism was determined by
Theodor Herzl. It was a matter of political negotiations and
propaganda. Herzl's failure to win support from Germany and
Turkey and the rejection by the Zionist Congress of England's offer of Uganda followed by Herzl's death closed that
chapter of Zionist history. The successors of Herzl were unable
to restore the political objective as the center of the Movement
until the beginning of World War I.

Wise was a political Zionist. It was Herzl's adventure and
mission which stirred his imagination. He thought of Zionist
leadership as associated almost exclusively with political propaganda. Of all Zionists in the first decade of the movement in
the United States he had the qualifications and the desire to be
of service in the political field. He became a political force in
American life. He associated with political movements. He as-
siduously cultivated American political leaders. He had a deep
interest in winning non-Jewish support for Zionism. In due
course he had a large circle of political friends in every party
and in all liberal circles, especially, who were sympathetic to
the Zionist views of their favorite rabbi. He was a political
friend of Woodrow Wilson as well as a leading democratic
campaigner in that period. His name went a long way to help
make Zionist ideals popular, although during that first decade
he was more often than not on less than speaking terms
with American Zionist leaders, whom he classified as *kultur*
Zionists.

He was never able to rid himself of the overwhelming influence of Theodor Herzl and the prejudices of that early period.
He regarded the spiritual Zionism of Ahad Ha-am as a form of
opiate for the Jewish masses, which would keep them in the
bondage of a culture that never would lead to political
rebirth. The fact that members of the faculty of the Jewish
Theological Seminary were the new leaders of American Zionism and that Judah L. Magnes was their spokesman did not

help to reconcile Wise with what he regarded as new trends
in Zionism. He sulked in his tent. He complained bitterly of
the influence of Magnes and the Seminary but made no effort
to counteract that influence. He went his own way as an ambassador without credentials, relying upon his own platform in
the Free Synagogue.

When Louis D. Brandeis came to Zionism and headed the
Provisional Zionist Committee, Wise returned to the Zionist
fold. He saw Zionism again becoming a political force. His
large influence in the Democratic Party and with President
Wilson had a great deal to do with the final decision of the
American Government to approve of the Balfour Declaration.
Wilson recognized the intellectual leadership of Mr. Brandeis,
but it was to Wise he looked for the political advocacy necessary
to win public opinion for the cause and the Democratic Party.
Thus Wise became one of the molders of Zionist policy in
the United States in one of its most critical moments. He was
its most outstanding propagandist in non-Jewish circles. He
was its most effective advocate with government authorities.
From 1922 until the death of Franklin Delano Roosevelt, he
was the most impressive Jewish public figure in Washington.
He had taken on at that time the leadership of the American
Jewish Congress, whose destiny he guided as well as the destiny of the World Jewish Congress which was organized in
1936. His great influence continued unabated through the Second World War, when he was the Chairman of the American
Zionist Emergency Council and later its co-chairman with
Abba Hillel Silver. When he withdrew from official leadership
in the Council, relinquishing his authority in favor of Dr. Silver, his voice was not muted. Again he reverted to his own
platform, to his own audiences, to his own circles of influence
and to the last days of his life retained his freedom.

He was an orator and preacher of the old school. His voice
was deep and resonant and changeable. He had the equipment
of a grand actor and used the platform not only for oratory but
to present a dramatic performance, always thrilling, always
moving and always loaded with effective phrases. He was capa-

ble of winning the applause of tremendous audiences. His name was on the list of speakers of many of the great meetings held in the largest halls for causes which stirred the whole country. He preached many a sermon well; he delivered many a eulogy with great pathos; he was good-humored and captivating at dinners at which he presided with grace and dignity; he was a tempestuous political orator comparable to the best in American political life. But he was superb when he freed himself of form and manuscript and gave unbridled sway to his emotions. He often missed the bull's eye of accuracy; his logic was faulty, but the range of his vocabulary, the power of his invective, the wrath he was able to pour into his polemics gave these improvisations the quality of incomparable oratory.

Who will forget the period of his angriest mood, when the sinister figure of Adolf Hitler broke through the crumbling walls of the Weimar Republic and the Nazis began their march of destruction with the silent consent of the world, and in the course of their horrifying progress destroyed millions of helpless Jews? He was beside himself with savage moral indignation, and spoke in thousands of meetings and "raised his voice" so that he was heard in every corner of the earth. At that time he was beyond question the unrivaled spokesman for the appeal and protest of the Jewish people in the greatest tragedy of their history.

He was allergic to discipline in the Zionist Movement. As was indicated, he regarded the spiritual Zionism of Ahad Ha-am as disloyalty to Theodor Herzl. He was won over to the leadership of Mr. Brandeis, and regarded any opposition to his leadership as deserving of public censure. He went along with Mr. Brandeis in the controversy with Dr. Weizmann. He was opposed to Dr. Weizmann's political methods for about fifteen years and believed that these methods were the cause of the failure to convert Britain to Zionist friendship. He was against the enlargement of the Jewish Agency for Palestine. He opposed the partition of Palestine in 1937 but was reconciled to partition in 1946. He played for a time in the orchestra under

Jabotinsky's direction and with de Haas wrote an indictment of British policy under the Mandate called *The Great Betrayal.* Very soon thereafter he reversed himself and denounced Jabotinsky for his attitude toward labor in Palestine in a terrific attack. He was a hard opponent, but was always prepared to admit error and make generous amends. When the heat of anger cooled, his natural friendliness and good humor returned. In the last years he walked side by side with Dr. Weizmann, ignoring past differences, seeking in loyal friendship to be of service. In 1931, he had joined in helping to unseat Dr. Weizmann, but in 1946 at Basle he stood with Dr. Weizmann's friends to prevent his defeat.

Although he seemed a man of storms, the word "peace" had a curious effect upon him. He hadn't the heart to resist appeals for peace and unity. Even while engaged in what seemed to be a relentless controversy, he regarded it as incidental, episodic, in the nature of an interesting game, unrelated to the real thing in which he was interested. He never was able to fight to the bitter end of decision. He always seemed to be praying for a peaceful way out of the difficulty, as eager to fight for peace as he was to break it.

He was not concerned with foundations or monuments. He founded institutions and organizations and gave little thought to their future maintenance. He organized the Institute for Jewish Studies as a national seminary for the training of rabbis; it was a rival to the Hebrew Union College. A few years before his death, it was merged with the College. He gave twenty-five years of his life to the American Jewish Congress and was its champion in many a public controversy, disturbing the barons of Jewish philanthropy, running counter to their efforts to dominate Jewish life. But gradually the Congress moved away from its original moorings. He could not resist the encircling peace movements. He could not maintain a stand of belligerency against men who were his personal friends; and so he left the Congress unprovided for, dependent in effect upon the generosity of the Welfare Funds. The Free Synagogue was the foundation of his life; it was not only a platform; it was a social service with a large program. Only a few years before his death was he able to ensure the erection of a permanent home for the synagogue he had created.

In its early years Zionism was a propaganda movement. The practical work in Palestine was resisted for political reasons. There were few activities in Palestine that made an appeal for financial support. But as the Movement grew and deeper interests were aroused, more and more appeals reached the United States. There was then the Haifa Technical Institute, the Bezalel Art School, the Merhavia cooperative colony, the Herzliah Gymnasium in Tel Aviv, and, of course, the Jewish National Fund. The Keren Hayesod followed in 1921. Wise was one of the most effective campaigners for Palestine funds. He served all phases of the work indiscriminately, overgenerously. He saw Palestine on a number of occasions. He greeted the beginnings of the homeland and then saw its later development. His name appears in the Golden Book of the Jewish National Fund. Thousands of trees have been planted in his name. A village has been named Gan Shmuel in his honor. Like Herzl, however, he adopted none of the institutions in Palestine as his own; he had no favorites; he served them all in an all-embracing love. He was always the unrewarded servant of the cause.

LOUIS D. BRANDEIS (1856–1941)

Louis D. Brandeis became a Zionist too late in life. His personality was matured and fixed, and his way of life was trained in habit. It was not easy for him to learn new ways of thinking or of living. His was a liberal approach to the problems of American life. He had been greatly influenced by Lincoln, by Emerson and the New England thinkers. He looked American, he lived American, and the future of his country greatly concerned him. He was already distinguished in that way of life as a fighting lawyer for public causes. In all of his past his Jewish heritage had played no real part except as auxiliary to his basic concepts. He had to be recalled to his memory of the Jewish past that lived in his subconscious self. He had to return to his own people. It was a long distance to go. He had to be reintroduced to their living counterparts. He had to be sensitized to the tragedy of their lives, to sympathize with their aspirations and their hopes. He had to rediscover the Jewish people. The unfortunate feature of his return was that his knowledge was acquired not directly at first-hand but through the interpretations of others. These things had to be translated to him; they had to be explained. His questions had to be answered by third parties unrelated to the content of his soul. Therefore, when he passed over to the Jewish side and joined hands with his own people, he met them with fixed preconceptions, habits of thought and of speech by now rigidly his own. He had to leap over the processes that led him back to the birth of Jewish traditions, of ideals, and relate them to the Jews of his own day. Clashes were inevitable, for his mind was powerfully aggressive and seeking clear answers to his pertinent questions. He could not easily be reconciled with the forms in which the Jewish revival was being incorporated; the methods and standards of which were foreign to his experience, to his language and his social behavior; out of harmony with his personality. He got more from papers than from people. He could penetrate the meaning of intellectual conceptions; he was adept in the use of logic; but an understanding of personal relations was quite beyond him. His briefs were intended for the High Court of Justice, not for a jury or a general debate. His first defeat in the Movement was therefore his last. He retired from the Zionist field with displeasure and grief which diminished only as the years passed and as he was more and more enfolded in the silences that grew with the years. In his last days he was a symbol of rectitude and wisdom. His foundations in character could not be disturbed.

Louis D. Brandeis was the leader of American Zionists during the First World War. He was born in Louisville, Kentucky, in 1856. His parents were of Bohemian origin. He was molded by American life and there were few alien mixtures in the quality of his personality. He was taken by his parents as a youth to Europe and studied in a high school in Dresden, Germany. He returned to the United States and entered Harvard

Law School. He was an exceptional student. He had a retentive memory and a keen orderly mind. He worked his way through the Law School and took his law degree when he was twenty. He went to St. Louis to practice law, but decided to accept the offer of a classmate to open a law office in Boston. His partner had many influential connections in New England. When Brandeis was thirty his reputation as a skillful and resourceful lawyer was already well established. When he identified himself with the Zionist Movement in 1912, he was rich in legal experience and his name was linked with liberal causes and public service.

The traditions and standards of New England were integrated in his character. He acquired the habit of "plain living and high thinking." He disliked luxuries and excess in comforts. He had no itch for personal possessions and was simple in his food and clothing. He was reserved and restrained in speech and gave the impression of not revealing the workings of his mind freely. He was a Puritan in spirit and conduct, naturally thrifty and cautious. IIe hated ostentation and pride all his life. He was thoroughly American, feeling himself a product of its history, grateful to its great men, and endeavored at all times to measure up to the obligations of American democracy. He emphasized in all his public addresses the distinction of America as not being in its bigness but in the quality of its democracy; its doors were open to all on a basis of equality. His democracy was not soft and abstract, but resolute and practical. He was a moralist. Boston was the hub of his universe; he always came back to it as his home. IIe was a Jew, but did not regard it as his duty to assert the fact unless a situation called for it. He belonged to no Jewish religious body. And yet unrelated as he was to all forms of Jewish life, unread in its literature and unfamiliar with its traditions, the heart and mind of this man were captured by the ideal of the rebirth of a Jewish State and he became one of the few American Jews who understood and appreciated the genius of Theodor Herzl.

The identification of Mr. Brandeis with the Zionist Movement lifted it out of a narrow circle and enabled it to take advantage of the new political conditions which matured during World War I.

A decade of Zionist work had produced a substantial layer of Zionist life among the new settlers and their children. But the settlers of the older period were hostile to the new trend and fought it with harsh resentment. They regarded it as a disturber of their peace of mind; it was an offense to their Americanism; it was an obstacle to Jewish adjustment in a democratic environment; it revived memories they wished to forget. The orthodox at that time were steeped in their traditions and rejected innovations; they believed in the Messiah and the Redemption of Zion, but God had to utter the word. The Jewish labor movement accepted the materialistic conception of history that came from the mind of Karl Marx; they had already written off Jewish nationality as one of the sacrifices the Jews would have to make for the world-revolution; and they regarded Zionists as benighted reactionaries. The Zionist pioneers in the American field found it hard to overcome this formidable triple-headed opposition.

Through his position in American life Mr. Brandeis was able to develop a Zionist Movement colored by American standards and ideals. He had made a place for himself in American life without emphasizing his Jewish identity. His return to Jewish ideals therefore had an enormous influence upon all Jews—orthodox and reform, labor and liberal.

He took command of Zionist affairs in 1914 and held his control until he was named by President Wilson to the U. S. Supreme Court Bench. He became the master of Zionist facts. With the single-mindedness and tenacity for which he was distinguished as a lawyer he made the organization of the movement his special task. By "organization" he did not necessarily mean a democratic organization. He meant establishing law and order, planning, securing the resources for action, depending upon masses of people. The brief was in his hands. All believers were expected to cooperate. He prepared himself to assume the responsibility. He read modern Jewish history. He heard witnesses who told him of the facts of Jewish life. He listened with great patience and remembered all he heard accurately. He met Aaron Aaronsohn, the discoverer of "wild wheat," who lost his life in the intelligence service of the British in the First World War. He had long and exciting discussions with Shmarya Levin, who was a sagacious analyst of Jewish thought and history. He met Nahum Sokolow, who had an inexhaustible fund of Jewish knowledge and recollection of historic fact, whose erudition made a deep impression on him. He knew little of the Jews of Eastern Europe or, for that matter, of Jews in general. He read up on Palestine and Zionist achievements. In general, he was a relentless cross-examiner and once he began questioning any man about Jewish affairs, his witness was in for a terrific raking of memory and a testing of its accuracy.

He was fresh and eager when he became head of the war-time Zionist agency which was charged with management of the larger part of international Zionist functions. The official world leadership had broken up; Sokolow and Tschlenow were in London; Shmarya Levin was in the United States; Victor Jacobson was in Copenhagen; Hantke and Warburg were in Berlin. Dr. Weizmann was not an official member of the leadership. He was the unofficial negotiator with the British Government on the proposed Declaration. Thus, Mr. Brandeis was the leader in fact of all Zionist affairs and procedures. The legal responsibility had been assigned to the Provisional Committee by Dr. Levin, with the approval of all Zionist authorities.

Mr. Brandeis took over with zest and enthusiasm. He would come to the Zionist offices in New York early in the morning and remain for hours, receiving visitors, questioning them and assigning tasks. He presided at the frequent meetings of the committee and won general admiration for the cogency and subtlety of his questions and the sagacity of his conclusions. He was innocent of vanity or conceit and unconventional in his behavior. He had a cordiality that won confidence. He was seldom direct in attack, but with rare subtlety insinuated the trend of his thinking into the discussion. But he could be merciless in judgment too, and his indignation could be devastating. You did not feel that he was forcing his views; he drove them home by logic and dominated the situation with tact and reason. He would take his coat off, loosen his tie, ruffle his hair, use his hands actively and twist his body in the chair as he carried on a hearty discussion with infinite patience.

The Provisional Committee assumed direction of every phase of Zionist activity. All Zionist groups were brought under its wing. Mr. Brandeis established a control over all funds. He set in motion a relief activity to reach remote corners of Jewish life in the war zones. He organized the sending of money from the United States to Poland and Palestine. The transfer department of the Provisional Committee was a large apparatus, occupying an entire floor in a loft building, with several hundred employees. He had a tremendous appetite for reports; nothing provoked him more than an executive who was reluctant to provide him with reports on request.

He joined Shmarya Levin on the platform and together they drew large audiences wherever they appeared. He was not an orator, but his directness and clarity, his moving sincerity, his use of illustrations drawn from American history made Zionism for the first time a matter of interest to all Americans and Jews. He was a controversialist on the platform. He challenged the opposition of the Reform Jews of wealth. He provoked to reply men like Jacob H. Schiff and Judge Mayer Sulzberger. He gathered a coterie of personal friends—men and women theretofore alien to Zionist and Jewish thinking—who served him with loyalty and reverence. He had Judge Julian W. Mack help him. Mrs. Joseph Fels became an interested member of the inner group. Men of affairs like Louis Kirstein and Eugene Meyers placed themselves at his disposal. Julius Fohs was interested to investigate the oil possibilities of Palestine long before oil was found in Arabian lands. Bernard Flexner, of Chicago, gave his skill and experience to financial problems.

He inspired confidence and optimism with rare skill. He believed from the start that the Allies would win and that one of the fruits of their victory would be the fulfillment of Herzl's program. He excluded all sympathies with Germany. He rejected every suggestion that came from German Zionists for testing German offers to give national group rights to the Jews of Poland. He barred pro-German and pacific Jews from Zionist councils. He had a British orientation all his life. He was deeply convinced of the Anglo-Saxon desire for justice and fair-dealing. To no Zionist was Britain's subsequent violation of its pledges as devastating as it was to him. He was unable to see the value of the American Jewish Congress until he realized that it could be used as an instrument to further the Zionist cause. It was at his suggestion that the Congress adopted the resolution inviting England to accept the Mandate for Palestine. He was opposed to the involvement of the United States in the Mandate. As early as 1914 he had received verbal assurances from President Wilson and the British Ambassador in Washington as to the intentions of the Allies with regard to Palestine. He was on terms of close friendship with Colonel House, President Wilson's confidant; with William Hard and Norman Hapgood, liberal democrats, writers and lecturers. He was the American correspondent of the Zionist group in London headed by Dr. Weizmann and every step taken in England in connection with the Balfour Declaration was cleared with him.

His closest adviser during these years was Jacob de Haas. In fact, it may be said that he was converted to Zionism by de Haas, who came to the United States in 1901, served as secretary of the Zionist Organization for several years and then went to Boston, where, in 1910, he had his first occasion to hold a conversation with the man who, at that time, was deeply interested in a plan for placing life insurance in the hands of savings banks. The conversations were protracted. Mr. Brandeis was led to inquire into the basic problems of Jewish life. The personality of Theodor Herzl was revealed to him through de Haas. Through de Haas he was prepared for Zionist leadership, and when he accepted the chairmanship of the American group de Haas was his closest adviser, seeing him more often than did any other man in the Movement. It was Mr. Brandeis' habit to call de Haas before breakfast, regardless of time and convenience. De Haas' life was no bed of roses; but he was dedicated to strengthening Mr. Brandeis' position in the Zionist Movement and in American life.

In later years, after de Haas had led his friends in revolt against the Zionist Organization and his alignment, to a degree, with Revisionist elements, Mr. Brandeis' close friends sought to break the spell of de Haas' influence. They did not succeed. In 1928, Judge Mack, then a past president of the Zionist Organization of America, wrote to Mr. Brandeis, suggesting that de Haas was using Mr. Brandeis' prestige for ends that led to separating him from his Zionist friends. The complaint was made that members of the group, including Henrietta Szold, were unable to discuss Zionist problems with Mr. Brandeis and were being referred to de Haas. This was a fact. Mr. Brandeis preferred to conduct his affairs so that all facts on any given problem could come to him through one person who knew his mind. Mr. Brandeis rejected Judge Mack's complaint and wrote to him: "No one whom I have met has been more devoted (than de Haas), more knowing and on the whole more clear-sighted in all the political aspects and in his judgments of a political character." He said that de Haas was responsible for his political views on Zionism and it would be the height of folly in the strenuous times ahead to get along without his knowledge and experience. He acknowledged his indebtedness to de Haas on a number of occasions. At 68, he called de Haas "his teacher and companion." He was conscious of no reason to doubt de Haas' reliability. De Haas was the first to reveal the mystic ideals of Zionism. He had touched the mantle of Herzl. He knew how the First Zionist Congress had been assembled; who were its leading figures; what were the issues. Mr. Brandeis was delighted to hear all de Haas had to say and kept it in his memory as the first deposit of Zionist instruction. The verbal extravagances of de Haas were an oriental quality, a part of his Sephardic heritage. There was something strange in the relationship. De Haas was the antithesis of Mr. Brandeis; he was complicated in his thinking; he could never tell a tale simply and made no effort to clarify his theme. He loved to dramatize political situations. But there is no doubt of the authenticity of the close personal relations established between these two antipodal men.

Mr. Brandeis went to Palestine with de Haas for the first time in 1918. The Balfour Declaration had been issued on November 2, 1917. A Zionist Commission headed by Dr. Weizmann had been sent to Palestine. The British Army was in charge of Jerusalem and British officials with experience in Arab lands were being assembled to set up the Mandatory Government.

Mr. Brandeis found Palestine a promising land, with much to be rebuilt, much to be created. He was amazed and distressed by the prevalence of malaria. He was disturbed by the anti-Zionist prejudices of the British officials. He found little encouragement in what the Zionist Organization was doing. He returned with an accumulation of devastating criticism. He found the Zionist group in London an assembly of refugees in a state of nervous anxiety, uncertain of the future, lacking funds and groping in the dark as to where the means could be found now that the road was open for the Return. The older Zionists seemed to be obstacles in the way of the new course Zionism would have to take. Their endless discussions exasperated and bored him. He wanted to cut the cackle and proceed to action. He was impatient with Zionist dialectics. He had become used to the terms employed by Herzl and was unaware of the burden of ideologies that already encumbered all Zionist thinking. He could not make order out of the "practical" programs submitted without any conception of the important factor of budget. He did not meet Arthur Ruppin, the pioneer of Zionist colonization, who had written what was to become the basis of the colonization program. Dr. Ruppin was in Turkey at the time. Mr. Brandeis had sharply criticized him for using the profits earned in money exchange with relief funds to bolster up the bankrupt Zionist corporations of prewar days.

He found himself in London for the first time in the center of a free Zionist discussion. This was new to him. Discussion in a real sense was not the habit in the American Zionist circle

dominated by Mr. Brandeis. His disciples expressed their
loyalty by agreeing or trying to agree with his conclusions. In
London, however, the European system prevailed. Everybody
talked at length without fear or favor, unconcerned by
threats of points of order. The long drawn-out debates in a
number of languages left Mr. Brandeis exhausted. He did not
understand them, nor did they know precisely the meaning of
the legal and political terms he used. It was difficult for him to
articulate his thoughts. He felt that he was talking to an alien
audience. He had the traditional English aversion for foreign
languages. He did not understand their conventions. He did
not know that agreement in private talks might be followed by
violent disagreements in formal discussion. He wondered how
American Zionists, and he more particularly, would be able to
exercise an influence upon an international body so consti-
tuted. His American mind revolted against the confusion,
against the dialectics, against the babel of languages, against
the European parliamentary system which placed a premium
on general debate and discounted the value of discussion of
details. He could not imagine himself tied to that "wagon of
Jewish renascence." He had a single-track mind; he saw
Palestine as the objective; he thought of programs and budgets,
of people and their redemption. He had been using the terms
of Jewish nationalism. For the first time, however, he appreciated the embarrassing problems arising out of the acceptance
of the nationalist ideal as interpreted by European Zionists.

His reactions were formulated in the plans later accepted by
his group when he returned to the United States. These plans
prepared the way for the controversy that arose between him
and Dr. Weizmann, which came to a climax at the Cleveland
Convention of 1921, when he and his group retired from the
Zionist Administration. His views are succinctly expressed in
his report on what happened in London, in the Zeeland document, in the memorandum adopted by the majority of the
Provisional Committee, and in a number of addresses he gave
at meetings of the dissident group which later organized the
Palestine Development Council.

He could not stand what seemed to him the disorder in Zionism. He wanted to be free to serve Zionism from Washington, rather than from London or Jerusalem. He accepted the division of the Zionist Movement into two or more parts, provided it left American Zionism, and himself as its leader, free. He was eager to accept the fact of the Mandate as sufficient reason for the liquidation of certain features of the Zionist program. He said in the Zeeland document that Zionism was no longer a propaganda movement "except the propaganda that comes from undertaking concrete enterprises." He said that the Zionist Organization as such should not assist, directly or indirectly, migration to Palestine! It was not clear what this meant, for he followed it with the statement that it might properly grant certain temporary aid to those who actually reached the country. The Zionist Organization in particular should not undertake to grant such aid, but the Joint Distribution Committee might be persuaded to do so. He thought Zionist political work in Palestine should come to an end. It was then being represented by a Zionist Commission in Palestine. In the appointment of Sir Herbert Samuel as High Commissioner, "true to the Jewish cause as well as the British cause," we had reached the culmination of political achievements so far as the present was concerned. All political questions should be solved through the Mandatory Government and its proposed Advisory Council on which Zionists and other Jews and Arabs would have representation.

He had no faith that campaigns for gift funds would produce the budgets for the rebuilding of Palestine. The forms used during the war had become obsolete in 1920. His judgment on this matter was not supported by subsequent experience. The Keren Hayesod campaigns (conducted in its own name or in partnership with others) produced ever-increasing returns from 1921 onward to 1949. He thought an appeal for investment funds would bring larger returns. He would have liked to have each local community adopt its own project. He thought individual Jews could be persuaded to engage in export and import, which would create the commerce of Palestine. He wanted to give his attention to the American end of the enterprise. He was looking for stability, fixed objectives and blueprints. That was what he was good for, but he was distressed by the emotional agitation of Zionists and their emphasis on sentiment. He found it difficult to adjust his thoughts to an international organization. The stage was too vast and too complicated. He did not accept the concept of Diaspora Nationalism. Once the Homeland was an accepted fact, the internationality of the Jewish people would be liquidated and merged in the liberated nationality settling down in Palestine.

All these ideas were the material out of which the controversy between Mr. Brandeis and Dr. Weizmann was born and developed. Mr. Brandeis was then on the Supreme Court Bench. He was not the attorney of record in the controversy at Cleveland which led to his retirement, but he was in fact its leader. He provided the strategy and the reasoning. His views were reflected in the documents issued by Judge Mack and his colleagues. His advice was freely offered and accepted without demur. He wrote many of their letters. He saw many people on their behalf. He was responsible for the drafting of the Memorandum, the adoption of which by the ZOA Administration led to the organization of the minority group. He was in no sense the "silent" leader. He did not appear on a public platform, but he was the director of the controversy until it reached its climax at Cleveland, when he and his associates retired from the scene. To assume that Mr. Brandeis was an impartial judge at that time, or for that matter at any time, when he was not on the bench, would be a misrepresentation of a great, self-revealing personality who in all his life never avoided a battle in which he thought he was right and who in this instance showed the same zeal, audacity, magnetism and polish he gave proof of in all the legal and public issues he fought before he left the practice of law for the Supreme Court.

His interest in Zionism came too late in life. He was already a man of fixed habits and acquired few new ones after sixty. Zionism was the one object of his affection and interest which he clung to and developed in the last two decades of his life. He refused the crown of world Zionist leadership in London when he was sixty-four. He then said that as a Jew he could not withdraw from a post in government upon which liberal opinion depended for the sake of Zionism which had better and more experienced men to lead it. When he donned the robes of his judicial office, he was deeply conscious of his obligations as a liberal and as a Jew, but he felt most his responsibilities toward the High Court of which he was a distinguished member. Privately he served Zionism and Palestine. He gave of his means with calculated generosity. He judged causes in Palestine on their merits and had no party interests or prejudices. He would not use the prestige of his office to further any cause privately, but he emerged on a number of public occasions to serve the Jewish cause. The fact of his association with Zionism and the Jewish people contributed to our prestige and influence through all the years of his life. He was the friend of Woodrow Wilson and Herbert Hoover. He was an elder statesman to Franklin D. Roosevelt who called him Isaiah. He made a deep and lasting record as a judge and was bracketed with Justices Holmes and Cardorzo among judges of that court who contributed to its prestige at a time of great change in American trends.

As the influence of Hitler in the world became powerful and the menace to Jewish life assumed appalling forms, his isolation from Jewish life, his physical absence from the battlefield, made his position more and more difficult. He shared the Jewish protest and indignation, but he was bound by his own way of life, now almost rigid. He maintained his position with dignity and reserve. He spoke with forceful words as the situation required and identified himself clearly and unmistakably with the destiny of his people. His visits to President Roosevelt seemed to the younger man like the appearance of an ancient Hebrew Prophet reminding him of what justice required of him. But Mr. Brandeis did not join the throng or the leadership. He was perilously near to living in an ivory tower except for the gusts of passion in the interest of his people which, on occasion, drew him out of his seclusion and gave refreshment to his soul for brief moments.

To the American public he was one of the great liberals of

his generation, one of the great judges of a great court. To Jews everywhere he was a superior moral personality whose heart and mind were engaged in the Jewish tragedy, who shared their grief and hopes. But he was bound by the chains of the conventionalities in which his American ambitions had led him and was always mindful with integrity and exactness of the position he had achieved in American life. His interest in Zionism never abated. To his last days he read the reports coming to him from Palestine, received visitors who told him of how Jews were reacting to British injustice, how they were establishing themselves in the land in spite of the mean-spirited and ungenerous conduct of the British Administration. He never forgot Zion.

He passed away in the fullness of years on October 5, 1941, just as Hitler began his career of destruction. It is doubtful whether Mr. Brandeis was able to foresee in all the confusion of the war, the possibility that out of the debacle would come the establishment of the Jewish State and the fulfillment of Herzl's dream.

JACOB DE HAAS (1872–1937)

Jacob de Haas was a Jewish journalist in London who went to the first Zionist Congress as a reporter, was named as one of its secretaries and subsequently served Theodor Herzl with diligence and loyalty as one of his general correspondents. He enjoyed a good quarrel. He was so involved in communal disputes in London that he decided it would be better to emigrate to the peaceful shores of the United States. Herzl gave him a letter of introduction to Professor Richard Gottheil, first president of the American Zionist Federation, in which he suggested that de Haas' organizing talent could be used for the Movement in New York. Professor Gottheil proposed de Haas' name to the Convention in Boston and he was elected unanimously as secretary of the organization. He was compelled to take over immediately. Professor Gottheil was never again seen at a Zionist Convention in the United States. The burden of the Movement was taken over by de Haas with unusual courage, for it was a flimsy organization that was handed to him. He carried on for a year or two, until Dr. Harry Friedenwald was elected as president, when de Haas came to the conclusion that he could not carry the burden any longer and should look out for himself. He went to Boston and acquired the Jewish Advocate *of which he was editor and publisher. I was his regular New York correspondent. He was a Herzlian Zionist in an environment which, in his view, was more cultural than political. He felt himself alone, and in spite of the efforts of a group of us to bring him back to the organization, he was at odds with the Federation until he met Mr. Brandeis and began conversations with him that led to his gradual conversion, which officially occurred when the Provisional Zionist Committee was organized. To be near Mr. Brandeis, who then lived in Boston, de Haas was appointed secretary of the New England Zionist Bureau and became Mr. Brandeis' confidant, guide and representative, finally returning to New York to become executive secretary of the Provisional Zionist Committee. Just as he had been a loyal follower of Theodor Herzl, so he now, in his middle years, became the disciple of Louis D. Brandeis. He had the tenacity of his Dutch ancestors, and once having committed himself to an issue, or a personality, was unable to relax or give up his position or change its terms. He fought against Dr. Weizmann until the last remnant of influence had oozed out of his hands. He was inexorable and probably fanned the embers of Mr. Brandeis' prejudices. De Haas returned to the Zionist Organization of America in 1930, remained for a year or so, but found himself an alien in an environment in which he had always been at home. In his desperation he joined the cause of Jabotinsky, but was too late to render effective service in the leadership of the Revisionist Party. Throughout all his years in the United States until the Cleveland Convention, we were close friends, but his star led him to follow Mr. Brandeis away from the Zionism which had its source in East European Jewish Life, and from which I derived my Zionist convictions. After the first Zionist Congresses, de Haas was never again able to identify himself with any Zionist Group or Party. He lost his interest in the Congress after Herzl's death. He lost his interest in the American Zionist Organization after Mr. Brandeis' retirement and could not contract a perfect loyalty to the Revisionist Party. His last years were darkened by disappointment and fruitless endeavor and protracted illness; but none doubted his integrity and the sincerity of his loyalties, and all deplored the ruin of a personality destroyed by excessive loyalties to personalities and dogmatic issues.*

Jacob de Haas was sent to the United States by Theodor Herzl on a Zionist mission, became an American citizen and lived ever after as an American. He was born in London in 1872 and was descended from Dutch Sephardic Jews. He attended the Stepney Jewish School and was an eclectic student in a number of high schools before he became a journalist. He remained English in manner and speech all his life; he never rid himself of the London fog in his throat. As a young man he was a member of the London Fabian Society, frequented public meetings and heckled the speakers, acquiring a talent for debate which was good preparation for a Zionist propagandist. He would take the "word" in Hyde Park on Sunday afternoons, breaking into the addresses of the free and easy haranguers in this forum of democratic discussion. He also attended Jewish communal meetings and participated in the discussions, carrying the same chip on his shoulder he had with him in Hyde Park into the Jewish community. He began to write for the Anglo-Jewish press and soon was a regular contributor to the *Jewish World* which was then the only rival of the more prosperous *Jewish Chronicle*. He was a rebel and took delight in attacking the conservative leaders of the Jewish community. He was contentious and loved to pick a quarrel. He was a restless romantic Zionist before Herzl appeared on the Jewish scene.

He was one of the first in England to respond to the call of Herzl. He went as a delegate to Basle and was named one of the secretaries of the First Congress. In spite of his contrariness he was a hero-worshiper. His first hero was Theodor Herzl. He accepted Herzl instantaneously as the great leader of his generation. He believed that Herzl was the embodiment of Daniel Deronda. He saw a mystic significance in every word Herzl uttered in his proclamations, in his books, in his personal appearances. He never was at a loss for a word from Herzl's writings in his conversation. He was proud to be one of Herzl's lieutenants. When he became Herzl's English correspondent it was a great event in his life.

When de Haas returned to London after the First Congress, the *Jewish World*, of which he became editor, was on the verge of collapse. He saw no place for himself in Jewish public life. He knew that he had powerful enemies in the community who looked upon him as a disturber of the peace. Herzl urged him to go to the United States to develop certain connections he had made. Herzl had opened a correspondence with Cyrus Adler and Oscar S. Straus. He had met a number of American delegates to the First Congress. He wrote a letter on de Haas' behalf to Richard Gottheil, first president of the American Zionist Federation. To de Haas' surprise, Professor Gottheil read the letter to the Boston Zionist convention in 1901, recommending de Haas' election as secretary, and thereupon de Haas became the administrative head of the American organization. Having secured a competent secretary, Professor Gottheil seemed to be anxious to rid himself of all official responsibilities at once, and before de Haas arrived, left for Europe on a summer vacation and remained away for many months, and thereafter was president in name only. De Haas had to carry the burden himself.

In those days de Haas was a picturesque figure. He made the most of a beard trimmed in French style. He carried himself with a Bohemian swagger, spoke of political affairs with mystic allusions to what he might reveal if he were free to speak, and had an endless fund of gossip about the leading figures in the Zionist Movement. He was a colorful talker and had decided views on many subjects. He put all Herzl's friends and followers on a high level and was cynical about the Zionism of many of the Russian Zionists who were not, in his view, political-minded or reliable. He smoked a pipe with savage intensity, drank beer like a German, and had a bizarre taste in matters of the theater. He had keen appreciation of the psychology of English men of affairs and discussed politics as if he knew the ins and outs of all the affairs of the Empire. His beard was trimmed down gradually to a mustache which, in turn, was clipped to a dark shadow and, finally, many years later, was removed altogether. The final mask was that of a New Bedford fisherman who could have served as a model for one of Rembrandt's paintings.

He was always a romantic Zionist, playing with political combinations. He was influenced by Disraeli's grandiloquent style, his oriental imagery, his fantastic mixture of the ancient and modern. Like many of the early Zionists, Zionism was to de Haas a great adventure in which he found place for self-expression that was denied to him in other areas of Jewish life. He believed that mystic influences played a large part in Jewish history. Romance and politics and mysticism were joined in a strange combination. He often dwelt upon the significance of numbers, the recurrence of historic events on the same calendar day, giving the impression that Providence was tied to numerology and coincidence, and through them, shaped the course of Jewish history. He often talked as if the Messiah were just around the corner waiting patiently to appear at a moment fixed in advance by the recurrence of a historic date. He saw portents in the sky. He used to confide that he saw meaning in the fact that he, himself, was descended from Don Isaac Abravanel who had found a haven in Holland and that one of his descendants had become Herzl's lieutenant to help in forcing the coming of the Messiah.

He loved to talk at night in cafes and spent much time at meals in restaurants in conversation. It was hard to tell what was truth and what was fancy in his discourses. He was easily provoked to informal discussion but was not so fluent on his feet. In those days I spent many evenings with him and Jacob Fishman of the *Jewish Morning Journal* in discussions of how Zionism was to be organized, how the communities were to be conquered, how the Promised Land was to be taken, about actors and plays, about decadent art. What impressed him most was what Herzl signified in the life of the Jewish people. With such a leader the long-awaited miracle could happen any moment. De Haas was a dissident by habit, but he had absolute faith in Herzl. His thoughts were usually involved and blurred, but in the midst of the fog there was always a glow of insight and imagination. He resented the pride of the mighty, but equally resented democracy when it did not go his way. When he seemed about to win the approval of the majority he began to doubt his own views and sought with all his skill as a dialectician to keep himself in that minority, which included himself and God. He felt safer in isolation.

He never thought that he would have to spend the greater part of his life in the United States and not return to live in England. He had brothers there and often visited them, but soon he felt more at home in the United States than in England. He fancied that one day he would perform his mission and return to Vienna and submit his final report to Herzl. He found himself, however, with a struggling organization on his hands, with few supporters in an uncongenial atmosphere. He continued the setting up of an administration, edited *The Maccabean,* and was on the way to freedom from worry when Theodor Herzl died.

The blow shattered him. It meant the frustration of his life. It cut the ground from under his feet. His eyes were no longer fixed on Vienna where the leader lived. He had lost his guiding star and Zionism was in eclipse. He wandered about in a wilderness of indecision. He was the secretary of the Zionist Organization, but did not know where the Organization would go after the death of Herzl. He felt that he was being encircled by Zionists who lacked his loyalty to Herzlian methods.

More and more, *kultur* Zionists were entering the movement. The "practical" Zionists were in the ascendance. The Jewish Theological Seminary was becoming Zionist-conscious, but not in the spirit of Herzl. Israel Friedlander, Henrietta Szold and Solomon Schechter were expressing themselves publicly on Zionist questions. Judah L. Magnes returned from Germany and introduced a new note which struck no answering echo from de Haas. Dr. Magnes brought with him the inspiration of German Zionist groups. De Haas could not adjust himself to the leadership of Dr. Magnes who became secretary of the Zionist Organization upon the election of Dr. Harry Friedenwald as president.

De Haas felt that his Zionist career was over. He was no longer at home in the Zionist circle. He returned to a few Zionist conventions but he was querulous, depressed and hopeless. He saw the "practical" Zionists taking over and the end of political Zionism. With Bernard G. Richards he edited a weekly publication called the *Chronicler,* which had a brief exciting life. He took a newspaper job on the New York *Commercial Advertiser* through the influence of Samuel Strauss, its publisher, but the speed of the American daily newspaper was too much for him to endure. He left for Boston and took over the management of a Jewish center. He made an attempt to enter Boston politics, but he was a Democrat in a Republican state. He became the publisher of a local Jewish periodical, the *Jewish Advocate,* which he conducted for many years. The turning point in his life was his encounter with Louis D. Brandeis.

He met Mr. Brandeis to discuss a plan for life insurance through savings banks. He became a regular visitor at Devonshire Street and in the course of time aroused Mr. Brandeis' slumbering interest not only in Jewish affairs but in political Zionism, and specifically in the personality of Theodor Herzl. It was amazing how eager Mr. Brandeis was at that time to absorb knowledge about Jews, how he remembered what de Haas told him—much of it touched with de Haas' vagrant imagination—how delighted he was with what he heard.

De Haas' imagination at once saw Brandeis as the inevitable successor of Herzl. De Haas, in turn, found his zest in life renewed by contact with the thinking of a man who was thoroughly familiar with the twists and turns of American political life and who, at the same time, was capable of appreciating the glamor of a leader like Theodor Herzl. Through Mr. Brandeis de Haas got to know Norman Hapgood, William

Hard and other liberals. He was able to persuade Mr. Brandeis to greater interest in the movement. In 1914 he enjoyed his greatest moment when Mr. Brandeis became the chairman of the Provisional Zionist Committee and leader of American Zionism. For some time de Haas continued to live in Boston as director of an office provided by the Provisional Committee, but acting throughout for Mr. Brandeis. Then he returned to New York as executive secretary of the Provisional Zionist Committee and Mr. Brandeis' "secretary of state."

De Haas believed that the coming war would shake the foundations of the civilized world and create disorders and changes out of which the miraculous would be revealed. He believed that we were destined to realize the slumbering hopes of the Wandering Jew, and that the Galuth would be liquidated. He directed and guided the spreading activities of the Zionist movement through the Provisional Committee. In the strenuous days when the Balfour Declaration was born, de Haas had moments of political clairvoyance. He organized the Jewish Legion that was sent to Palestine to fight with General Allenby. With Henrietta Szold he assembled the Hadassah Medical Unit. The S.S. Vulcan was sent with provisions for Jews and Arabs in Palestine. He expected that when General Allenby took Jerusalem the keys of the city would be handed over to the Zionist Commission and that the Jewish flag would be unfurled over the Tower of David.

Mr. Brandeis was the second hero of his life. De Haas found in him a reincarnation of Theodor Herzl. With Mr. Brandeis he believed that he could take over the whole Zionist movement. He thought of Mr. Brandeis as capable of the same devotion and service that had characterized Theodor Herzl. He established a mystic bond of brotherhood with the Puritanic Boston lawyer and thought he could create the leadership Herzl would have exercised had he lived.

But Mr. Brandeis was not of the same material as Theodor Herzl. He was not of the same age or temperament or background. Mr. Brandeis was not a poet led by his imagination, nor could he understand the psychology of a whole people as Herzl got to know it through his experiences. Mr. Brandeis shattered de Haas' hopes when, in 1920, in London, he rejected the mantle of Herzl and decided to remain on the Supreme Court Bench. At that historic meeting Mr. Brandeis heard the convincing, cold voice of Felix Frankfurter. He did not hear the voice of de Haas or of the entire American Zionist delegation. At that fateful moment the purpose for which de Haas had lived ceased to be real. He saw the collapse of his dream. De Haas was responsible for defending Mr. Brandeis' position at the Cleveland Zionist convention in 1921. He deceived himself into thinking that the Zionists of America would not reject Mr. Brandeis, that they would remember what he had done for the Movement during the difficult years of the war. De Haas was mistaken. All his calculations were wrong. A two-thirds vote overruled the position advocated by Mr. Brandeis who with all his associates, including de Haas, retired from the Zionist Organization.

The disillusionment of de Haas found expression in the same drift toward non-conformity and protest with which he began his Jewish career. He thought Theodor Herzl would bring the Messiah; Herzl died before his time, disappointed. He thought the Balfour Declaration was the fiat of destiny. But when fulfillment of the Mandate lingered far behind and Mr. Brandeis stepped over to the sidelines, the frustrations of de Haas issued as revolt along the whole course—against the faithless Mandatory Government, against the leadership of Dr. Chaim Weizmann who was the cause, in his mind, of Mr. Brandeis' retirement, against all Zionists who disagreed with his analysis of the situation. He stood away from the organization he had helped to establish. He questioned methods he had helped to create. He lost faith in prophecy. He felt that through another instrument he might give expression to the tragedy of the Great Betrayal. He came closer to the Revisionists, but never could merge with the heated, viscid climate which was so peculiarly the emanation of that party.

In his recoil from the ideology which had maintained him in his youth, the glamor of his personality was obscured. When he returned to a coalition administration of the ZOA in

1930 and appeared once more in a Zionist convention, few of the delegates knew or recognized him. His sojourn on the fringe of opposition had blurred his imagination, hardened his will, cooled his ardor and enthusiasm, and after two years of effort in an attempt to take the lead in the organization, no longer supported by the mind and name of Mr. Brandeis, he retired to isolation and opposition with fewer friends, sheltered by no organization, a free lance. He wrote *The Great Betrayal,* in which he poured invective against Britain. He wrote a brief life of Herzl which was, in fact, his memoirs of the First Leader. He wrote a brief life of Mr. Brandeis. Even the flame of wrath burned low and feeble, and he found slight comfort in what the pioneers were achieving in the Jewish National Home, which was not as he would have had it. The Homeland did not look like home to him.

The picture he thus painted of himself showed a man of dark features and dour forebodings—a man exalted by mystic influences that made it possible for him to reach out and often touch the fringe of the robes of the Messiah, and often depressed him into the bitterest reflections. He had few moments of exaltation. He seldom let his prejudices mellow; his dogmas were as hard as rock and he clung to them with obstinacy and resentment. He was a defeated man, whose defeat was reflected in everything he did or said or wrote. He could not forgive the non-Jewish world for its betrayal, nor could he be kind to the Jewish people who had disappointed his ardent dreams and plans and prophecies. His frustrations killed him in the sixty-fifth year of his life.

JUDAH L. MAGNES (1877–1948)

I met Judah L. Magnes when he returned from his studies in Germany, probably in 1903. I was advised by Mrs. Philip Cowen, the wife of the publisher of the American Hebrew, *to see an American young man who should interest me as a curious personality. I met Dr. Magnes the next day in a kosher restaurant on Canal Street. He insisted that it be kosher. He was a tall, spare young man with a light beard, who smiled*

*generously with an easy friendliness, and confessed without
provocation, that in Berlin he had been converted to orthodoxy, that he had attended a Zionist Congress and knew Theodor Herzl, and that he was born in San Francisco. He was a
charming man and wanted to see what was going on on the
East Side, and in the Yiddish Theater. Soon he was speaking
at Zionist meetings. Soon he knew all the celebrities of the
East Side, including Chayim Zhitlowsky, a famous revolutionist
and Yiddishist. We asked Dr. Magnes to speak at the Cleveland Zionist Convention, where he made what was regarded
as a militant speech. Against whom? It must have been against
Russian Pogromchiks. His theme was "Jewish Self-Defense,"
which he had also picked up in Berlin. In the course of a few
months, he succeeded Jacob de Haas as secretary of the Zionist Federation, and one year later abandoned that post to a
young reform rabbi. It was evident that he could not be kept
down to routine. He was greatly excited by life. He liked to
be free and to change his music. His next public venture was
to lead an organization, the New York Kehillah, which he regarded as a further reversion to Jewish tradition. He was
probably the first popular hero of the Zionist Movement in
America and was greatly admired by all classes of Jews. To
the surprise of all his friends, he made his way to the pulpit
of Temple Emanu-El, resigning that post shortly in a clash of
opinion on liturgical practices in the temple. The Kehillah was
the first expression of Jewish Democracy in America but Dr.
Magnes was persuaded to give away its educational program
to the Benefactors who were to provide its budget if they
would be allowed to control education through Dr. S. Benderly,
to which Dr. Magnes light-heartedly agreed, and thought the
world was a nice place to live in. It was the first step in the
wrong direction for Dr. Magnes. It led him to joining forces
with the American Jewish Committee against the American
Jewish Congress. It led to his withdrawal from the Provisional
Zionist Committee of which Mr. Brandeis was the chairman,
and to his devotion to the Jewish Relief Movement, which was
regarded by Zionists as competition to the Movement. The
Zionists were pro-Ally; Dr. Magnes was pacifist. When peace*

came, he left for Palestine where he represented Hadassah in-
terests for a time, and then became interested and identified
with the Hebrew University on Mount Scopus, an interest
which occupied the rest of his days. For all practical purposes,
he never encountered Zionism again except as the head of the
University, and as the leader of a small group of Jews in Pales-
tine who were interested in Arab-Jewish peace. He was a
stranger to Zionism in Palestine as well as to Zionism in the
Diaspora, but his pacifism was indivisible; he never fought
with Zionists, or Jews, or Arabs. He lived all the days of his
life in what seemed to be a state of wishful peace, except that
when asked to describe what he meant by peace, you could
not guess from his answer the meaning of the blissful state
which for him reconciled the existence of all hates and all
prejudices, all differences and interests.

It is difficult to interpret the contribution of Dr. Judah L.
Magnes to Zionist history. For about ten years after his conversion he was nobly excited by its ideals and prepared to
make Zionism his mission in life. Then he withdrew and was
a habitual non-conformist and critic. His activities took a
mild controversial form. He walked on the other side of the
street and seemed to be moving toward the same goal but in
a leisurely way. His life was an endless contradiction. His
Zionist faith collided with what the Movement planned to
achieve in practical terms. He made the impression of being
insensible to the political and human realities of the Jewish
position. He had an aversion for the Movement as if he could
not endure the clash of ideas, the dialectics of parties, the
dynamics emerging from ideological struggle; and his personality seemed to reject democratic responsibilities. He could
not achieve an articulated ideology. You could never get him
to understand the meaning of a nationalist Zionism. He was
above the tumult of the struggle. He was more the preacher
of morality than the practical statesman or propagandist.

At the same time, of all American Zionists he was the first
to accept loyally its implications as a guide in life. He shaped
his practice to accord with his ideal. He was a convert to

Zionism in a real sense. It brought him closer to the Jewish religion, its piety and its practices. It did not mean merely affirming the Basle Program. He spent the last two decades of his life as a resident of Jerusalem. He was at home there and glorified the beauty of the Holy City and the kind of Jewish life one could live there. He brought up his family there. He became the head of the Hebrew University and gathered around him a group of sympathetic men and women devoted to the cultural and intellectual life of the community. He was integrated with its domestic affairs.

Without harsh words, peaceful in tone and manner, his political views—if they may be regarded as such—ran counter to Zionist tendencies in every crisis. He was a pacifist in the prophetic manner. He wanted to avoid struggle and violence. He thought it nobler to shed one's own blood than to shed the blood of another; to take a blow rather than give it. He advocated a bi-national state of Jews and Arabs in spite of the fact that there was no evidence that either side believed such a state was possible. He organized a small group called the *Ihud*, printed a number of pamphlets, wrote letters to the press, testified before political commissions, and gave the impression that he was convinced that in God's own time—and in an easy way—the solution of peace and good-will would prevail. He lived long enough to see the Hebrew University on Mount Scopus occupied by Jordan troops; the Arab majority disappearing in streams of flight; and the State of Israel established in a part of Palestine. The consummation of the Herzlian idea in that form was the bewildering climax of his life. It was a complete reversal of what he had advocated without abatement from first to last. Not that way did he expect Zion to be restored.

Born in San Francisco in 1877, Magnes was typically American. He loved American sports and was interested in American baseball games even when in Jerusalem. He read the juvenile stories of Horatio Alger, Oliver Optic, Harry Castleman and Edward Ellis. He loved to talk about these books as a fond memory of youth. (I was reading the same books at the same time in Rochester, New York, where I was born.) Instead of entering a local university, he decided to go to Cincinnati where he could get his secular education and, at the same time, attend the Hebrew Union College and become a rabbi. The College was founded by Isaac M. Wise, a vigorous opponent of Zionism all his life. It was then being conducted in the spirit of its founder.

Before settling down to the life of a rabbi he went to Germany to pursue his studies further. He was a postgraduate student at the Universities of Berlin and Heidelberg, and obtained his doctorate in Berlin in 1902. In Berlin he came in contact with a new Jewish world. He was gregarious by nature and sought company among congenial persons who could instruct and interest him. He made friends of Berthold Feiwel, Shmarya Levin, Martin Buber, Ephraim Lilien (the artist), Heinrich Loewe (the librarian), and others. He was fascinated by every manifestation of the Jewish renaissance. He read *Der Jude,* a magazine published by young Jewish literati. He felt that he was being reborn and initiated into a mystic brotherhood. He was impressed by Hassidic lore, by the philosophy of Ahad Ha-am. The old Hebrew prayers moved his spirit. He was attracted to Theodor Herzl and attended one of the early Zionist Congresses where he served as translator of the German and Hebrew addresses with great success. He was praised for this by Israel Zangwill.

His sojourn in Europe transformed him. When he returned he seemed like a man who had put on the shining armor of knight errantry and was eager to conquer the world. He wore a beard and observed the dietary laws. Everything Jewish seemed to fascinate him. In New York he found the contemporaries of the kind of men he met in Berlin (on a miniature scale). He frequented the East Side and saw Yiddish plays. He read the Yiddish newspapers with eager curiosity. He admired the Yiddish poets, Morris Rosenfeld and Yehoash. He formed the Society of Jewish Art which had a short life. His conversion was amazingly thorough. He joined the Zionist Organization and became one of its most popular orators. He was the secretary of the Zionist Federation from 1905 to 1908. He became the rabbi of Temple Israel of Brooklyn and drew young people to hear his sermons. He often spoke on the East Side.

It was a travesty of consistency that Temple Emanu-El of New York, which in the past had rejected as its rabbi both Stephen S. Wise and Max Heller because they were Zionists, should now extend a warm hand of welcome to Magnes to become its religious leader, although Magnes was the glowing embodiment of a form of Zionism that contradicted all the tendencies of Reform Judaism. His success was due to the charm of his personality. He was a speaker with a pleasing, sentimental approach, disarming in its innocence. He used simple and direct language and had a flair for poetry and abstract ideas. He avoided controversy and recrimination, and loved peace. He won public favor by his modesty and not through organized publicity. He radiated goodwill and sincerity. But in spite of the impression of softness he was capable of great determination. He may have been helpless in argument but it was hard to get him to change his mind once it was fixed. His life followed a simple pattern and remained consistent throughout. He took life easily. The years did not change him much. He had the same youthful spirit when he was seventy as when he was thirty.

In the heyday of his youth he seemed to be concerned about organization. His leadership in the Zionist Organization led to that unique anomaly in American Jewish life which was called the New York *Kehillah*. This was the first attempt to organize a democratic community, pressured by the Yiddish-speaking group. Magnes' enthusiasm lacked the revolutionary spirit without which it was not to be expected that the philanthropists of Jewish life would agree to the introduction of democratic procedures. Magnes was excited about the *Kehillah;* it reminded him of a remote tradition; but he lost interest as soon as its problems were blurred by popular demonstrations, newspaper controversies and the insistent demand that the "masses" should have a determining voice in its affairs. These demonstrations were not to his taste, nor did he know how to manage the difficulties arising from them. He was at the mercy of controversialists and ideologists, and the practical side of the institution confused him.

As the *Kehillah* faded away it was followed by the Jewish Congress movement. As the Congress gained momentum Magnes found himself in a dilemma. His wealthy friends were opposed to the movement as a blatant exposure of Jewish nationalism. The Congress idea could not come in peace. It had to be forced upon a determined opposition. Magnes decided to take sides against the Zionist elements and to support the American Jewish Committee. He wanted to delay facing the issue for a later day. He was averse to any form of revolution. He did not like popular demonstrations or sensations in the press.

The *Kehillah* was Magnes' last experiment in leadership. Never again did he attempt to be a leader of men. When Temple Emanu-El refused to accept his proposals for a radical change in its ritual he tendered his resignation and withdrew to minister to the needs of the Congregation B'nai Jeshurun which had an orthodox tradition. But he soon lost his interest in preaching. He had already lost his interest in the Zionist Organization, the leadership of which had been taken over by others. He turned to the bureaucratic efficiency of the Joint Distribution Committee.

Magnes' peculiar relations with the Zionist Movement deserve special consideration. He never was a Herzlian Zionist. The glamor of Herzl's personality impressed him, but after Herzl's death political Zionism was in eclipse. When the Turkish autocracy fell and a new constitutional government was formed, Magnes proposed that the Basle Program be cast aside and that the Movement should adjust itself to a program of settlement in Palestine on the basis of equality of citizenship. His resolution to this effect was accepted by the American Zionist convention—with seven negative notes—but the resolution did not survive a fortnight of scrutiny. When the Zionist group supported the American Jewish Congress, as indicated, Magnes stood by the side of Louis Marshall, the president of the American Jewish Committee, in active opposition. When the Zionist group, under the leadership of Louis D. Brandeis, held that Zionist, as well as American, interests required a pro-Ally orientation, Magnes was a pacifist and, in a sense, a pro-German sympathizer. He sponsored the activities of a German Zionist who came to the United States to persuade the Zionists to accept a German "declaration" favoring Jewish national rights in Poland if and when Germany won the war, in place of the Anglo-American Balfour Declaration. The First World War presented an opportunity for the first time in Zionist history to raise funds for Palestine work. Magnes gave his support to the American Jewish Relief Committee and helped to organize the Joint Distribution Committee which was, in effect, a counterbalance to the Zionist effort, emphasizing the priority of relief against constructive work in Palestine. He was opposed in his own mild way to the Brandeis regime. It was he who publicly challenged Mr. Brandeis on the propriety of a Supreme Court Justice participating in controversial Jewish issues and thus was the indirect cause of Mr. Brandeis' retirement to "silent" leadership.

It was Magnes' fundamental dissent on Zionist policy with regard to Arab relations which revealed his tragic incompatibility during the years of the Mandate regime. Over a period of twenty-five years he persisted in urging a bi-national state in Palestine, by agreement, on the basis of equality of all parties concerned. During this period the Jewish community of Palestine suffered bloody anti-Jewish riots at the hands of the Arabs. They had to deal with the malignant influence of the fanatically hostile Mufti of Jerusalem. During this period the Peel Commission's report recommended the partition of Palestine, which was shelved by His Majesty's Government; an Arab-Jewish conference was held in London with the British Government meeting the Jews one day and the Arabs the next; the Mandatory Government issued the White Paper of 1939 in which the Arabs were assured of majority control of the whole of Palestine; Hitler assembled his power and let go at all Jews in Germany, extending the empire of his malevolence over the whole of Europe; from 1940 to 1948 the Mandatory

Government maintained its inhuman blockade of Palestine ports to prevent the refugees fleeing from Germany from reaching their only haven of refuge. But without varying his proposals in any appreciable way, with the same unruffled and naive spirit which was evinced when he first began his propaganda, Magnes urged again and again that the problem be solved by a bi-national state in the whole of Palestine; he submitted his views to the Anglo-American Committee of Inquiry on Palestine in 1946 in Jerusalem, and was in no way deterred from reiterating them down to the day when the State of Israel was proclaimed.

He believed—looking beyond the realities—that the Jewish people could achieve their aims through an appeal to the ideals of peace and justice. He believed that right was on both sides and that peace could come only by agreement. He wanted to keep on reminding both Jews and non-Jews of the ideals of peace and good-will, while those who should have harkened to his lofty words were trampling humanity under their feet.

Magnes spent the last years of his life in a troubled Palestine, administering the affairs of the Hebrew University, speaking of peace while his students were enlisting in the underground Haganah. He was devoted to the University. He was devoted to the Hadassah medical work. He lived a simple, modest life with no discernible ambition and with an easy mind. He was angry with the Nazis, he was disappointed in the English, he resented the Irgun underground and condemned their bloody deeds. He was accepted as a good man, fair in dealings, upright in character, clinging with remarkable loyalty and guilelessness to conceptions that had lost all meaning in a world in which genocide had become the pattern of life for the Germans whose civilization had greatly influenced his youth. His mind was revealed as a mold that had frozen, and which he could not adjust to the changing world in which he was condemned to spend his last years. He was not a party to the jubilation of the citizens of Israel when the State began its life. He did not join in the anniversaries that were being celebrated. He was not elated or hopeful. He died while on a visit to New York.

SOLOMON SCHECHTER (1849–1915)

Solomon Schechter was an imposing, white-bearded, tousle-haired man with a ruddy complexion, whom Rembrandt would have loved to paint. He was absent-minded, but had a prodigious memory. He loved to talk, seldom listened and was a rough participant in discussions. Fragments of his provocative conversations may be found in his biography written by Norman Bentwich. The echo of his voice lingered for many years in the halls of the House of Learning he presided over in New York City. He was an interpreter of ancient manuscripts, a student of the Bible and its commentaries, a teacher of teachers, an essayist with a distinguished style, and an advocate of universal, traditional Judaism. Of greater interest here is the fact that he made a substantial contribution to the growth of the Zionist Movement in the United States in its early period when it was encircled by opponents.

He was born in Rumania and educated in German universities. He was fortunate that, subsequently, he was greatly influenced by his life in England and by the thirteen years he spent in the more unconventional environment of democratic America. The core of his personality was Rumanian, which abided with him throughout. He had none of the talents of the religious or clerical functionary. According to the best authorities, he was not a pre-eminent Talmudist nor a master of Hebrew; but what he knew radiated from a luminous, humane personality, the universality of his knowledge and his strong desire to inspire a love for truth and piety, which gave him distinction. What interfered with Schechter as a scholar in the field he made his own was his active imagination and his exuberant interest in intellectual life generally. He saw beyond the text of the Genizah manuscripts he studied; and was able intuitively to perceive the implications of the clues that lead to discovery. Although a bookman, he was not bookish. He loved light as well as heavy literature. He was not a cataloguer, a librarian, a specialist interested in the biography of books. He looked for the writer's personality and would read a poorly written book because of his inquisitiveness as to how it came to be written and who was the man who wrote it.

He was at his best when he gave expression to spontaneous opinions; he was at his worst in formal arguments. Facing a dialectician he was helpless. He was a *Chassid* chafing against the rigidity of the text. He could not accept contradictions. His affections as well as his dislikes were abiding. He did not relish tameness in love or in hate.

He was orthodox because he felt at home in the Jewish way of life. He respected authority, which he found in the practices of orthodox Judaism. He avoided the practices his reason could not accept, but in the main he lived in the orthodox way. He was willing to waive intellectual acceptance. Join in the synagogue services, observe the Sabbath and the dietary laws and you will come to believe in the principles of conduct underlying them. And if, in the last analysis, faith should not come, what have you lost?

He did not appreciate, however, the mechanical observance of the Law, and had no affection for theology as such. He had no liking for the rabbinical "profession," although he trained a generation of rabbis. His love went out to the pious, unlearned man, who believed in God with simple faith and went about the business of being a Jew with devotion, confidence and humility. He was not frightened so much by ignorance as he was by lack of piety. He was not interested in what the Priests in the Temple were doing. Let every man be his own rabbi, do his own praying; keep his own account with God. Be satisfied with coming out at the end of your life with a fair balance to your credit. In the final reckoning there will be cause for rejoicing.

He was not at home in the formal life of his Seminary. His amiable wife always had to keep him in line with convention. He was impetuous in speech. Even when his hair was white, he was the redhead he was born; quick in anger; capable of keen sarcasm and good humor; hot in attack on sham and hypocrisy; but his anger quickly passing and leaving him contrite. He took pride in nursing his prejudices, which he regarded as a weakness to be tolerated. He was pious, but not bigoted. It was because he loved the ordered life of the religious Jew that he observed the Law, that he chanted the prayers, that he sang the traditional melodies. He had no grudge against the ungodly; he felt compassion for them. All his life he lacked the feeling for money values. He knew what poverty meant, but was not humble in poverty. He was humble only in scholarship and in piety.

Schechter was never a "regular" Zionist. He always resisted regularity. His Zionism was a reflection of his religious faith. It was the incarnation of the Promise. The Return was the expression of God's mercy; the sinful people were to return to the Land Promised and to be re-enfolded in the arms of the forgiving Father. He loved the Hebrew language and its literature; it was a "sacred" tongue, and therefore should be immunized against alien dross. He knew that the writers of Hebrew could also practice a sort of idolatry. He had a dislike of the Hebraists who poured into the old vessel the disintegrating influences of the modern world. He hated the pornographists who wrote in Hebrew.

Although for some time he made no profession of interest in the Zionist Organization, he exercised a paternal influence upon the young men who came to the Seminary to study for the rabbinate. He gave them the feeling that the great tradition of Jewish scholarship was the shield of their Zionist faith. His fresh, hearty, rude voice breached the wall raised against Zionism by the "Reform" graduates from Cincinnati who were presumed to be going the American way and not the way to Zion. In those days Zionism—whatever there was of it— came from the quarters of the newer settlers through their Yiddish press, their own social life, their own customs derived from the old country. The Anglo-Jewish press was dominated chiefly by Reform rabbis. The pulpits where English was spoken disseminated the ideals of a Jewish mission, but provided no missionaries. Every manifestation of differing Jewish life was condemned as disloyalty to the Land that had received them as refugees.

In spite of his sharp criticism of Reform Judaism, however, Schechter won the admiration of many of the Reform rabbis who derived their culture from Germany. In fact, they admitted that the crown of Jewish scholarship deserved to be placed on the head of the rough and ready Rumanian who came to the United States via theological seminaries in Germany, and more than that, clothed in the scarlet robes of a Cambridge doctor. They could not easily resist him. He crossed swords with many of them in the English manner of controversy. He won respect for his erudition, his literary skill in English and his genuine faith. Thus Schechter weakened the ideology of the mission the Reform movement preached. The mission finally became an empty phrase.

But he remained the scholar in Zionism, restless and eager to enter the field of dignified controversy. He was not a joiner or endorser of causes. His friends in England were never able to enlist his interest in the Zionist Organization. He waited until 1905 before he joined the Zionist Organization in the United States.

He raised the tone of Zionist discussion in the United States at a time when Zionism was sealed off from the gentile world. He was not reluctant to reply to Jacob A. Schiff's frequent letters to the *New York Times*. He always wrote such letters with great care, as he did all his correspondence. He made not only the students of the Seminary his disciples, but for a number of years spent his summer vacations in a summer resort where the Zionist conventions were held, and loved the company of the young people he met there. The unclerical atmosphere pleased him. He knew no order of business and interrupted the proceedings whenever the spirit moved him. In conversation with them he was overbearing. His disagreements were frank and unconventional and sometimes cruel. He disported himself in Zionist company on such occasions with an amiable gruffness which deceived nobody, for they knew he enjoyed the rough and tumble of debate and could take a vigorous reply just as comfortably as he could deliver a savage verbal attack.

Whatever Schechter wrote had a personal style which was easily recognized. He was, of course, a foreigner, but he acquired English idiomatic forms with keen understanding and without the slightest error. Philosophical discussions were enlivened by his wit and humor. He never hit an opponent in controversy with blunt, harsh words; he made his effects sharply but with tenderness.

His first words about Zionism were written in a preface to a volume published shortly before his death.

"Speaking for myself," he wrote, "Zionism was, and still is, the most cherished dream I was worthy of having. It is beautiful to behold the rise of this mighty bulwark against the incessantly assailing forces of assimilation, which becomes the more dangerous, as we have now among us a party permeated by Christianizing tendencies, the prominent leaders of which are ever clamoring for a recognition of Paul, the apostle to the heathen—not to the Jews. These tendencies which, it must be said in justice, would have been strenuously opposed by the founders of the Reform school, are now thrust upon us on every occasion, and Heaven knows where they might have landed us but for the Zionist Movement which has again brought forth the national aspect as a factor in Jewish thought.

"But the dream is not without its nightmares: For in their struggle to revise the national sentiment, some of the Zionist spokesmen, calling themselves by preference Nationalists, manifest such a strong tendency to detach the Movement from all religion as can only end in spiritual disaster. There is such a thing as the assimilation of Judaism even as there is such a thing as the assimilation of the Jews; and the former is bound to happen when religion is looked upon as a negligible quantity. When Judaism is once assimilated the Jew will surely follow in its wake and Jew and Judaism will perish together. All this is a consequence of preaching an aspect of Nationalism more in harmony with Roman and similar modern models than with Jewish ideas and ideals. However, nightmares are fleeting and evanescent—the vision as a whole still remains glorious. The aberrations will, let us hope, be swept away quickly enough as soon as their destructive nature is realized by the majority of the Zionists, whose central ideas should and will remain God and His people, Israel."

Schechter's death was hastened by the First World War. He was a sick man when the war came. He could not bear to read of the first German victories. He detested the arrogance of the Germans. He hated imperialism of all kinds and of all ages. In his youth he was attracted to the liberalism of Germany, but soon discerned that although the Jews had been emancipated in Germany they had accepted an intellectual and spiritual inferiority. All the trends in German philosophy, history, literature and science were being used to depreciate the nature and organization of the Hebraic and Jewish contribution to civilization. He was enraged by the supercilliousness of the Higher Critics. He reacted against them with fervor. He rejected the attempt to make the Son the equal of the Father, the Second Chapter as the more authentic Revelation, reducing the First to the status of a *plagiat*.

He felt more at home in England. He was impressed by its conservatism and stability, its respect for tradition. He loved the atmosphere of Cambridge, its professors, its students, the scholarly dignity removed from the tumult of secular life. He said that "what interested me most (during the war) was the glorious prospect of England annexing Palestine, with God's help. This is the only solution for which we should hope. England is a Biblical country, reverential and practical, kind to our people and able to understand their aspirations for and in the Holy Land. Any other power would secularize it soon enough. England in its sincerity and reverence would serve as a model to our radicals, and would save us from all sorts of assimilation."

But he loved America most and saw in its history, and more especially its attitude toward immigration at that time, signs of providential intention toward the well-being of Jews.

America was the apogee of the democratic revolution; it was the ideal testing ground for a democratic life in which respect was accorded to varying cultures and religions.

He was a voracious reader of American literature. He knew intimately the history of our wars—the war for independence, the civil war. The personality of Abraham Lincoln had a peculiar fascination for him. He found in American history, in its early days, a revelation of personality which had in it traces of Hebraic influence. He thought the way should be found to natural recognition of common origins, the Hebraism of New England, the influence of the Old Testament, the Hebraic coloring of the Christian religion. When he thought of the Jewish "mission," not as mere doctrine of reform, he considered how properly trained Seminary rabbis could become a defensive force in the process of reconciliation.

He made a study of the life of Lincoln. He used to tell how the figure of the Great Emancipator became known in Rumania when he was a youth through the medium of Hebrew journals. He was attracted to the "Rail-Splitter" in whom he recognized a likeness to Hillel, who, legend has it, was engaged in the occupation of wood-cutting. In a lecture delivered in 1909 at the Seminary, he quoted a characterization of Lincoln by Alexander H. Stephens that "the Union with him (Lincoln) in sentiment rose to the sublimity of a religious mysticism." Schechter said of Lincoln's mysticism:

> No religious hero ever entered upon his mission to conquer the world for an idea and creed with more reverence and a deeper feeling of the need of divine assistance than did Lincoln when he was about to leave his home and his old associates and associations, good and evil, for his new home and his new life in Washington as President.

Religious mysticism, said Schechter, has the defects of its quality. From these dangers Lincoln was preserved by his training and not less by his "divine" humor. His sublime faith in the cause of the Union, which he considered God's cause, made real despair impossible in the trying days of the Civil War.

Schechter died before England was given the Mandate over Palestine. He was spared the sight of England's double-dealing with the trusteeship over the Holy Land in which he had great hopes. He never heard of the Nazis and Adolf Hitler. The future of the Promised Land seemed assured under England's guardianship.

HIRSCH MASLIANSKY (1856–1943)

Death found Hirsch Masliansky dignified and honored in old age. He was reconciled with that status and spent his last years in sheltered peace. From time to time, unable to resist the temptation, he would return to the Stage, but he got to be afraid of what he might do and say there. It was pathetic to see the Grand Old Man watching his step, hesitant in speech, feeling for the right word and worried because he could not always find it. Finally, he raised the White Flag and was seen no more by the great public that loved him. Unless he was one of the speakers, he had no interest in appearing on the platform. In his home, old friends came to see him; he was warmed by the affection of his children and grandchildren. He read the Yiddish newspapers; he went to his schul in Boro Park; he raged and wept when he heard of the tragedies of Jewish life in the Hitler days. He wanted to raise his voice to console his people; he wanted to blast the enemy with blistering speech. But he could not risk the excitement. Nor would the desired words come at his bidding. Toward the end, it is said, he had one complaint—he was living too long.

The story of his life begins in Russia with the rise of the movement to settle in Palestine and, simultaneously, the great migration to the United States. He was a young man when the May Laws of 1880 fell upon the Jews in Russia, when the *Chibbath Zion* blossomed, when the Biluists went out to found the first Zionist settlement. He saw thousands packing their belongings and crossing the great ocean to find new homes in "godless" America. He became a teacher and made his first talk in 1881 in the *Beth-Midrash* of Pinsk. It was realized by the leaders of the *Chovevei Zion* movement that he had a

way of speaking which could command wide attention. He
had power and imagination. So he began to address Zionist
circles and was sent into the provinces of Russia to stimulate
interest in Palestine and Zionism. He was always at home in
the synagogue; he had a natural piety, but his ideas and
methods could not be confined within the limitations of
the synagogue. He never liked to be called a *Maggid*. He did
not want to be an itinerant preacher; he wanted to have a
home and live attached to the Jewish community; but he was
not free from some of the mannerisms of the *Maggid*. He had
his own style of speaking, which clung to him all the days of
his life. He had interludes of description and anecdote; he
drew easily upon the Midrash and the Bible; he even had his
own chant for many years. But there was also something
worldly in his approach to the subjects of his discourses. He
had to have a broader platform. He needed space for movement. He wanted to be free, while speaking, even of the
restraints piety and synagogue convention might impose
upon him. As a preacher, he was also an agitator and a propagandist.

I remember hearing Masliansky over fifty years ago in
Rochester. He came to the schul, which was the schul my father
and mother were part of. I cannot remember when I became
a Zionist. It must have been so with me always, for I had an
instinct for Jewish books in which Jewish identity, Jewish
character, Jewish tragedies and hopes, and the incongruities
of Jewish life were dealt with. These disturbed me greatly.
The Hebrew print of Yiddish newspapers fascinated me and
provoked curiosity. My father had a large Hebrew library
which was circulated among the Maskilim. His conversation
brought to life the novels of Smolenskin and Mapu and what
he read in the current Hebrew and Yiddish newspapers. I
lived in two worlds. Side by side with books of English and
American literature were these books that brought into my
life bearded alien Jews, redolent of memories of a distant
past, whose descendants were now living in the incongruous
American present.

In spite of all this, Masliansky had the fanciful idea that he had made a Zionist of me. As one would say, "It was I who made a man of you." It would be hard to prove that, but there was truth in his claim in a deeper sense. I remember how he looked, how he talked, and what he said in the synagogue that Sabbath afternoon. I have never forgotten that experience. He was so thoroughly alive as a speaker. He raked his audience fore and aft with invective, sarcasm, lamentation, sentiment, and with appeals to faith and loyalty. He drew pictures in vivid words of what had been in the old country, what was to become of us here, what was to be the Jewish future. He spoke of *Golus* and Zion, of wandering and return. He alternated from comedy to tragedy, varying his tone, the tempo of his sentences, and in interludes, rested in a soothing chant. Time has blurred the details of what Masliansky said that day, but nothing in later years changed the pattern of that picture of a great and moving speaker, nor that feeling he gave of establishing contact through him with an endless Jewish tradition.

Thousands who left Russia brought the fame of Masliansky to the United States. That was the time when imported goods were greatly relished in our community. When he left Pinsk, he traveled through Europe and went to London. He received the acclaim of that poor Jewish community, but its poverty and its climate distressed him and made him unwilling to remain there. He had started out with a longing for free America and he could not rest until he had found his home in the land Columbus had discovered. When once he rested his feet on American soil, he became its most loyal patriot and most extravagant panegyrist. He never had any difficulty in painting a picture of Zion that brought back animated memories of regal pomp and majesty; he could tell stories of the past with quaint charm and intimacy, never troubled for lack of words; but he never had words enough adequately to describe what a blessing America was to Jews. He had the naivete of a peasant in this respect; and his wonder never ceased. He used to contrast the furtive meetings in Russian cities, the dread of visitations by the police, the censorship of speech and press, with the freedom of movement, of speech and press here in the United States. He might be speaking of Golus in a spiritual sense, but there was not a trace here of the dreadfulness of the Golus in Russia. Everything that was spread out before his eyes was a gift from God and he was genuinely grateful for it. He overlooked all the blemishes in our democracy. He chanted praises for his heroes, Jefferson, Lincoln and Theodore Roosevelt. He appreciated American democracy with Walt Whitman's exuberance and fervor. Nothing, ever, shook this faith.

Soon after his arrival, he made a tour of many of our large cities, was the guest of many congregations, received the adoration of many groups he had known in Russia, and set up his platform in the Educational Alliance, where arrangements were made for him to speak on Friday nights. At that time, the Jews of the older migration—the so-called *Yehudin*—believed that the immigrant Jews should be made to accelerate their adjustment to the American way of life. They were afraid that assimilation was not going on fast enough, that the uncouthness of alien methods and dress and speech—the abnormality and congestion of the East Side—was not good for public relations with the *goyim*. They hit upon the quaint idea of having Masliansky use his talents to inspire the aliens with a proper understanding of what America expected of them. Masliansky was asked to serve as the interpreter of Americanism to the Jews of the East Side.

They builded better than they knew. He accepted the commission, for he believed in having Jews build their lives here on an authentic American foundation. His platform in the Alliance became a weekly forum for the review of all things that passed through the minds and souls of Jews in the great community. He fought against the radicalism of the day that scorned and derided the Jewish tradition. His was the one noble and dignified voice that protested against the vulgarities of godlessness and the crude violation of tradition. A whole generation of Jews, who received their spiritual and intellectual sustenance through Yiddish, found in him a source of continuing delight, instruction and inspiration. Hundreds of them came week after week, never satiated, never bored, but always glad to hear Masliansky speak again. His pulpit in the Alliance was not intended for Zionist propaganda. But it served as the best Zionist pulpit in the United States, to the chagrin of those who had elevated Masliansky to this position. Masliansky became a Jewish institution all by himself, like the Yiddish press or the Yiddish theater.

It was in the Zionist Movement, however, that he found his complete freedom. Many Jews who had come here during that period remembered the old country, its customs and traditions, but their memories of the past were being blurred and forgotten by the softening influence of the new world. The new life distracted and misled them. They were prepared to discard the old gods and to accept the shoddy ideals of a hurried, superficial life. Masliansky had to make their memories live again. He did not want Jews to throw themselves into the melting pot without retaining the virtues and qualities that were the Jewish contribution to modern civilization. He reminded them of Zion, of the prophets, of Jewish law, of Jewish legend, and he attuned them to the vision of a new Zion and a new freedom. He made them conscious of the ties that bound them to the millions who were living under the oppression of Europe. He appealed to them to remember Zion and to strive for Jewish freedom. Masliansky was the symbol of all the implications of *Chibbath Zion*, its sentiment, its vision, as well as its hesitating practicality. He lifted Jews out of the slums of the East Side and made them see the new Jerusalem Jews were rebuilding in verification of the ancient prophecies.

For years and years—four decades—at propaganda meetings, at dinners, and at anniversaries, at Zionist conventions and conferences, at protest meetings of all kinds, Masliansky gave the light of his presence, his spirit, his remarkable artistry in oratory. He improvised his thought and the pictures he used to illuminate it were drawn from an inexhaustible fountain of knowledge and experience. His affection for his people was never tarnished by doubt of their quality, and he never lost faith in Jewish destiny. His name, his voice and gestures—the stories Masliansky had used, the epigrams Masliansky had made—became a colorful feature of American Jewish life. He was heard on every occasion of crisis and commemoration. He led in the Kishinev protest, that first American Jewish manifestation of protest. He participated in the *Kehillah* movement and the organization of the American Jewish Congress. He was always the favorite eulogist at the annual meetings of the Hebrew Immigrant Aid Society and the Hebrew Free Loan, for whom he had a special affection. Time and again, he went out on long, fatiguing trips for Zionist propaganda and Palestine fund-raising. He was one of the celebrants in the glorification of the Balfour Declaration and of the San Remo decision, and in all the protests against the violations of the covenant England had made with the Jewish people. He led in the mourning, and he led in the rejoicing, of his kinsmen in America, over a period of forty years.

The seeds of Zionism were transplanted to the freedom of America from the lands of persecution. These seeds were hidden in the baggage of many an alien, who had forgotten to throw them into the sea. The remembered voice, the printed word, the ceremony in the synagogue, brought Zionism to life in our midst. Herzl and Nordau, Ahad Ha-am and Pinsker, had many a disciple here whom they never knew, but whose spirit and mind and faith were sustained by their inspiring words. Many of these creators of Zionist spirit came to us in person and fructified the seeds that were sleeping in our consciousness. Their names are registered in the Zionist history of three continents—Palestine, Europe and the United States. Among these are the names of Chaim Weizmann, Ben Zion Mossinsohn, Nahum Sokolow, Menahem Ussishkin, and Vladimir Jabotinsky. They were with us and of us for a time. Heading the group were Shmarya Levin and Chaim Nachman Bialik—Levin who spent years among us, enriched our lives, gave Zionism three-dimensional proportions, and turned a sleeping idea into a ball of glowing fire; Bialik who came later and not so often, but whose personality glowed in our hearts long after he was called away from us; and Weizmann who was both speaker and statesman.

Masliansky belonged in that gallery of Masters. He too was more than a voice, more than a message, more than a guide; but of all who have been named, he was the only one who was never a stranger, merely paying us a visit. He came, he saw, and he was conquered, never thinking of leaving the hospitable community that provided him with home. He was a neighbor and friend. He was a coworker and fellow-citizen. He was a dash of vivid color that became part of our American landscape. He never had any pretensions; he never assumed that he was a philosopher or the discoverer of new thought. He was an artist who communicated the emotions of a man greatly excited by the prospect of Jewish life being recreated in an ancient mold. He painted pictures even the simplest could see and understand. He made the whole Jewish world the frame of his adventures—from Pinsk to London, from London to New York, back to Zion, to Warsaw and Pinsk and Kiev, and returning always to rest in his home in Boro Park.

He was not merely a speaker of Zionism; he was the chanter of its song. He was a Zionist by birth, an optimist by nature, sentimental by temperament, and a man of great faith. He did not live to see the Jewish State, but he came mighty close to it.

ABRAHAM GOLDBERG (1 8 8 3 – 1 9 4 2)

Abraham Goldberg came to the United States from Russia where he was born in the town of Yarmolinetz (Ukraine) and spent his life as a writer and speaker in the land of his adoption. He spoke Yiddish for the most part with a unique sparkle and fluency, but in his latter years, when Yiddish in Zionist circles was waning, he preferred to speak and write English in which he was not so proficient or successful. He was a genial *yeshiva bocher* delighting in casuistry, always cheerful and optimistic. At an early age he threw off the *yeshiva* attitudes and rushed forward with youthful enthusiasm to conquer the new world—the world of Jewish labor, the Yiddish newspapers, the Yiddish theatre.

He was one of the few American Zionists who had made a

place for himself in the old country as a speaker and writer. He never forgot, however, that home was where you found a *minyan* of Jews, but he loved to browse in alien fields. On his travels he found Jews to hobnob with in London and Paris, in Berlin and Vienna, in Warsaw and Vilna. At the same time, he was curious to know how the other half lived. He went to theaters and museums and restaurants and night clubs. He read foreign books and magazines, knew about their writers and artists, but he never rid himself of the impression that however well he knew them, they remained *goyim*. The better he got to know them, the more certain he was that the world was divided into two unequal parts. The larger part was *goyish* unmistakably. Equality would be achieved only when we Jews had a state of our own; there we too would fill a stage —a small one—but our own.

The cause of all causes was, of course, Zionism. That was his settled dogma and the source of his life. He stood on a Zionist platform and subordinated all other interests to the ideals of the Hebrew writers he cherished, the learning he imbibed in the *yeshiva,* the instruction he received from friends of his youth. Zionism was the mother who took to her bosom all Jewish interests. From the Zionist platform he held out his hands to all Jewish causes and made them his own, in his own frame, and integrated them in his conception of the Jewish renascence.

In his youth he was a partisan. The practical aspects of territorialism then advocated by Israel Zangwill captured his interest, fed his tongue and pen, and excited him no end. When he was a workman in New York he was a territorial Poale Zionist and tried to reach a formula that would put him at ease for the rest of his life. He did not like to live in a cauldron of partisanship. The discipline of party was really not for him. He was too good-humored and eager for popular acclaim to bind himself to the decisions of a caucus. He had a facile imagination and a quick mind. He was the victim of logic that often led him to heresy. These made his sojourn within the walls of any party an unbearable restraint and embarrassment. He was a Socialist, but could not accept the yoke of Marxian discipline. The lure of Zion led him to abandon the strict logic of the territorialist, and he soon found himself in the vast freedom of what was called "general" Zionism. What that meant he did not pursue too far lest it lead him into difficulties. When once he entered that heterogeneous company he looked back at his first loves with wonder, thinking of them as the aberrations of youth, for he was not born to be loyal to any dogma or doctrine except in the broad open ways of Zionism—the more abstract the better.

He found the freedom he needed in the non-party form of Zionism then prevalent in the United States and from about 1912 until his death he stood with the Center. The Center was (and probably always will be) the eclectic party. It made its decisions as circumstances dictated, but was always controlled by what was regarded as the interests of the whole. It swerved now to the right, now to the left, and always maintained the balance, becoming the stabilizing factor in the Zionist movement. Power, however, went over to the parties who talked much of ideology, but won through the labor of the pioneers. Their ideology was a screen for more practical objectives.

First in the Federation of American Zionists, then in its successor, the Zionist Organization of America, Goldberg played the various parts to which his talents entitled him, but he always claimed that he was never given his rightful position. He was the editor of *Dos Yiddishe Folk* for many years. He was one of the founders of the Histadruth Ivrith. He was a popular Yiddish speaker who became known in every city and hamlet throughout the country. He was a messenger of enlightenment, the analyst of policies, the commentator on personalities. He spoke before the meetings and after them late in the night in the cafeterias. He served for many years on the Zionist Actions Committee. He attended many Zionist Congresses and spoke in the "general debate." At Vienna in 1925 he was the chairman of the *Permanenz Auschuss* (general committee or steering committee) which he regarded as a great distinction.

Many times he went to Palestine and spent months loitering

about, familiarizing himself with the land and the people. He was an advocate of "practical" Zionism and approved many practical enterprises which he himself promoted with embarrassing results. He spoke to Jews week in and week out on the platform, in *Dos Yiddishe Folk*, in *Hadoar*, as a regular contributor to the *Jewish Morning Journal* and *Der Amerikaner*. He showed early promise as a poet, but he deserted the Muse for easier forms of expression. In the midst of these specifically Zionist activities he was always found with *landsleit*, serving them, advising them, participating in their festivals and their funerals. He was one of the prime movers in the organization of the American Jewish Congress and the People's Relief Committee during World War I. He was always at the beck and call of the Federation of Polish Jews. But wherever he went and whatever he did there was never any mistake about his being a Zionist primarily. He wore the Zionist insignia on his sleeve. His name appeared in the telephone book as "Abe Zionist Goldberg" to be sure that nobody made any mistake about it. It was that he was most proud of. He was a lover of people and could not resist the appeals of people when they came to him with their complaints. But, as he said, his greatness was never apparent to his closest friends. He never could get to the head of the procession.

He loved books but loved the writers of them more. He enjoyed the company of the creators of the literature of his people, in Yiddish or Hebrew or English, and regarded as priceless moments the hours spent in conversation with kindred literary spirits. He would go out of his way to find—in Vienna or Warsaw, Berlin or London or Tel Aviv—the men who wrote the books for which he was grateful. He was prodigal in praise of his heroes and in a quaint manner loved to be praised by them, fulsomely if possible. He often resented the lack of reciprocity in this respect, saying that generosity on his side called for an equal degree from the other side in order to balance the account. He overpaid in praise, expecting a balanced return.

His love for people led him to being a chronic peacemaker. He loved controversy, but disliked seeing brothers interlocked

in controversy that could not be settled in peace and come to
an end. Every war had to have its peacemakers. He got to
think that all differences could be settled by men of good-
will. All you needed was a peacemaker with *sechel*. And that
he had in abundance. He tried his hand at the game time and
again, often succeeding, but often giving up the job as
hopeless and receiving the pay the peacemaker usually re-
ceives. Thus in the Zionist controversy with the American
Jewish Committee, at the time of the first American Jewish
Congress, Louis Marshall was the head of the Committee.
Goldberg admired Marshall and believed that because he
had a good Jewish heart you could come to a compromise
with him on every Jewish question. He believed that having a good Jewish heart, Marshall was, of course, almost a
good Zionist. Goldberg sacrificed much at that time to this
thought, which the Zionists rejected. In fact, he lost the editorship of *Dos Yiddishe Folk* on account of it. Later, when Marshall went to Versailles and pleaded the general Jewish cause,
and Dr. Weizmann set out on his efforts to create the extended
Jewish Agency with the non Zionists, Goldberg was one of the
zealous partisans of this Zionist compromise. To him, every
compromise was a victory.

But Goldberg's zeal for peace led him into courses of action
later on that gave him great pain and, in turn, grieved all his
friends who loved him in spite of his waywardness. He
wanted to make peace with Soviet Russia. He thought he
could do it single-handedly. He was afraid that the Jews
of Russia would be lost. To the amazement of all his old Zionist friends he became, in fact, a "fellow traveler" in the last
years of his life. He persisted in his efforts regardless of the
friends he lost and the queer new friends he won.

He was the victim of a subtle communist who was a lawyer
who had once studied in a *Yeshiva*. Goldberg became the tool
of that intriguer at Geneva in 1936, when he volunteered to
get the American Jewish communists admitted to the World
Jewish Congress. The effort failed. When Goldberg returned
home, it was noticed that strange friends provided his com-

pany. Then he appeared at a few "fellow Traveler" meetings, then his writings betrayed traces of communist aroma. Then he was making trips in the interests of Jewish communist organizations.

When I went to speak in Detroit at a Goldberg memorial meeting, quite a few Zionist friends were present, but the strange voices of his last friends were heard, to the embarrassment of the Zionists.

He was never at a loss for a word or an argument, fighting for his ideas, quarreling about them, but always striving to hold together friendships and good-will. He would always ask for the floor the moment he entered a meeting even before he knew what was being talked about and before he knew what he himself was going to say. He would push his way to the front, run his hand through his curly hair, hesitate only a moment and then speak freely and eloquently without regard for time. The words gushed out of his mouth. He was short and stocky. He had a round face crowned with black hair, and always looked cheerful. He was young in spirit and dreaded the thought of old age. He served the Zionist cause with prodigal enthusiasm and all the talent he had.

He felt that he could go on and on for countless years. There was so much work to be done; there were so many things to be said; so many articles to be written; so many political combinations that could yet be made. He was more away from home than in it and was thinking of the day when he could change his way of life and get to know his children better. They were growing up rapidly. They were entering the professions. They were getting married. His family was crowding in on him and he would soon have to make a final decision— should he cling to the "road" or prepare to stay at home for good?

He was destined not to face old age, not to feel the weakening of intellect and body. He died young at 59 in June 1942. He died looking eagerly forward. He was about to take a train to make a speech in Detroit. Death closed his eyes quickly. It was so sudden that his friends felt his spirit marching with them years after he had left them.

JOSEPH SEFF (1864–1919)

The nineteen years Joseph Seff spent in the United States did not fulfill the hopes he had when he left Russia. He expected to be a Zionist missionary to the *Galut* of America. When he arrived, he was not hailed by crowds in America as a great speaker nor was his path strewn with roses. His life was a hard, bitter, rancorous struggle. He was in exile and, in effect, his American years were the twilight of his life.

Seff was born in Slavuta, Wohlynia in 1864. His father was a man of means who sent his son not to a *Yeshiva,* but to the *Realschule* in Rovno nearby, where he acquired a solid Russian education. He found his own way to Zionism and Hebrew. He went to Vienna and conversed with Perez Smolenskin, the Hebrew novelist. He joined the Lovers of Zion movement and became a belligerent partisan. Unlike other Zionists of the time before Herzl, who thought of returning to the soil, of the renascence of Hebrew, he grappled at once with the political aspects of the Jewish problem. His mind turned to the Turkish Empire in which Palestine was not so profitable a province. He thought the time was ripe for revolution there. Although not provided with funds, he went to Constantinople on his own and lived there for over a year. His aim was to organize the Jewish-Turkish youth who were already infected with revolutionary ideas. He frequented coffee houses and newspaper offices, and acquired a mass of information which he integrated into a plan for Jewish action. He had a hard time of it. He had plenty of ideas and plans, but was short in funds and friends. He could get no support from associates back home; they were afraid of illegal schemes.

He left Constantinople defeated and returned home where he was hailed as a man of great spirit, but privately regarded as a high-class *schlemiel.* He went about telling of his experiences and convictions. He had influence enough to secure an appointment as Crown Rabbi in Old-Konstantin, which he used to extend his Zionist activities. He talked at great length of what might happen to Jews in a reformed Turkish Empire. He saw a Zionist chance in the anticipated revolution. Many American Zionists who came from the other side remembered what a powerful speaker he was at that time. He spoke Yiddish and Russian with equal passion and descriptive power. He deprecated the *Galut* as all Zionists did at that time. He led his hearers into the new world of international politics. He came to know all workers for Zion. He was a visitor in the home of the parents of Bialik, the Hebrew poet. He was not a friendly man, but his intellectual equipment commanded respect and admiration.

When Herzl published *The Jewish State,* Seff's mind flashed instantaneous recognition. He accepted everything Herzl stood for. He became Herzl's loyal and devoted partisan. He supported the "call" for the Zionist Congress. He traveled about in many cities speaking at mass meetings and urging the election of delegates. He himself was elected a delegate from Berdicheff. When he left Old-Konstantin for Basle, he never returned to Russia.

He met Herzl at Basle and was advised to go to the United States. (The same advice was also given by Herzl to Jacob de Haas and Boris Katzman.) Herzl was sure that a man of Seff's talent would be able to organize Zionism in the United States. As Seff told the story, Herzl gave him a letter to Richard Gottheil, then president of the American Zionist organization. The letter was never delivered. It was stolen or lost on board the ship. To his dismay Seff found his wallet also was gone. The handicap of coming to a new land without "papers" or pocket money was the tragedy of his life. He used to say that if he had come to Professor Gottheil as Herzl's representative, if he had established himself in a good hotel, he might have had a chance. He would have been accepted as an official Zionist speaker, as a delegate to the First Zionist Congress, as the Crown Rabbi of Old-Konstantin, as one of Herzl's disciples. But he was unsponsored. Who could vouch for his identity in this godless country? He could not blow his own horn and there was no one around to do it for him. He had two strikes against him from the start.

He made the best of his embarrassment. He found lodgings

on the East Side. He suffered great privations and humiliations. He was always clumsy in money matters. He did not
know how to negotiate a small loan nor did he have the crust
to ask for a large one. He was reduced to having someone pay
for his meals and to speaking at local Zionist meetings, calling
the chairman aside after the lecture to tell him his hard luck
story. His American career was conditioned by this miserable
start. He was never able to recover the position lost. He started
out in life, he said, as a dubious character, without a Zionist
"passport."

As we knew him then, Seff was a tall, blackbearded man
with a magnificent head, who had a talent for controversy and
partisanship. He was a rapid talker. He was the first real political Zionist we knew. He was adept in Oriental politics. He
had the intrigues of the Sultan's court at his fingertips. Those
were the days when the Charter was the key Zionism was to
use to unlock the door to Palestine. He was a relentless political Zionist. He denounced those who would take less than a
Jewish State. He believed a Charter could be gotten, if not
from the Sultan then from the Young Turks who would over-
throw him, which they did a few years later, but they had their
own reasons for not giving the Zionists a Charter. He wanted
a Jewish army organized underground, located perhaps in
Cyprus. He took scant notice of what was going on in Palestine, although he had paid a brief visit to the Judean colonies.
The territory was to be Palestine, of course, but that was the
lesser part of the problem. His mind operated only with the
political situation. That was what excited him when he lingered over his memories of Herzl.

He was a stubborn opponent of orthodox rabbis. He had a
great desire always to pick a quarrel with rabbis and religion
in general. He brought that allergy with him from Russia
where the rabbis were his inveterate opponents. He also quarreled with modern Zionists who disliked his caustic and cynical references to piety and religion.

He lacked a relaxed touch and a friendly spirit. There was
not a drop of humor in him on the platform or in private life.

He was full of gall and bitterness. Life had not treated him
with kindness, so he retaliated. He soon acquired an easy use
of English. He did not want to be known as a Yiddish speaker.
He was at home on the East Side and frequented Zionist
meetings. His aim in life was to speak at large mass meetings,
to be counted as one of the leading Zionist speakers, but it
was hard for him to make the grade. There was something for-
bidding in the way he spoke, in his resentment and criticism
of his audiences, in his harsh voice and gauche manners. They
felt a cold wall between themselves and his words. You never
could tell what he was going to say or how he would say it. He
was more Russian than Jewish. He was envious of the popu-
larity of Hirsch Masliansky. He was an intimate friend of
Abraham Goldberg, but regarded him as a young upstart. He
could not endure Joseph Barondess, who came to Zionism as
a convert from the trade union movement. He regarded every
secretary of the Zionist organization as his mortal enemy,
standing between him and the platform he wanted to stand
on. He sensed a conspiracy against him in which all Zionists
were joined and found solace only with a few journalists or
Zionists from the old home who remembered his great past
and sympathized with his grievances.

The Kishinev pogrom aroused American Jews for the first
time to the thought of helping Jews abroad in an organized
way. Of course, the new settlers sent help to those left behind
and assisted in their reunions; they also remembered their
home towns. But the pogroms were the turning point in
that they aroused public demonstrations and public relief
measures. The American Jewish community as a whole was
concerned about the Jewish victims of the pogroms. Out of all
proportion to the damage inflicted by the pogrom in Kishinev,
they were excited and disturbed and went to mass meetings
determined to give public expression to their feelings and to
make their contributions. It was a time of great trouble when
all personal differences and partisan quarrels were overlooked.
Seff was active in these demonstrations. He seemed to undergo
a serious psychical disturbance. He would give hysterical

descriptions of the pogroms, telling with brutal realism what had been reported, shocking the sensibilities of his hearers beyond endurance. Women fainted at his meetings. Men reviled him for his brutality and left the hall. His persistent conduct along this line made it necessary to call him to book.

"Do you have to speak that way?" he was asked. "Your words are shocking." He said: "When I begin to speak I tell myself, 'Be calm, don't get excited.' But when I think of the horrible crimes committed against women and children, my indignation gets the best of me. I feel a moral satisfaction in telling exactly what these crimes are. I feel as Bialik felt when he wrote *The City of Slaughter.*"

He lost his status as a speaker. In fact, he could find no place at all in the Zionist world. He wandered into the field of American politics. He became an admirer of William Jennings Bryan, the great "Commoner," whom he resembled in features and was proud of it. He joined the Democratic party and Tammany Hall. He hobnobbed with Irish politicians and Jews who lived on the fringe of the political machine. He was taken by some of them to be a rabbi. Finally, he got himself a job as an interpreter in the courts and was assured of a measure of security for the rest of his life.

His rejection by American Zionists made an orphan of him. Now and then he made a startling appearance on a Zionist platform, looked morosely upon the audience and lost himself in the lobbies. He lived on the fringe of the growing Zionist community. He never had a family or a home. He seemed unable to keep money in his pockets. There were a few friends who listened to his complaints, loved to hear him talk about Russia and the people he knew there.

But he was a figure out of the past long before he died. He had a habit of vanishing from view for stretches of time. His beard was removed early. Then it was possible to see his face and to observe how life had traced deep lines of suffering on his features. His lips were thin and drawn. His nose was long and sharp. He lost all his teeth and never replaced them with plates so that when his mouth opened in speech, an empty cavern was revealed. There was no truth in the slander that he drank or took drugs. He protested that he was not well and he certainly did not look well for years before he passed away. He was reduced to a shadow of the virile, eager, ambitious personality he was when he first came here.

He died in 1919 and was buried in a Brooklyn cemetery. A stone was placed on his grave by a group of Jewish journalists who thus paid their last respects to the man who was an eloquent pioneer of Zionism in Russia, and had been given his Zionist credentials by Herzl. Nobody ever saw his credentials.

CYRUS ADLER (1863–1940)

It may be incongruous to include Cyrus Adler in any gallery of Zionist profiles. He would have resented it and requested its exclusion. He was Zionism's critic from its beginning in 1897 to beyond the Balfour Declaration; and when the extended Jewish Agency came into being in 1929—and he had had some share in its creation—he thought he was entitled to heckle a movement in which he had had no creative part.

He was a man of faith. The tradition of Zion and Jerusalem was woven into his Judaism, but as happened to others, the projection of the reality of the tradition was too much of a shock, and his first reaction was to reject it with anger. He should have been a Zionist by reason of his faith, for he was a Sephardi. There were many Sephardim in the American movement who affirmed Zionism, like Henry Pereira Mendes, Sabato Morais, or Meldola DeSola of Montreal, who could get terribly excited about Sabbath observance or *kashrut*. Cyrus Adler loved the formal, the ritual, the traditional; but emotion seldom shook him.

Therefore he was a stranger to the birth of Zionism and always resentful of its existence and its successes. It was something he regarded as illegitimate, premature, out of order, not ordained. He disliked Theodor Herzl from the start and, having lived in Constantinople for some time, he derided the notion that Turkey could be persuaded to consider granting a charter for Jewish colonization in Palestine. It irked him to think that a Viennese litterateur who was in no way recognized by him as Jewish was being hailed as a Messiah. The only thing that recommended Herzl was his beard, which was a Viennese convention.

Dr. Adler achieved prominence early in life as a social worker in educational enterprises and as a quasi-political observer of Jewish life. He was connected with the management of the Jewish Theological Seminary, with the American Jewish Relief Committee (the Joint), and in the affairs of the American Jewish Committee. He functioned under cover of various institutions. He was the editor of the *Jewish Quarterly Review*. He was the president of both the Dropsie College and, after the death of Solomon Schechter, of the Jewish Theological Seminary. He was the active chairman of one of the most important committees of the Joint, which dealt with the relief of Jewish religious institutions in Eastern Europe. After the death of Louis Marshall, he succeeded to the presidency of the American Jewish Committee. He was a very successful heir-apparent. At one time he was connected with the Smithsonian Institution in Washington. He must have regarded with embarrassment an aberration of his youth in the form of "Coffee House Sketches" written with Allan Ramsay about life in Constantinople. But through the affectionate interest of his uncle, Judge Mayer Sulzberger, he entered the field of Jewish educational enterprises. He had an aptitude for administration and great respect for order, plan, budget and sober deliberation—slow thinking, slow acting. He was first interested in the Jewish Publication Society, to whose modest beginnings he made a major contribution. He was what could be called a first-class managing director. He was the right-hand man—for specific tasks—of Judge Sulzberger, Jacob H. Schiff, Louis Marshall and later of Felix M. Warburg. Through association with these leaders in Jewish affairs and in loyal service rendered in the promotion of causes in which they were interested, Dr. Adler rose to the position of leadership.

Although in no sense of the term a theologian or scholar, he

lived his life in association with the Conservative forces in
Judaism. He resisted innovation. He refused to lend himself to
any form of action in which overemphasis or sharp distinction
or controversy was an ingredient. He felt that in any change
in Jewish forms basic principles would be disturbed and
washed away in time. He believed in ceremony and the
habitual and hesitated to acquire new habits and to direct his
life into new paths for fear that he might lose his way. He
was old when he was young and became mellow when he was
old. In his youth he was a cynic on general principles. He
discounted the value of adventure or novelty or revolution
in either intellectual or social affairs. He was a conservator,
not a creator. Thus in the Jewish Theological Seminary he
did not venture to replace Dr. Schechter, nor did he seek
to dominate its intellectual life. He rendered great service in
maintaining to the best of his ability the institute of learning
Dr. Schechter had created and added greatly to its equipment
and buildings, its library, its faculty and its endowments. He
was the guardian of the temple of learning, not its prophet or
priest.

He resisted Zionism for fear that it would lead to the secu-
larization of Jewish life. He would have avowed his love for
the Holy Land in the old traditional ways if there were no
Zionists to take advantage of his confession. He was reluctant
to be seen in their company or to be mistaken as a member
of their fraternity or as an admirer of any of their leaders,
even, for that matter, of the American leader, Brandeis,
whose conversion to Zionism he always regarded as motivated
by personal ambitions. But these negative views did not check
his interest in and affection for every trace of Jewish influence in the Holy Land—his interest in the Yeshivot, its
learned rabbis, its archaeological records, the Wailing Wall,
about which he wrote a memorandum in 1930 submitted to
the League of Nations on behalf of the Jewish Agency. Nor
did it prevent his giving generous support to the new creative
Jewish life in Palestine, especially those aspects that appealed
to his religious sensibilities.

He refused to go along with the democratic trends in Jew-

ish life. He favored the formation of the American Jewish
Committee on a strictly personal basis. He deprecated the
Kehillah movement, which aimed to organize the New York
Jewish community on a democratic basis. He denounced the
American Jewish Congress and was angry indeed when the
World Jewish Congress was formed in 1936. In American
politics he was a liberal Democrat and protested his liberalism on many occasions. But he seemed to think that democracy was an alien notion in Jewish life. In Jewish matters he
was controlled by a communal tradition integrated in religious practices and in forms of defense that had their origin in
the Middle Ages. He seemed to think that Jewish life should
be ordered in the spirit and mood of a religious service in a
Sephardic synagogue, where ritual and ceremony are hallowed
by time and Divine sanction and where disorder and controversy are an offense to sanctity. It seemed to him that Jewish life had to be lived unobtrusively, bending before storms
and avoiding struggle, and relying upon Divine guidance and
intervention in all mundane existence. Where God presided,
majority votes had no binding effect and should be disregarded as a matter of piety.

But all this did not restrain him from following the lead of
Louis Marshall in supporting the Versailles demands of the
committee of Jewish delegations with regard to Jewish minority rights. Dr. Adler was there unofficially for the American
Jewish Committee and could not resist the influence of the
Jewish nationalists and Zionists. Nor did he hold aloof from
the efforts of Dr. Weizmann to enlarge the Jewish Agency for
Palestine. Here, too, Louis Marshall set the pace, but Dr.
Adler followed with a genuine personal interest and later became a devotee of the program of the Jewish Agency. In his
later years—more especially after the untimely death of Marshall—he participated in a number of Zionist enterprises
and was aligned with specific Zionist policies in matters
bearing upon British interpretations of the Mandate. He soon
was not so keen in dissociating himself from the ideological
implications of his new course. He gave his name and support
to many Zionist protests against the violation of our rights in

Palestine and evinced a keen interest in every phase of Zionist development. But he continued to disclaim Zionism. Even the term non-Zionist irritated him. He did not know how to escape from his dilemma. Finally, he gave up trying. There was involved in his thinking a chain of ideas nurtured in the days of his youth that ran parallel with the second chain of ideas born out of the secular experience of a lifetime. He loved the old concepts, the old ways; there was sentiment, there was all that he venerated in life, and he could not let it go. But life also had its pressures, so he often turned away from the traditions of his youth and compromised with reality.

While leader of the American Jewish Committee, Dr. Adler did not maintain the vigor and forensic skill which was the distinguishing trait of Louis Marshall's advocacy of Jewish causes. In discussion Marshall was splendid when he took the offensive, but in defense he was often complicated and confused. Dr. Adler, however, was not an advocate. He could marshal his case in writing with great effectiveness. He built up a better administration for the American Jewish Committee. He extended its program and influence and kept his group constantly within the lines originally laid out in its earlier days. He never ventured in a big way and never gained much for the record. But he also never receded from a position he had once taken. He refused to bend to democracy. He was faithful to the old staid procedures. He disdained open struggle in domestic affairs, although his world seemed to be crumbling and new forms blocked his way more and more.

In his last years he sensed that a new world was being born, but he seemed content to continue his old habits without protest during the remaining days of his long life. When he was young he was critical and caustic, dictatorial and intolerant, but with old age a desire controlled him to live among his brethren in an atmosphere of peace. He became friendly with old adversaries, enjoyed a whiskey and soda in the English manner and was a good conversationalist. He hated *pilpul*. Once the writer sat with him at a meeting of the Jewish Agency and heard his comments on the speakers. Dr. Adler wanted the right to intervene and make a motion to close the debate. When he was told that to move to close the debate while the list of speakers was not yet exhausted would be a hazardous undertaking, he snorted and said, "What *are* we really coming to!" He could not imagine Jews having a parliamentary procedure of their own. He did not know that Zionist procedure was taken from Austrian practices.

epilogue

The objective of the Basle program was, in a measure, achieved on May 14, 1948 (5 Iyar 5708) when the representatives of the Jewish community of Palestine met in Tel Aviv, under the chairmanship of David Ben-Gurion to proclaim the State of Israel.

The Proclamation was written under great stress and in haste. General Zionist opinion was divided. Leadership in Palestine wavered and swayed back and forth. Government authorities in the United States strongly advised against the proposed action. They feared the consequences in view of Arab threats. For these reasons the text of the Proclamation lacked the classic form and the lofty tone of a great historic document. It reflected the indecision that prevailed in Israel. It was calculated to serve an immediate purpose. It conveyed the views of the provisional government on matters of urgent political concern. It was intended to be communicated with dispatch to all nations who should hear what the new State had to say on the day of its birth. Speedy advantage had to be taken of the opportunity to give assurances to friends and to allay disturbance in hostile circles. There was no time to consider rhetoric or style.

On the record, a political victory was registered at the United Nations, but Israel had to be provided with the organs of state life. The world had to be told of its democratic intentions. It had to be impressed by Israel's aspirations for peace and justice. It had to convey faith and confidence in the promise of a useful future. The Proclamation served these purposes well. It is regarded as a document worthy of a great occasion. What is basic and relevant eight years after the event is herewith appended.

The Land of Israel was the birthplace of the Jewish people. Here their spiritual, religious and national identity was formed. Here they achieved independence and created a culture of national and universal significance. Here they wrote and gave the Bible to the world.

Exile from Palestine, the Jewish people remained faithful to it in all countries of their dispersion, never ceasing to pray and hope for their return and the restoration of their national freedom.

Impelled by this historic association, Jews strove throughout the centuries to go back to the land of their fathers and regain their statehood. In recent decades they returned in masses. They reclaimed the wilderness, revived their language, built cities and villages, and established a vigorous and ever-growing community, with its own economic and cultural life. They sought peace yet were prepared to defend themselves. They brought the blessings of progress to all inhabitants of the country.

In the year 1897 the First Zionist Congress, inspired by Theodor Herzl's vision of the Jewish State, proclaimed the right of the Jewish people to national revival in their own country.

This right was acknowledged by the Balfour Declaration of November 2, 1917, and reaffirmed by the Mandate of the League of Nations, which gave explicit international recognition to the historic connection of the Jewish people with Palestine and their right to reconstitute their National Home.

On November 29, 1947, the General Assembly of the United Nations adopted a Resolution for the establishment of an independent Jewish State in Palestine, and called upon the inhabitants of the country to take such steps as may be necessary on their part to put the plan into effect.

Accordingly we, the members of the National Council, representing the Jewish people in Palestine and the Zionist movement of the world, met together in solemn assembly today, the day of termination of the British Mandate for Palestine, by virtue of the natural and historic right of the Jewish people and of the Resolution of the General Assembly of the United Nations, hereby proclaim the establishment of the Jewish State in Palestine, to be called ISRAEL.

We hereby declare that as from the termination of the Mandate at midnight, this night of the 14th to 15th May, 1948, and until the setting up of the duly elected bodies of the State in accordance with a Constitution, to be drawn up by a Constituent Assembly not later than the first day of October, 1948, the present National Council shall act as the Provisional State Council, and its executive organ, the National Administration, shall constitute the Provisional Government of the State of Israel.

The State of Israel will be open to the immigration of Jews from all countries of their dispersion; will promote the development of the country for the benefit of all its inhabitants; will be based on the precepts of liberty, justice and peace taught by the Hebrew Prophets; will uphold the full social and political equality of all its citizens, without distinction of race, creed or sex; will guarantee full freedom of conscience, worship, education and culture; will safeguard the sanctity and inviolability of the shrines and Holy Places of all religions; and will dedicate itself to the principles of the Charter of the United Nations.

We offer peace and amity to all the neighboring states and their peoples, and invite them to cooperate with the independent Jewish nation for the common good of all. The State of Israel is ready to contribute its full share to the peaceful progress and development of the Middle East.

Our call goes out to the Jewish people all over the world to rally to our side in the task of immigration and development and to stand by us in the great struggle for the fulfillment of the dream of generations—the redemption of Israel.

With trust in Almighty God, we set our hand to this Declaration, at this Session of the Provisional State Council, in the city of Tel Aviv, on this Sabbath eve, the fifth of Iyar, 5708, the fourteenth day of May, 1948.

The Partition decision of November 1947—the climax of the turbulent history of nine years—was backed by legal and moral authority. But it did not reflect the firm intention of the United Nations to see that what had been agreed should be realized in fact. It came as the result of a political squabble that ended in a favorable majority vote. What is agreed to on such occasions may sound convincing at the time, when the vote is taken under stress of passion or sentiment or intense self-interest, but when the irrevocable action is imminent, timidity and fear take over and a scramble ensues to undo what had been decided to be done, if retreat is at all possible. The Palestine problem had been one of the most difficult controversial items on the agenda of the United Nations. It was a football of international politics. It was the center of conflicting national interests. It was being used as the object of the vindictive and relentless policies of the British Foreign Secretary, Ernest Bevin. Opinion had swayed from right to left, from Yes to No, from loyalty to pledges to a frantic desire to undo a decision arrived at. The U.S. State Department was bedeviled by pro-Arab and pro-British officials. No sooner was the vote on partition taken than forces were released to set in motion plans for retreat, revision, and the reshuffling of the cards with a view to inhibiting the success of any solution that might bring to life a Jewish state. It was doubted that the British at any time had a serious intention to solve the problem. They relied upon chance. They were waiting until the very end, thinking that something different would come up if they could only continue to muddy the waters of political action. It was not believed at any time that the British genuinely intended to evacuate Palestine. Many friends of Israel in the United States were frightened by the British and Arab propaganda. For the record, they had done what they had been called upon to do, but they had not anticipated the violent repercussions that shook the lobbies of the United Nations and the international press. In Palestine there were clashes between British and Jews, between Arabs and Jews. The disorder was tantamount to civil war.

At this time of hesitation the retreat was led by the United States. A Temporary Trusteeship was to be substituted for partition. The idea was to go back to where they had started. The trusteeship would undoubtedly bring Great Britain back again to the driver's seat in Palestine, supported by friendly governments. But by this time world opinion and especially the free discussion in the United States had become so incensed and inflamed with the obvious chicanery of changeable "statesmen" and their irresponsible behavior that steps had to be taken without delay to set up the plan for the partition of Palestine.

Foreseeing that there would be an interregnum between the Mandate and Partition, a Commission of five was appointed by the United Nations for an orderly transition from the Mandate to Arab and Jewish states. The British in Palestine rendered the efforts of the Commission ineffective. The British rejected its request to open a port for Jewish immigration or to permit the organization of Arab and Jewish militia to maintain order after the British withdrew. The British would not permit the Commission to enter Palestine before May 1 on the ground that its presence in Palestine would lead to divided authority and stimulate Arab disorders. The British removed Palestine from the sterling bloc countries and its assets in Great Britain, amounting to 100 million pounds, were frozen in British banks. A large grant from the Palestine treasury was made to the Arab Higher Committee for the "religious" purposes of the Mufti of Jerusalem. The huge oil refineries in Haifa were closed and a fuel famine was imminent. Imports of essentials were suspended; railway traffic was halted; telegraph services were discontinued. The Lydda airport was closed and international air traffic came to an end. As the day of final evacuation approached, huge quantities of dispensable military vehicles and other equipment were either destroyed or sold by British soldiers to Arabs or Jews. Barracks, military camps and police stations were either abandoned or turned over to the Arabs. Ernest Bevin refused even to consider at that time President Truman's proposal to let 100,000 Jewish refugees into Palestine. The victims of Hitler were blocked at the ports of embarkation. They were harried on the high seas, on the beaches, in the air.

The Arabs were preparing to take advantage of the situation the day the British left Palestine. They stood at the frontiers with their armed forces like vultures ready to strike at their victims and tear them apart. They warned the local Arabs to vacate the fields where the battles might take place. They advised them to get out of the way when the bombs burst, when the tanks rolled in, when the planes struck. They were promised a rich harvest of loot when they returned home after the infidels had been driven into the sea. What Great Britain had built up over a period of three decades was virtually dismantled and ruined before the last Englishman left the Promised Land an May 15, 1948.

The Arab states gave notice to the United Nations, to the press, through all the media of communication, that they intended to make war on Israel the day the British left. And sure enough, on May 15 the army of Egypt crossed the frontier of Israel. The United Nations failed to react. On the following day the Syrian army, reinforced by the Iraqis and the Arab Legion of Jordan, marched forward to seize the Jordan Valley from Lake Kinnereth to Beisan, and then to cross the Emek to Haifa. After a few minor victories the loud threats of the Arabs failed of their purpose. The Iraqis were routed and fled back across the Jordan. The Syrians were repulsed and fell back with heavy losses. In the north, the Lebanese suffered a prompt defeat and ceased to be a factor in the war.

The battle for Jerusalem was the most crucial and desperate struggle of all the incidents of the war. When the British left Jerusalem the Jews took possession of nearly the whole of the New City. They hesitated to attack the Old City, for nearly all the Christian holy places were there, and to attack them would evoke world repercussions. Likewise, the defense of the Old City under these circumstances was impossible. On May 28 the few remaining Jewish defenders gave permission to the leaders of the community to surrender to the Arabs. There were then only 39 Jews in the Old City capable of bearing arms. But the critical front in the Battle of Jerusalem was still the road to Tel Aviv. The Arab Legion, holding Lydda, Ramle and Latrun, sealed off the road. It was clear that unless food, water and fuel as well as arms and ammunition and reinforcements could be kept flowing to the city, beleaguered Jerusalem,

with its 100,000 Jews, was doomed. The city was saved by the
fortitude of its people and by the ingenuity of their defense.
They managed to change the character of the siege. The army
of Israel hewed out a track through the hills south of Latrun
and around a ten-mile arc about Bab-El-Waad which they
held and along which vital supplies were carried by jeep and
mules and men through the city. They called it their "Burma
Road." The work was done at night and in secret, and only on
the eve of the cease fire did it become known that the siege of
Jerusalem had been outflanked through this improvised road.

Israel's defense of its sovereignty and freedom lasted for
eight months. There were periods of internal conflict, alternat-
ing with cease-fires ordered by the Security Council. In the first
period, from May 15 to June 10, the Arabs felt certain of a
swift and decisive victory, but they were checked on every
front during this period. The first cease-fire was ordered on
June 10 and continued to July 9. The war then continued for
ten days, and again a cease-fire was ordered. When the second
cease-fire was agreed to, Israel held more than 800 square miles
in addition to the area included in the Jewish state under
Partition. The second cease-fire lasted officially until the sign-
ing of the Armistice Agreements. The Armistice Agreements
were arrived at in various stages. On February 25, 1949, after
six weeks of negotiations on the Island of Rhodes, Egypt and
Israel signed an armistice agreement which left the disputed
Negev in Israel's possession. In March of that year Israeli
forces moved down to Elath, near the southern tip of the
Negev on the Gulf of Aqaba. The Gaza coastal strip remained
in Egyptian hands, but the strip had never been included in
the Jewish State. An armistice with Lebanon was signed on
March 23, and with Jordan on April 3. The armistice with Syria
was not concluded until July 20, 1949.

Since its troubled beginning Israel did not see peace in any
form. It was a nation under siege. It was encircled. It was compelled by vociferous and active enemies constantly to give
thought and to spend resources on its security. The Armistice
Agreements were honored more in the breach than in the
observance. Systematic infiltration continued from Jordan,

Syria and Egypt. The infiltrators were official emissaries of the states of which they were citizens. They engaged in murder and the destruction of property. Their intrusions were not the acts of individuals; they were part of a design in which all the Arab states were partners. All the Arab states were concerned in the boycott of Israeli goods. The boycott of the Suez Canal, conducted by Egypt, was an enterprise which depended for its success upon the cooperation of other Moslem states. The boycott reached out to all countries that might have commercial or cultural dealings with Israel, and the progaganda in connection with this boycott took on the color and aroma of the domestic anti-Semitism that prevailed in each country. Israel among the nations practically stood alone. When it was attacked no member of the United Nations regarded the incident as its concern.

The situation went from bad to worse. The Arab propaganda, centered in the United Nations and in Arab embassies in many countries, derived great comfort from the appeasement policy of the United States. It was being strengthened by the generous support of international oil interests, who felt that helping the Arabs was in fact helping to protect their own material interests. The hirelings of the oil companies were recruited for service in the cause of the Arabs.

The techniques of the Arabs improved, though latterly they may have overreached themselves. The American and British intention to finance the great Aswan Dam was frustrated by Nasser's seizure of the Suez Canal, which set the Arab world aflame with patriotic ardor and alarmed the British, who felt that this was indeed the unkindest cut of all, for this to be done to Great Britain after she had already abandoned the canal and tremendous accumulations of military supplies to the Egyptians! The canal incident even confused John Foster Dulles, who persisted in thinking, on the basis of intimate reports from Ambassador Henry Byroade, that Nasser might still be regarded as America's best friend in the Middle East. The presence of the Communists in Cairo was not encouraging, but in all probability Mr. Dulles would win another victory for peace by persuading the British and French to appease the

Russians a little bit more. After all, the Russians were already
at home in Egypt, so what harm would there be in giving them
a hearty welcome under the American flag?

Israel was no longer master of its own fate, but that was the
fact for sometime past, so why complain now? It would have to
rely upon its own inadequate military forces, on whatever help
its kinsmen in America might be able to give; and it would
have to await the miracle it had always relied on, but which
seemed never to come at the right time.

DAVID BEN-GURION (1 8 8 6 -   )

In concluding this volume, dedicated chiefly to profiles of
Zionists who have passed to their eternal rest, I am constrained
to break its pattern by including the man who was the leader
on the day the State was proclaimed and who, at this writing,
continues with unabated vigor and courage as the Prime Minister of the Government of Israel.

David Ben-Gurion worked his way up in the Zionist movement through the period following the death of Theodor Herzl.
His distinctions in Zionism came originally from the labor
movement, which he first nurtured in Poland, then organized,
led and tyrannized over in Palestine. From his first days on he
had his own dogmatic views on problems of Jewish life and
of Zionism. It was never easy to dislodge any notion he had
latched onto. He was a savage fighter who took advantage of
every opening in a debate and remained unrelenting until bat-
tered down by a more powerful antagonist. All he knew of life
he learned in the close comradeship of the labor movement.
His education came from his experiences in that narrow world.
He drew his inspiration from a keen knowledge of the ways of
Jewish life, its history and its folk tradition. Although it is said
that he was engrossed in the study of Greek and Greek literature and philosophy, the alien influence did not show in the
pattern of his life. The student was not there. Least of all his
comrades was he ever a disciple of the *goy* Karl Marx, whose
doctrine he outlived years ago. He fought side by side with
labor comrades in a common cause, but above and beyond

that cause the oracle he consulted most came from Jewish life, its wisdom and loyalties. Zion was his lodestar.

He was exiled from Palestine by the Turkish authorities when The First World War erupted. He came to New York and here, as elsewhere, devoted himself to the labor movement. Strangely enough, he was persuaded by Pincus Rutenberg to join the Jewish Congress movement and in the preparations for a Jewish Legion to join General Allenby against the Turks. Marching side by side with Isaac Ben Zri (now President of Israel), tall and lanky and awkward, he returned to Palestine and helped remove the debris of war when peace came. He also spent two years in London and then returned to Tel Aviv, which was his home from then on.

In the Homeland he was propagandist and leader of power. He was a doughty fighter in partisan struggles. He was the most aggressive one of the brilliant group who created the Histadruth and its economic and cultural enterprises. He was not a theorist like Boruchov, or Dr. Nachum Syrkin, or A. D. Gordon. He was not a scintillating journalist or a personality of charm, and winning manner, like Berl Katzenelson. He was not an adroit political analyst like Chaim Arlosoroff. He was not a Yeshiva student, turned practical, like David Remez. He seemed to think that most theorists were bores. But he had what none of the others had—a vision of where he was going. He elbowed his way through opposition and always expected to come out the victor. But when he lost he retired to his tent, licking his wounds, sulking, and preparing for the next round. He was obsessed by his work and could not be diverted. His mind followed one track. In fact, he was born to be a tyrant, but fortunately he was bound in discipline to the party of which he was the leader, whom he could swear at, berate unmercifully, but with whom—that was his fate—he had to live as a brother-in-arms. His tyranny had to bow to the democratic spirit of Palestine, which gave a dissident the right to answer back, to swear back and to denounce the man whom he acknowledged as his leader. That was what made Ben-Gurion a leader in office or out of it.

His hold on the Jewry of Israel came from the fact that he had the right to appeal to a higher court. The interests of the nation were above the interests of Jewish labor and the interest of Marxian socialism. He believed labor to be the instrument for the fulfillment of prophesy. Without labor, the co-operatives and the collectives, without labor as the crown of the State, one was bound to fall into the morass of competitive struggles in which Jewish national destiny would find a miserable death.

He gradually worked his way into the larger interests of Zionist authority in Palestine. He was driven in that direction by the tragedy of Jewish life. He foresaw that the Hitler massacres would inevitably lead to the opening of the doors of Palestine to the refugees and also inevitably bring about the creation of the Jewish State—in the whole of Palestine or a part of it. Its size did not concern him. If not big enough at the beginning, then later it would expand to provide welcome to those who needed sanctuary.

The first labor representative in the Jewish Agency was Chaim Arlosoroff, who accepted the political portfolio with Moshe Sharett as his assistant. Eliezar Kaplan graduated from the Histadruth and became the Treasurer of the Jewish Agency. David Ben-Gurion seemed to be free-lance in the Jewish Agency, then became its Palestine Chairman and served as liaison with London. He was once on the verge of a pact with Jabotinsky, which his party rejected. He and the labor movement went along with Dr. Weizman through the enlargement of the Jewish Agency in 1929 and the Partition resolution at the Congress in 1937. But it soon became clear that David Ben Gurion's hot blood, his uncontrollable indignations, his egotistical drive, his impatience, could not long endure the moderation of Dr. Weizman. He wanted the Jewish people in its pain to cry out and to denounce the betrayers of the Promise. He was unable to accept restraint as a policy or patience as a virtue. He was unable to accept Dr. Weizman's timeless program, his reliance on faith and his readiness to carry burdens endlessly while waiting for the redemption. Still, Dr. Weizman remained the political leader until 1946. He was honored as the elder statesman and President of Israel until he passed away. But David Ben-Gurion was the *de facto* leader of the Jewish settlement through the period from the White Paper of 1939 to 1946, when, with an intensity and ruthlessness difficult to understand, and against the will of over half his own party, he forced the official retirement of Dr. Weizman and became the Chairman of the Executive of the Jewish Agency at the Basle Congress in 1946 and then the head of the State in 1948. It is a heavy crown that rests on his head.